i

ACT LESS, BE MORE!

Notes on Acting for the Screen

by

Anthony Perris

Published by
HOUHOULI BOOKS
13 St. Catherine Road
Timour Hall   Plumstead
Cape Town 7800

houhoulibooks@gmail.com

Layout	Koji Nakashima
Illustrations and Design	Werner Meintjes
Editorial and Layout	Joanne Huysamen

ISBN   978-0-620-52167-3

Printed and bound in the Republic of South Africa
by

Acknowledgements

To

Aletta Bezuidenhout. Her creative, performance and teaching skills are awesome.

She has given me a greater awareness and deeper appreciation into the actor's art.

And

Helen Bizos, my sister who was always there with unconditional support through both the good and difficult times.

Contents

Part 1

What does it mean "to care" in a performance?

Part 10

Part 11

FOREWORD

This is an Actor's working companion. I have used these notes and insights at times when I got stuck with interpretation.

It's a terrific reference book – it covers every aspect of acting in the movies. It's not only valuable for actors, but for writers and directors as well.

I highly recommend it if your passion is the movies and television.

Aletta Bezuidenhout

Part 1

We shall not cease from exploration
and the end of all our exploring will
be to arrive where we started - and
know the place for the first time...

- T.S. Eliot
FOUR QUARTETS

Acting

You probably want to learn to act because you want to become a professional or part-time actor. Maybe you even see acting as a way to become rich and famous and you find that exciting. Maybe you'll succeed. However there are more valuable things that will benefit you when you learn about the finer details of acting.

If you're really serious about learning to act, you'll gain knowledge about *yourself*. You'll increase your self-assurance. Acting will teach you a professional discipline and you'll develop your speaking and communication skills, which you can use with confidence in other ways to take advantage of life's opportunities.

Most people don't realize how *complex* an actor's job really is. An actor works on many levels. Some of them are:

- To entertain: to touch people's emotions (happiness, laughter, joy, excitement, sadness, anger, etc.).
- To inform and educate.
- To communicate ideas/ideals/values/propaganda. For instance: commercially, socially or politically.
- To change perceptions in society. This can be either positive or negative.
- To reflect life in all it's nuances. To interpret the good and bad in social and cultural values. You do this because when you perform as an actor, you stand up as a mirror for people to look at themselves.
- To transform society, whether society is ready or not for change.

An actor also bears a personal responsibility:

- To enhance his/her self awareness as a human being.
- To be flexible to change - and not to stagnate.
- To understand the emotional and potentially volatile nature of many acting situations, and therefore to keep your acting life separate from your personal life and to know and respect the difference.

Know Yourself

It is essential for a person to know themselves intimately if they wish to pursue a career as a professional actor. An actor constantly works from their feelings. If the actor is not in touch with their feelings, then it's difficult for them to feel empathy for a character they have to interpret or portray.

The better one understands oneself, the better one is able to appreciate another person's point of view and the character one is playing.

Specific techniques have been developed to help actors access emotions for a performance. They encourage the actor to come to terms consciously with their feelings.

When you study acting, you'll discover qualities about yourself. You'll learn that self discovery and self acceptance is a continuous healing process and fundamental to the actor's craft.

Discipline

The dictionary defines it as: *a mental and moral training; a system of rules for conduct; to bring under control:* **'to be obedient to yourself'.**

You've probably heard uninformed people say that acting is not *real* work and when you've expressed a desire to become an actor, or tell somebody that you are an actor, you've probably heard at one time or another something like, 'Don't do that! It's a waste of time!'

Well, that kind of a comment is totally misleading. Acting *is* real work. It's very demanding work. It takes effort and focus to understand and learn lines and to work within the technical, artistic and production demands of the profession.

It's *physically* demanding! *Creatively* demanding! *Intellectually* demanding! *Passionately* demanding! *Emotionally* demanding! *Psychologically* demanding!

It demands total *discipline!*

It can take years of training, combined with practical experience, for you to become successful and really good at it.

You might even have to make personal sacrifices.

You only get out of something the amount of *effort* that you put into it!

You cannot be successful at something if you don't have the necessary *discipline* to make the effort that is required to achieve it.

Learn to discipline yourself!

HOW DO I COMMUNICATE WITH YOU?

Let me count the ways:

*I communicate to
the limits my
body,
mind and spirit
can reach.*

*I cannot speak of
communication
without me in it,
because my
communication
is me. Because
I communicate
I am...*

*...and when I stop
communicating,
I shall be dead
in mind if not
in body,
in spirit if not
in mind.*

- E. Barret Browning

Sensuality

*"...of sense or sensation; the capacity for enjoying the
pleasures of the senses; the quality of being pleasing to
the senses; relating to sensation and the sense organs..."*

- The concise Oxford dictionary

You have five sense organs:

* You have eyes so you can see.
* You have hands and skin so you can feel and touch.
* You have ears so you can hear sounds.
* You have a tongue so you can taste and talk.
* You have a nose so you can smell.

You use your senses to absorb information from the outside world, from your fellow actors and from circumstances and situations.

That information can come to you in different ways. It can be very subtle or it can be very pronounced.

You also use your senses to *project* or communicate information to the outside world - or to your fellow actors - to create information, or to respond to circumstances and situations.   For example:

* *In the way YOU SEE (perceive) things.*
* *In the way YOU SAY things or MAKE SOUNDS.*
* *In the way YOU FEEL things physically, emotionally, psychologically, intuitively, subconsciously, erotically.*
* *In the way YOU HEAR things.*
* *In the way YOU RESPOND to the way things look, feel, smell, taste and sound.*
* *In the way YOU APPEAR and SMELL to people or to other living things.*

Smell is one of our most powerful senses. In real life you respond instinctively to the odor of people and other smells in the environment around you. Even in the slightest way they affect you every day in pleasant or in disagreeable ways.

And the way *you* or your environment smell can cause a similar reaction in another person. Your smell reflects your state of mind, emotions, surroundings and cultural conditioning to people and other living things.

But most people aren't even aware of how deeply they're affected by the smells that surround them.

For example, think about how people from some Mediterranean and Middle Eastern countries use generous amounts of garlic in the food they eat. Don't you think that someone from a conservative or different gastronomic culture would pick up that smell and feel uncomfortable around that person, whereas someone from inside that culture might not?

Smell can also trigger past memories in you. In special moments what images or thoughts might you recall from your life if you suddenly got a whiff of an erotic smell emanating from sweat on your lovers body? How would that affect you?

How would the musty scent in an old book store impact on you as you enter it? The sterilized stench of a hospital? The fragrance of fresh-cut grass on a dewy spring morning? The animal and agricultural odors on a farm? The aroma of fish and chips coming from nowhere as you're standing on the beach? Hamburgers being grilled outdoors on coals at an unforgettable sports event? The sudden hint of fresh baked bread as you pass a bakery?

What kind of emotions or memories might these examples trigger? Take a moment to think about that and see what you might remember?

When you're in an acting situation and if the circumstances are appropriate, consider using the physical, emotional and psychological power of smell to stimulate you as a character. An alert actor will use the quality of smell in the environment or from the natural body smells of other actors to stimulate an appropriate response in a scene.

Accomplished actors have learnt to develop and *use* the natural facilities of *all* their senses as they interact with what is happening in a scene.

To lead you into the appropriate emotional, physical and psychological requirements of any acting situation, learn to use all your senses:

> In your daily life experience...
> When you work on exercises and improvs in class...
> When you rehearse or work on scenes...
> When you perform in films, on TV or on the stage...

To learn more about the power of smell, read *Jacobson's Organ and the nature of smell* by Lyall Watson, especially Part 2 – The Fragrant Ape and Part 3 – The Most Human Thing.

Observation and the Actor

Everything consists of energy. The world around you is made up of energy. So when you *observe* something, all your senses are receiving energy from that subject.

The dynamic or power of that energy depends on how sensitive your senses are to receiving that energy – as well as on the *intensity* of the energy which the subject is radiating back to you.

You sense and receive that energy in the form of *information* and each time you do that, you learn something which you didn't know before about the world, yourself and the subject you are observing. A lot of what you know about things, yourself and people comes from observation and much of that information is communicated subliminally.

As an actor, see what you can use in a performance by consciously observing the different qualities in yourself and of people and things. Try to understand what makes something or someone *to be* what it or that person is.

The purpose of the observation is to find *inspiration* from the subject you are observing and to bring elements of what you have observed into the character you are playing. It's not to imitate what you observe, *but to identify with and to make the information you have chosen from that observation your own*. What you use in a performance must come from a very real place in your own passions and feelings.

When you observe a subject, it's important that you are *interested* in what you are observing. When you are interested in something, your senses are sharper and you become aware of details that you would not normally notice when you are not interested in something. You pick up information on a conscious level and you become more focused on what you are observing.

Try to capture the fundamental nature of the character or thing that you are observing. What do you think the unspoken information might be that is being communicated? **Observe** *why* and *how* that information is transmitted and communicated. For example:

- What does a person's body language such as gestures, accent, physical expressions, posture and actions suggest about them?
- What is a person's attitude and temperament when they are confronted by different challenges in different situations? How does that person respond and react?
- What are that persons different moods and mannerisms? Why are they like that? Can you identify with that in yourself?
- What kind of emotion does a person's voice project? How does he/she breathe and speak? Fast, slow, panting, boring, energetic, fearful, boldly? Can you empathize with what that person might be feeling at a particular moment? Why?
- What does their body odor suggest and how would you react to that? For example, it's well-known that animals can pick up the scent of fear or courage or friendship or the state of health in a person when they smell them. In a similar way people pick up different emotional and physical qualities in each other. Is the smell attractive or repugnant?
- What are the characters habits, demeanor and thinking processes? What do you think his/her history, circumstances and social standing might be? How does that person's environment affect their circumstances?
- How intimate is their relationship with different people? What is the attitude and reaction of other people when they interact with them? Why?

How observant are you about yourself? How aware are you about your own habits, emotions, psychology, physical features and body odors and attitudes?

How do you communicate and respond in your interactions with people, your environment and in the situations and circumstances that affect you? For example, as an exercise in observation *consciously* try to become aware of the following in observing yourself:

- How do you sleep? Eat? Caress and kiss your lover?
- How do you wake up in the morning?
- What is the first thing you do when you wake up?
- How do you brush your teeth, shower or bath?
- How do you feel in the morning, depending on what you did and how you felt the night before?
- How do you get dressed?
- What are your first thoughts?

What other aspects about yourself are you aware of in your everyday life?

Look at the various things that you do automatically each day and become conscious of what you do and how you do it. An alert actor will be aware of even the smallest detail of their life experience and use that in an appropriate acting situation.

Make it a habit to consciously observe people, places, situations and the things around you. When you begin to consciously observe your experiences, you will eventually be able to apply much of what you have observed into an acting situation.

Defining an observation: To observe something or someone means that you need to look closely at what it is you are looking at: to discover; to be on the lookout; to notice.

Due to our personal life experience and cultural conditioning, we all carry some form of discrimination in one way or another. However, as an actor you cannot hold prejudices when you make an honest observation. You cannot be small minded or have a narrow point of view. You need to be neutral about what you observe.

You don't have to agree or disagree with what you observe, but if you're not tolerant of other peoples' customs and habits you cannot be an objective observer and learn from that. To be tolerant means to have a willingness to bear with the *differences* of others; to put up with them – especially when it deals with politics and social, sexual, cultural and religious matters.

Voice

Your voice is a valuable tool which you have to communicate as an actor.

You use your voice to verbalize and express thoughts, ideas, attitudes and different emotions so that an audience can hear you clearly, understand what you're saying and feel the emotions you are feeling in the sound, energy and texture of your voice when you're playing a character.

Breath is life. Without breath there is no life. The way an actor is trained and uses their breath, determines the power and intensity of the emotions that are projected through the actor's voice.

Most people take their breath for granted. For many of us, it's a totally unconscious act.

The basic power of your voice resonates from the diaphragm which is situated below your solar plexus. When they communicate, many actors don't know how to use this power. They speak in raspy, squeaky, weak or soft voices which strain their throat and vocal chords. It's often hard to *hear* or *understand* what they're saying.

It happens many times in casting sessions when actors audition for a part. An actor could look physically perfect to win it, but as soon as they open their mouth to speak, the quality and energy of their voice and accent lets them down, so they lose out on what they might have had.

Strong actors speak in rich, clear tones which make people *want* to listen to them, even when they're playing or mimicking the sound and texture of different types of characters. They have recognizable voices that set them apart from everyone else.

When they speak, they have a conscious retention and control of breath, which after much training and practice becomes second nature.

Just like the muscles in other parts of your body that need to be regularly exercised to keep you fit, the muscles that resonate inside your mouth – that create the sounds of your voice – also need to be developed, strengthened and frequently exercised to keep your voice fit and in good tone for what is usually many hours of intense film, TV and stage performance.

Voice Exercises:

These prepare the actor to perform in a way that doesn't *strain* the vocal chords and trains actors to tune into different levels of intensity and emotion when they speak in a scene. They're also beneficial in helping to neutralize a harsh or unpleasant cultural accent you might have, or to coach you into an appropriate foreign accent for a particular part.

Like any musical instrument or tool that one uses in life, an actor's voice is also considered to be an *instrument* which needs to be kept fine-tuned to perform at its best. You go to the gym to exercise your body and fine tune your muscles into shape. Likewise, learning to do voice exercises will benefit you as an actor to attain and strengthen that fine tuning in your lips, breath, tongue and throat muscles when you communicate *verbally*.

Voice coaching is a very specialized field. Bad voice coaches can do more harm than good. Like finding a good gym coach, connecting with a good voice coach is vitally important. Ask around before you commit to one.

Sound

We're surrounded by sound. When air is disturbed in any way it moves and creates sounds. Sound is one of the ways in which we communicate, and all living things make sounds that may be meaningful to each other.

Sounds affect our emotions and they're also useful to us for our survival.

We can hear a car approaching and that warns us to be careful crossing the road, or we can hear an explosion and that warns us of danger. It's also important for us to make sounds to *release* our emotions, and screaming and shouting sometimes seem to happen automatically without us even thinking about it. So obviously there are some built-in instincts that we have that cause us at certain times to make sounds.

We might shout for joy when something pleasant occurs in our lives, or gasp in pleasure when we are aroused, or yell in fear or choke in shock or sorrow when something traumatic happens around us.

Making sounds is also part of the way we *express* our emotions to others. When you look at what we've learnt to do with sound, things like music and especially language, then sound becomes an extremely valuable communication tool in our lives.

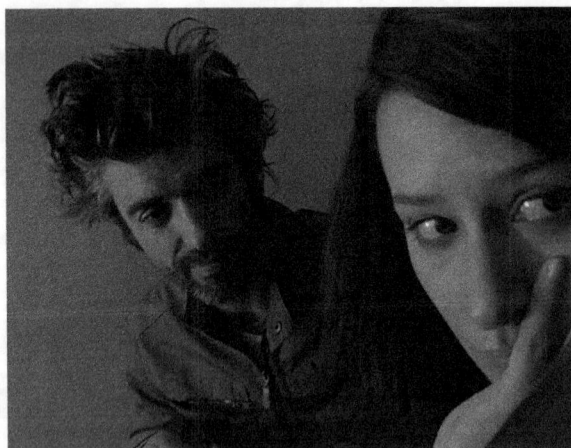

The way we talk to each other has shown us that when we look at each other as we speak, eye contact is very important and some of that has to do with *monitoring* the other person's expressions. So obviously our face seems to be revealing the state of our mind, it reveals our emotions, how we feel at any given moment.

By the same token, you could say that the emotional tone and pitch of our voice, whether we're sad or excited, calm or nervous, loud or soft, or speaking quickly or slowly, does the same thing. So we've evolved to become very good at paying attention to the *tone* and *texture* of each other's voice as we speak to one another, because obviously there's a communication and survival value in knowing how another person feels.

Sounds affect us in different ways. Some sounds we call noise. Noise is any sound that's loud, monotonous, confused or disturbing. It's irritating to listen to. The rhythm and timing of that type of sound feels out of harmony. It jars our emotions and annoys us.

Other sounds we call music, and we usually think of certain types of music as sound that's pleasant, stimulating, erotic or exciting to hear. The rhythm and timing of the sound might be harmonious and in sync with our feelings at a particular moment. It satisfies our emotions. We associate music with mood and we can feel music that's happy, light, romantic or sad, rushed, or has suspense, drama or tension to it.

We cannot underestimate the emotional impact that sound has in our lives. For example, before the invention of sound movies there were silent movies. Without sound, the emotional experience of the people watching a silent movie was lacking.

That's why they had people creating sound effects behind the screen to compliment the action the audience was looking at and live piano players playing the piano in front of the silent movie to create a musical mood. It was a natural thing to have sight and sound together. Even if the audience couldn't hear the actor's voices, a good piano player could still sort of mimic the feeling of the actor's emotions with the type of music that they played.

The audience could get a *feeling* for the action, comedy or drama in the way the music was played. Even today, music is still used to compliment the mood and feeling of the action in a movie.

Many actors are alert to sounds and use what they hear around them to react appropriately to a situation in a scene, because they're aware that different qualities of sound and music are tied very closely to their emotions and that they affect them in different ways. They might even use a suitable type of sound or music to set them in the mood when they prepare for a particular role.

Do you want to play an irritating, nervous character? Listen to disturbing sounds that will begin to annoy you. Do you want to get into a romantic or erotic mood? Try becoming stimulated by listening to an appropriate type of romantic or rock music.

Music opens the mind to transcendent reality,
to the world behind the world of sight, touch,
smell and other mundane phenomena, drawing
the listener away from himself and, some will
claim, closer to God.

- Alexander Waugh
  God

Eyes

The eyes of men converse as much as their tongues.

- Ralph Waldo Emerson

He speaketh not, and yet there lies a conversation in his eyes.

- Longfellow

The actor's eyes are probably their most important sense organ. With your eyes you see to gain information from the world.

Your eyes also reflect to the outside world the *feelings* that are happening inside you.

Eye contact is vital when you communicate. It's been said that the eyes are the window to the soul. You can read a lot about a person or another character when you look into their eyes.

When you look at people on Reality TV or on the news of real life events, their eyes tell a lot about how they are feeling. You can see how happy, painful, angry or sincere they are about what is happening around them.

The same should apply to acting when your characters emotion is appropriate to the circumstances in a situation. The camera will pick up in your eyes how you, the actor, are feeling and how truthful you are about the things you are saying and reacting to.

In an acting situation, when you are *internalized* and communicating emotionally in a truthful way, there will always be some *energy* reflected in your eyes. The camera will pick up even the minutest *sparkle* seen in your eyes that will communicate an inner life, feeling and thought process to an audience of what is happening inside you as a character.

It will pick up the *quality* of the energy that comes out of you. When you are feeling erotic, excited, pleasure or are frightened, your pupils might dilate and widen or moisten. Your eyelids might flutter or twitch in a nervous way. When you are feeling soft and loving inside, your eyes might look blurred or gentle and moist.

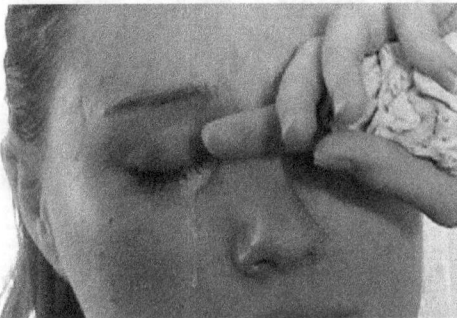

When someone is aggressive or looks angry and menacingly at you, we say they have "eyes like daggers cutting through me..." When someone is stoned, their eyes look glazed, or lifeless. When they're feeling tired, lethargic or stressful their eyes might be itchy and reddish.

A person's eyes might contract, enlarge or become damp when certain emotions are felt. For example, tears build up and people usually cry when they're feeling sorrowful, emotionally hurt or in deep physical pain.

When someone has something to hide or is being dishonest, they usually look shifty eyed and tend to glance away rather than look directly at you as they are communicating, and something similar might happen when you are feeling uncomfortable or insecure about something.

So our daily experience in real life always goes through different moods and changes from moment to moment and we usually react and respond to circumstances and situations subconsciously, intuitively and spontaneously as they occur and we communicate much of what we are feeling in the energy that's reflected through our eyes.

That energy is a *natural* reaction coming from the emotion happening inside *you,* and not something artificial that you are trying to act out.

When an actor tries to "act out" an emotion rather than feel it, their eyes will not register the appropriate energy of that emotion convincingly on camera. On the screen any unnecessary, repetitive, nervous, twitching or other distracting, insincere and over played eye movement can look exaggerated and disturbing to an audience, especially when the actor's eyes are seen on the screen in close-up.

An exception might be if the actor is playing a specific type of character who displays a particular type of physical habit or neurosis and even here, whatever that habit or neurosis is - to play it out believably – it must still be projected in an honest way from inside the actor.

Likewise, keep eye contact when you're interacting with another character in a scene and read the emotion that's reflected in their eyes when they're interacting with you from moment to moment. Then respond with an appropriate emotion of what you are feeling inside you as a character.

Emotions / Body Language

Defining emotions: *Emotions or feelings are your reactions. They're the way your body feels as well as the way your mind feels. It's all your anticipation of what's going to happen in a situation.*

And then the thing happens, and it's your reaction to it. What happens inside you is your feeling about the thing.

It would be strange if you went through life and felt good things only, or just bad things because that would make your life very narrow to have just one feeling inside you all the time.

The same should hold true for the character that you as the actor are interpreting.

Many actors have difficulty creating *real* emotion in a scene. Much of this has to do with a person's lack of emotional focus, which is also to some extent a result of a person's social, cultural and defensive conditioning.

When a person changes their way of thinking and responds *appropriately* in a situation, they get closer to freeing themselves to express the requirements of a performance.

It's been said by many actors that when you experience a real emotion in a performance, "it vibrates through your whole body and you'll feel it tingling everywhere. You'll know that your performance was connected and true, without needing anyone to tell you. You'll feel the *rightness* of the energy".

That is a very valid observation. When you're acting, as in real life - your emotions should lead your body. Your body should respond to - and reflect - your true inner feelings inside the character you are interpreting.

People pick up on your feelings. It's not so much the things people say, but often it's what they don't say that can be more meaningful in both an interaction and a communication. What they don't say, can be closer to the *truth* of what they're *really* feeling.

Even non-feeling is a form of feeling. Some people are very good at blocking or hiding their feelings, but the very fact that they are hiding them, communicates a certain type of information about them.

For example, haven't you ever walked into a place and people looked at you and you looked at them and immediately a *feeling* was given off and you sensed that people were angry, afraid, depressed or happy and positive about something when not even a word was spoken?

Or when you met someone for the first time you talked, but for some reason you felt there was something about that person you liked, or didn't like?

Through your body language and the sound of your voice you communicate to an alert and observant person what you *truly* feel or don't feel from moment to moment.

We communicate our feelings in many ways. Smiling is a form of what you might be feeling about someone or something. Or you might reach out and touch someone – or kiss – and the way you do that is a physical demonstration of a feeling that's inside you, and it's one of the most intimate ways that people know how to physically display a feeling that's inside them.

How you hold your body expresses your feelings. It can reveal your feelings about events – and how interested you are about what's happening around you.

It can be in the way you dress, style your hair, or decorate your face and body, which is dressing off to attract attention to you. Or about people - how much you like or don't like them. It can show others whether you agree with an idea or not, and it can help you to take your place in a hierarchy. You can even observe this in the way that animals communicate with each other.

Our feelings are not that different from one another. The way we humans look at things, they're so similar.

With a screen performance, it should also happen the way it does in real life. When you generate *real* emotions of anger, crying, love, desire and other feelings, the camera will *pick up* the truth or the lie of it. The camera will see what's reflected in your body language. The camera will even see the subtle color changes and perspiration happening on your skin.

For instance, when you feel excited or passionate about meeting someone you like for the first time, you might suddenly blush and your skin will change color. You might sweat when you're afraid. When you dislike someone or are uncomfortable talking to them, you might avoid looking at them. Or your hands or feet might fidget when you're nervous about something.

As an observation exercise, study people and become aware of how they express through their body language the way they're feeling in different situations.

Integrating Voice and Body Language

Recap: *The camera will pick up all the subtle information about the way you honestly feel as a character when you communicate your performance from a real emotional place. It captures your changing moods and feelings.*

Within the context of what is happening in a scene, the emotional intensity and tonal qualities of the actor's voice cannot be separated from the feelings and energy that the actors eyes and body language are projecting.

If your emotions are not true, the one will feel false from the other. There has to be harmony within all the parts that are you. Without that, the realness of your character will not play out.

Too often, the lie is seen in actors. Through experience many have become good at faking external body language, but their voice gives them away when they speak. The lie is caught when there's a lack of character and subtlety in the voice, and when there's blandness in the sounds they project.

Working with actors, it becomes easy to pick out when they're not real. And even without intellectually understanding why, most audiences also do.

If you are *not* truthful about the emotions of the character you are playing, it becomes extremely difficult to give a believable performance.

Connect your performance with the *FEELING* of something. If you can do that, then your performance is more likely to stay with the audience.

Do Animals Have Emotions / Feelings?

How observant are you? Can you draw lessons from the communication skills of other species? For example:

An antelope   Elephant   Dog   Cat   Horse   Monkey   Ape

Any other animal or bird…?

How do they communicate without words? How do they use sound, smell, sight, taste, touch and hearing? How do they act, react and respond when:

> Happy
> Sad
> Angry
> Frightened
> Bereaved
> Sexually aroused
> Panicked
> Determined
> Competitive

Do they:

Cry? Make happy sounds? Use body language? Sweat? Smell? Show love? Affection? Confusion? Humor? Hate? Jealousy? Anger ? Curiosity?

Is there an emotion or spirit or some kind of change reflected in their eyes or in the sounds they make? How do they express such attitudes?

How do they see you? How do they communicate with each other in their environment - even under water or in the air - through their body language, movements and the sounds they make?

So look into the eyes of a dog, cat or a pet if you have one.

What do you see? Do you see life energy there?

Do you see some kind of intelligence or a life form that projects a feeling or communication of some kind?

It's been recognized that the martial arts, various dance forms and many other disciplines were inspired and developed by people observing the communication methods of other species.

So if you are serious as an actor, observe and learn from the experience and communication skills of the living things around you.

The late South African Producer-Director Jamie Uys brilliantly captured the humor and drama of how animals communicate with body language and sound in his 1974 feature length documentary *Beautiful People*.

Anyone who wants to learn about acting and communication should study it.

Improvisation

The dictionary defines improvisations or 'improvs' as: *"to do something on the spur of the moment...without formalizing or intellectualizing about it"*

Improvisations are exercises and techniques which have evolved over many centuries to help actors break through personal barriers and mental blocks. They are used in "spontaneous acting situations" to stimulate an actor's creativity and imagination, and to assist the actor to fine-tune their performance skills. They are also a useful tool for other reasons:

• During rehearsals, they allocate actor's, director's and writer's *time* and *space* to experiment with story "situations"- and to create and develop a character's action and dialogue.

A director might move the actors through an *improvisation* of a scene before a shoot to generate energy in the actors and to get a feel for the story and the emotional dynamic that might be required in their performance. For example, the improv might be structured around the relationship which the characters have with each other, and the conflicts that motivate the interaction between them.

• By improvising the situation *outlined* in a scripted scene, it assists the director and actors in getting a feel for the timing, pacing and rhythm of how the scene *could* work. It gives them a *feel* of how it plays or should not play. To *hear* how it sounds or should not sound. To get *a sense* of how the characters should interact in the situation.

Through improvs, actors gain knowledge about themselves and from each other. *Without thinking* about what will happen, they learn to *listen, respond* and *interact intuitively* and *spontaneously* with other actors in a given situation.

Through peer feedback, improvs can also be useful lessons in how to absorb criticism in a constructive way. Actors realize things about themselves as others see them, and learn to look at things with a positive and objective attitude.

Improv Exercise

Imitating and becoming another Species

If you were cast in the movie version of the musical plays *The Lion King* or *Cats,* how would you approach the part? Or as *Catwoman* or *The Penguin* in some pulp fiction movie?

How would you imitate and "become" the animal you were cast for, or even an "alien" from another universe if you had a role in a sci-fi movie?

How *truthfully* would you be able to communicate those parts?

In this improv, choose to play a life form from another species such as an alien being, an animal, reptile, bird or insect. Something that appeals to you, and take us through a few moments of that life forms day.

The improv is an acting exercise. Its purpose is to encourage you to:

- Experiment emotionally and physically with the extra-ordinary.
- Release your inhibitions.
- Apply in a practical situation what you've learnt through the observation of other life forms.
- Try and identify with the personality and lifestyle of another species.
- Project communication as another species would through the sounds it makes and the body language it projects.
- Identify and empathize with the *feelings* of another species, so that you can identify and come closer to understanding your own.

Consider this:

- How would one species interact with a species that is different from itself - or with one of its own kind?

- What would its needs be? Sex and procreation? Food? Conquest? Survival? Companionship? Peer support and acceptance?

How would such needs be expressed and fulfilled? When, why and how would it respond when: Angry? Fearful? Desirous? Embarrassed? Compassionate? Loving? Sexual?

How would two or more males interact with each other in different circumstances, or two or more females, or males with females?

In the improv, how would the species you have chosen to be interact with a different one that was chosen by another actor?

How would each of you communicate your attitudes and needs to each other without words but through action, sounds and body language only?

Listening

LISTEN - Or your tongue will make you blind.

- A North American Indian Proverb

What does it mean to 'LISTEN' when you're acting? It's like observation - but to be consciously alert and aware emotionally and physically as a character to what you are hearing and to what is happening around you from moment to moment.

- To really listen means that you must be *totally* centered, interested, attentive and focused on what you are "hearing".
- It means that you must *hear* not only what the other actor is saying - but also empathize with what their character is meaning, feeling and experiencing.
- It means that you must also hear the voice that comes from *inside you*!
- It means moving with each moment in a scene, being inside it and *responding* to a situation with a suitable attitude that's generated from the way your 'character' has been socially and culturally conditioned and *feels* at the moment in a particular set of circumstances.
- It means *letting go* of your inhibitions and of everything else that surrounds your performance space and to really *live* what is unfolding around you.

Much of what happens in acting is basically the result of *Listening* and *Reacting (Responding)* appropriately as a character to the information that's generated around you in an invented or imaginary situation.

In real life when you respond to a situation it's usually intuitive and triggered by what you've learnt through your life experience and the information, as you see and understand it, that's created around you.

Apply the same dynamic to acting. Learn to listen. *Trust* your experience and your feelings and *flow* with the scene that's unfolding around you.

That first impression or intuition that you sometimes get in a situation is usually the correct one to follow when you're acting.

Defining intuition: What is it? How does it work? Why should you trust it? What does it mean when someone tells you "to trust your intuition?"

The Oxford dictionary describes it as *"the power of knowing the truth without reasoning; insight; instinct, a hunch; a sixth sense"*.

People have tried to describe their experience of it in different ways. Bob Dylan said: *"I just write a song and I know it's going to be alright. I don't even know what it's going to say"*.

Henry Miller said: *"I only obey my own instincts and intuition. I know nothing in advance. Often I put down things which I do not understand myself, secure in the knowledge that later it will become clear and meaningful to me. I have faith in the man who is writing, who is myself, the writer"*.

It's that gut feeling that you sometimes get that makes you *sense* that what you want to do or what you feel about something is just right – no matter what your intellect, or what other people say.

I know from my own experience that during the times when I tried to force creativity to happen and over prepared myself intellectually for the days shoot, I usually stressed out and blocked myself from letting the energy flow unhindered and spontaneously through me. As I learnt to let go, things just came together and my best work came from that.

Today, before I do a shoot I can walk onto a set and get a *feel* of it, even if I've not seen it before. I let my intuition take over and somehow without realizing it, I seem to adapt to the situation more easily and know what to do, how to work with the actors and how to set up the scene and block the camera positions. I don't stress about it the way I used to.

I don't know why intuition works like that, but I suspect that somehow it has to do with knowledge that each of us accumulates throughout our life from the moment when we're conceived, as well as from social and cultural information which we inherited from past generations that's encoded in our genes.

And perhaps it's also connected to something even deeper than that. I think we all have access to it and can tap into whatever it is. And maybe it's been programmed into us as some kind of survival device.

Anthropologist, paleontologist and marine biologist Lyall Watson described it in a similar way in his book **Supernature:** *"Most often intuitions are the product of past experience – memories, wishes, hopes and fears that have been stored in the subconscious, but sometimes they may contain completely new information, perhaps obtained by telepathy"*.

The next time you're blocked by something, try to let go of trying to force something to happen. Let the *feeling* of what you might be sensing inside you flow freely through you and don't try to understand it, or intellectualize it or block it. You might not be able to put it into words, but somehow you'll know the "rightness" of what you're feeling.

And respond to that.

If you are ever in doubt – trust your intuition. Trust that feeling.

Touching

Most of us have a deep-seated need to touch and to be touched by others. Some people even project that need to the pets they keep.

- The pleasure we find in physical intimacy is probably rooted in our need during infancy for protective, caring, reassuring body contact with a parent or caregiver – most often our mother.

- When people touch - or even when animals do - feelings or non-feelings between them come together and subtle messages are exchanged on a psychological/emotional level.

You've heard expressions like "I felt electricity when she touched me…" or "I didn't feel anything…it was like he was dead or something. There was nothing there…"

Some people respond positively, while others react negatively when they're touched. What message could someone be projecting in the way they respond when you touch them? Why? What would your attitude be in *the way* that someone touched you? Under what circumstances would the feeling be good, bad, disgusting, pleasant, unpleasant, sexual, painful, uncomfortable, pleasurable?

Does your body tense up, or relax?

Remember, that an actor's job is to reflect life in all its shades, colors and nuances. An actor therefore, cannot afford to be shy or fearful of physical contact with other characters in a performance – unless its part of the characters personality in the story.

Physical intimacy and body contact with other actor's is inevitable in one way or another during an actor's career.

The way that an actor might touch another story character depends on the emotional and psychological background of the character the actor is interpreting. For example, think about touching or being touched by someone and try to *feel* **who** it was and **why** and **how** you would react in different circumstances when you're playing a character in the following scenarios:

Physical contact reactions / exercises:

- You're in an unfamiliar place and are accidentally touched by a sympathetic - or unsympathetic stranger.
- You're with relatives or friends and hug each other for comfort because someone close to you has died. How *intimate* is your relationship and the feel of the touch?
- You hold hands with a male or female friend in a platonic relationship.
- You touch your lover gently, reassuringly, caressingly - or perhaps in a way that sexual delight is aroused, signaled and exchanged.
- You stroke your lover tenderly or passionately. What does the texture of the lover's body feel like? Is your touch clumsy or aggressive? Soft or hard? How does your lover respond?
- Someone touches you in a sympathetic or loving way but you sense that the feeling behind it is insincere.
- Someone shakes your hand, hugs you or rubs noses to express their gratitude, pleasure or just simply to greet you. What is their cultural and social background, and how would you respond to that? What is their attitude, and what is yours? Why?
- A rapist or someone you don't like touches you. Where? How do you respond?

How would *you* touch another person in anger or with caring or love in any of the above scenarios?

- How do you touch and feel *other* living things or inanimate objects?

Now explore these situations in an acting class.

Motivation:

In real life, there is usually a *reason* which causes something to happen and makes you respond in a certain way to a situation. The same applies when you're acting. In acting we call it a *motivation* – it's the thing or incident that triggers an action to happen.

It's the act of giving somebody a *purpose* or *incentive* to do something. Other definitions for motivation might be to excite, stimulate, provoke, or inspire something to occur.

In an acting scenario, try to understand what motivates or causes your character to respond to different situations in a particular way. How would *you* respond, and under what circumstances?

The Character is you. You are the Character.

Recap: *When you perform, you have to be totally honest and objective about yourself. You must trust yourself and accept the rightness of how you understand things.*

If an actor cannot be honest with themselves, they can't be truthful and real to the audience watching them.

Internalize your performance energy. Draw the emotional and performance dynamics of the scene from the truth of your own life experience.

Project from who *you* are and from what *you* know. Don't "pretend" to play a scene with dynamics that you don't know. Don't try to become a character that you can't recognize. Don't try to 'imitate' another person's life experience or psychology.

Don't try to be what you're not, what you don't feel and what you don't understand. For example, don't try to "act" sexy because you see others in movies or on TV do it a certain way, and you think that is what you must also do.

Don't try to "act" childish or cute, when that is already a natural part of your personality. Use what comes naturally from you.

Often, beginners who enroll in acting classes "want to be" like some well-known actor they admire. That's a mistake. You can never "be like" any other actor you look up to. They are who they are because they are unique, and that's what made them special.

You may empathize with them. And you can learn from them by studying their technique and how they use their qualities, attitudes, body language, voice, speech patterns and mannerisms and how closely they can mimic some well-known personality they might be interpreting. But you can never *be* like them or like anyone else. The deeper emotional and psychological elements of the character you are interpreting still need to come from you.

The most powerful quality that you have is *you*. When you express your own life experience, and *adapt* it to the character you're playing, you'll be closer to connecting with the part you're performing.

Part 2

Emotions are what make us human – make us real. The word e - motion stands for energy in motion. Be truthful about your emotions, and use your mind and emotions in your favor, not against yourself...

Be an observer, not a reactor to your emotions. Learn to use your emotions to think, not think with your emotions...

                    - Robert T. Kiyosaki
                    "Rich Dad Poor Dad"

Energy in Performance

Energy is Eternal Delight

- William Blake

We now understand that everything you hear, touch, see, smell, sense and verbalize is a form of energy. The world around you is made of energy. Your emotions are a form of energy.

Emotion: It's what we e-mote or "give out". It's an energy that we release or receive at different times from people and things.

An emotion can be anything from robust, powerful, contained or weak - lacking movement and life - depending on our mood and circumstances at a particular moment in time.

All living things pick up on the "vibe" (vibrations) of each other's energies/emotions. It's like a kind of subconscious flow that transmits and receives "messages" on a subliminal level from and to all life forms.

[**Recap:** *Have you ever noticed how animals pick up the feeling of when you are fearful, hostile or friendly?]*

Sometimes, we might become more consciously aware of this when we watch a dynamic performance which excites us on TV, in the movies or on the stage and we intuitively refer to it as "having high energy", or that some actors have "magnetism", which is also a form of energy.

If the dynamic of a performance is flat and not integrated as a whole, we say it "lacks energy" - or that the actors don't have magnetism. It means that they're not *alive* with an emotional energy and are not transmitting an emotion/energy to the audience.

Believable or powerful acting involves an appropriate exchange and interaction of energies/emotions between the story characters in a controlled and imaginary situation which is outlined in a script and interpreted by the actors and other creative people involved in the making of a movie.

Accomplished actor's use their emotion/energy in a positive way and apply it to bring life to a performance, as well as to the character they're playing.

Emotion/energy is an essential dynamic of acting.

> "VITALITY"
> *"the state or quality of having life..."*
> *"principle of life..."*
> *"keeping the essence of you alive"*
> *"animation...movement"*
> -   Oxford Dictionary

In acting talk, having *vitality* is what we really mean when we talk about the *energy* in a scene.

"**Energy**":   Don't confuse or misinterpret "performance energy" as meaning that you have to be "hyper-active", forceful or loud all the time.

There are *appropriate* moments for that.

"Energy" as we generally mean it or use it in acting, is more in the *focus* you have and the *emotion, vibe* or *intensity* that you project in a scene.

It's about *what* you do and *how* you do it. It's about how you *listen, absorb* and *react* to the stimuli and information moving around you.

It's the *process* of what is happening to you mentally and physically as a character interacting with other actors in a situation, and responding inside that situation appropriately.

It's about being totally *involved* and *interested* in the role you're performing.

It's about how you *lose* yourself in the part.

In the way that we also project energy in real life, "performance energy" can be generated even in moments of silence or static action. It can be in a reaction or look that cinematically tells the audience that something meaningful or emotional on the screen is happening to the characters *internally*.

Even in the stillness and silence, if the actors are totally focused and feeling the character in a situation, the audience too will *feel* the actor's power moving inside them in the energy that's generated through their eyes and body language.

It's about how the actors transmit the *intensity* of a character's inner feelings and thoughts to the audience and make the audience connect with what they are experiencing emotionally.

Personal Exposure

In real life when you enter a strange environment for the first time, what do you *feel*? How do you *react* to people you don't know? How do they size *you* up? How do you size *them* up? What vibes about the place do you pick up and through which of your senses?

Think about some good or uncomfortable experiences you may have had in your interactions with people. For example:

When you talk to somebody and they don't respond to you, but insult or ignore you, don't you feel drained or some other negative emotion? If this keeps going on, in a relationship perhaps, wouldn't there be emptiness about it? Wouldn't you begin to feel there is nothing there?

Or think about when two lovers interact and one keeps "giving" and the other gives nothing back to nourish or feed the other emotionally, spiritually, sexually or physically. Wouldn't that person feel unfulfilled, resentful, hurt, uninspired - perhaps even angry?

Think of other examples and how you may have felt from your own life experience when people haven't *given* to you – or *received* from you when you tried hard to reach out to them.

Think about that. But what happens when you begin to open up to someone and they open up to you? Do you become more comfortable in the situation? Do you begin to trust and become *involved* with that person? Do you begin to find some common interest that you can share with them emotionally or in some other way?

As you begin to drop your fears and defenses, does some form of *communication* begin to happen? Does energy begin to move between you? It might be very subtle at first, but do you sense that something is definitely there?

As you feel more *comfortable*, you might notice that there's lightness in your interaction because you're *allowing* yourself to become more *interested* and *involved*.

You *expose* yourself a little. You *give* of yourself, and when they give back something to you, you *receive* something in return.

That exposing, giving and receiving of yourself, is one of the first steps that you have to take to become an accomplished actor. The more you *give of yourself* and the more you *allow* yourself to *receive* - and the more *truthful* you are about it - the more *real* you'll be as an actor.

It's not easy to reveal yourself on the stage or on the screen where millions of strange people can watch the most intimate things about you. You make yourself vulnerable when you expose your emotions, thoughts and physical being.

But exceptional actors do that. Al Pacino, Robert de Niro, Michelle Pfeiffer, Nick Nolte, Leonardo Dicaprio, Martin Sheen, Charlie Sheen, Olympia Dukakis, Jessica Tandy, Meg Ryan, Andy Garcia, Tommy Lee Jones, Will Smith, Antonio Banderas, Benicio Del Toro, Kevin Kline, Jennifer Lopez, Halle Berry, Kate Winslet, Sharon Stone, Demi Moore, Meryl Streep, Cate Blanchett, Glenn Close, Johnny Depp, Brad Pitt - think of many others - they all expose themselves when they act.

Study their films. Observe how they give and receive from each other in a performance and put something of themselves into it. And when they do that, their honesty and courage touches something deep inside the emotions of an audience.

Have faith in your own life experience - and in the character you're playing.

Expose something of *yourself* in a performance.

Creative Acting: The Rehearsal Process

A major part of your contribution to the creative process is to first *find* and then to *bring* your story character to life.

Rehearsals give you the opportunity to experiment and attempt new things, and to work out the faults you've made in trying to connect with your character before the actual performance or shoot begins.

- When you enter a rehearsal space, *feel* the atmosphere of your work area and the vibe of your fellow actors. *Move* into the space and *claim* your place as a character in it. You do the same thing in real life subconsciously in surroundings that are familiar to you and where you are comfortable.

Fear holds most inexperienced actors back from claiming their "space". Usually this is because they may fear failure or even ridicule by the "experienced" actors they may be working with.

Experienced actors have sometimes been known to play psychological games on new actors. These are usually power trips calculated to test the temperament and determination of a new actor in the cast.

- Make *suggestions* to the people you are working with about the way you have *interpreted* your character. Most inexperienced actors don't do this.

In acing talk, to *interpret* something means that you can choose to create a character from your own personal point of view and decide to perform your character's body language and dialogue in a scene in one of many different ways.

It means that you have a *choice* to develop something from your own understanding and feeling about it.

- Don't expect the director to explain every detail of your performance to you, or even how and when you should speak your lines. The director's job is to *guide* you, based on the character interpretation that you give.

In most instances the director will give you the basic blocking of a scene in the way they want to see it performed, as well as some performance and action guidelines and the vision they have of the character, the story, as well as other technical and creative instructions building on what *you* contribute to the part.

- Each actor is responsible for their performance. When you see really wonderful actors focused in a role, it seems that they bring something into a character that's grown beyond even what the writer's original vision and intention was. They make the character their own.

- Allow your acting intuition and passion for the character to take over. When you connect with the right *feel* of what you're doing, become consistent in your performance.

- Sometimes you may want to try slight variations from one rehearsal to another as you feel your fellow actor's response to the way you are playing your character. That may be acceptable, provided you communicate your intention to the other cast members and the director, and as long as you maintain a continuity in the part.

  But don't ever throw your fellow actors' focus, timing and rhythm off unexpectedly in a scene. They also need to adjust their performance to your changes.

However, there may be some situations when an allowance can be made for this. For example, it might be used as an acting technique by one actor or a director to force an "emotional shock" response from a "blocked" co-actor.

Don't be afraid of making mistakes, especially during rehearsals. Mistakes are the *experience* you build on. You become afraid or fail only because *you* decide to.

That's partly what it's all about.

Attitude

How much do you desire something? How badly do you want it? How much emotional, psychological and physical effort would you put into becoming skilful at it? What would you sacrifice to get it?

To accomplish something, you must have the right attitude. Having the right attitude is especially necessary if you want to become an accomplished actor.

Attitude begins each time you enter an acting class, rehearsal space, attend an audition or work on a performance.

A "right attitude" in a professional environment is:

- Generating *interest, enthusiasm* and giving out energy each time you perform.

- Not being dull and lethargic - whining, complaining and being unresponsive when you work on a project or when you're challenged to try something different. That type of attitude drains the energy of the people working with you. It affects a performance, your part in it and everyone around you. It breeds resentment.

- Having the courage and willingness to put all your energy and focus into trying a different or uncomfortable acting approach in a class, rehearsal or performance. It's not blocking yourself before you've even *tried* to break into something new. It's accepting the lesson in the *effort* you make each time you try something different.

It's listening and centering on what other people are trying to accomplish in a class exercise or on a production. Even when you don't agree with an approach give it space to prove or disprove itself. Or build on it. A properly focused attitude is usually the way breakthroughs are made.

It's preparing yourself emotionally, physically and mentally with each new challenge. It's *flowing* with the unexpected and turning it into an opportunity to explore and discover something new.

It's encouraging your fellow students, co-actors and the people you are working with into *UP* attitudes, not downers. Each time you're personally feeling low energy or lethargic, try to find a way *through* it and bring yourself *up* for the class or the performance. You're responsible not only for your own attitude, but to some extent also for contributing to a positive working environment.

Know that each time you accept an acting assignment it means it was *your choice* to do so. Once you take on the role, commit yourself fully to it. Nothing less will be acceptable in a professional environment.

Focus / Concentration

You can't bring your personal problems or a tired attitude into a performance. It will interfere with your focus and concentration. Each time you perform, it requires your intense focus and concentration. Without your intense focus and concentration, you cannot give an honest performance.

We know that the camera will see through you when you're distracted and unfocused on what you should be responding to in a scene. The camera will pick up the lack of those emotional details, textures and qualities that are basic to your performance.

When you forget your lines, it's usually because you're not fully concentrating on what is happening around you. When you're thinking of other things or are trying to remember your lines, you will obviously not be feeling the spirit of the scene, listening to the other actors and responding appropriately on what *you* should be doing at a particular moment.

Your unfocussed attitude will affect negatively on the dynamics which the scene will require. You will look unprofessional. You will gain an unfavorable reputation in the industry and people will not want to work with you.

Your lack of focus and concentration will cause delays during the shoot and upset the production budget and disturb tempers in the crew and other cast members. It will cause an *interruption* in the process of what *they* have to do and your disruptions will cause everyone else to loose their concentration and focus. Energies will become depleted and misdirected into the wrong direction.

Your attitude and lack of focus will touch on everything around you. It's vital that you do your homework and know your part and your dialogue thoroughly, and come onto the set each time prepared for the days work.

Experienced actors do relaxation exercises to release any tensions they carry. Just like athletes and dancers, they warm-up to loosen their bodies and mind-set before they do anything difficult because the same physical, emotional and psychological demands also apply to actors when they are performing.

Pacing Scenes

Slow-moving, lethargic and drawn-out scenes look deadly on the screen.

But there are different methods you can use to find an appropriate pacing, rhythm, timing and energy for a scene. For example, one method is:

- Perform the circumstances, relationships and conflicts in the scene first in improvised or free-flowing practice runs. By doing this before you commit the performance to camera, you can explore different energy qualities that might be workable for the scene in a rehearsal.

Improv exercise:

Begin performing the scene at a slower pace than normal and gradually as you rehearse the scene over and over, tighten your response / action / reaction time without losing the scene's emotional requirements.

Interacting with the other characters, continue doing this and start to sense an energy moving between you.

Carry on tightening the action and dialogue between you even more, not taking as long each time to move the scene forward.

Make your physical and vocal actions happen quicker till the rhythm, pacing and timing of the scene begins to resonate for you with just about the right *feeling* and *energy*.

Tight pacing is especially important in comedy and sitcoms where the energy, pacing, rhythm and timing of scenes is required to flow much faster than in drama.

Transitions

Transition: *a process or period of change, in which something or someone undergoes a change and passes from one state to another; to undergo a change of status or condition.*

Like a good piece of classical music, every role and scene in a comedy or drama is made up of different transitions or changes. Like in real life, characters in a story at different times and in different situations and at different moments go from one state of activity and from one emotion, mood and rhythmic change, to another.

For example, in a volatile situation when two characters become primed up for a fight a series of transitions might happen between them, beginning with their emotional state of arguing the cause of their conflict with each other, to physically fighting, to where they stop and calm down and experience the aftermath of that fight.

A transition is also a complete change that happens from the circumstances and setting of *one scene to another.*

When a transition is required in a character, something important that affects the actor emotionally and/or physically has to happen in the performance to make them *move* from one change to another.

What affects the character's transition might be anything from a subtle look projected by another actor that has some meaning, to a comment or a physical action or even something that is triggered by some deep-seated memory locked up somewhere in the character's cultural, social and psychological background that *motivates* or causes the change.

When an emotional change happens, there is always a bridge, link or crossing from one situation or feeling to another.

Think about how it also happens to you - even in real life. You take that **instant in time** to first realize what caused the change, and then you *respond* to it. You take in and *absorb* the information that affects you. You move *through* the change. You *feel* it, *experience* it and *deal* with it emotionally - before you make the transition to the other side.

In acting talk the point or instant when the transition or change is realized or happens, is also referred to as a "moment".

Don't try to "tell" the audience what you are feeling or experiencing at any moment if it's not happening inside you.

Just *be* it.

Forcing an emotion and making an unmotivated transition will appear false to the audience. The rhythm and timing of the transition will be inharmonious with the emotion you should be experiencing. Many actors, especially when they've been theatre trained try to "tell" the audience what they're experiencing emotionally in a performance by acting it out.

For example, the dialogue might say "Oh, what a beautiful day". Then for some unexplainable reason, the actor might "act" that out by making funny facial gestures of "pleasure" and indicating at the sky to "show" us what a beautiful day it indeed is, when we have already seen and accepted that information visually in the scene.

And then the actor might make some mellow-dramatic pause into some other unjustifiable emotion.

Think about this:

In real life you might be in a situation where you may perhaps be motivated to say, "I'm not afraid" to try and convince another person that you are heroic. But if you were really afraid the subtext in your body language would contradict this by sending out signals even in a subtle way, that you actually *are* afraid.

It will be seen in your eyes, facial expressions, in beads of sweat, twitching or perhaps in a tension in your body in spite of the words you are saying.

Apply the same in acting. Don't imitate laughing, fear, crying, happiness, sorrow or any other emotion if you can't feel it in a scene. If you can, move yourself first into the feeling of the emotion and then shift into the transition.

Your job is to *really* make that experience happen on the screen, not to act it out.

Scenes and Moments

A movie is made up of various scenes and when they're structured, connected and combined into some sort of logical sequence, they tell a story. The blueprint or plan of this structure of scenes is laid out and written in the screenplay.

The story might be presented in a humorous, adventurous, frightening or dramatic way, depending on the genre and style of the movie in which it is being told.

The scenes are comprised of different rhythms, timing and pacing which are important in the way the story is meant to unfold.

When each scene is played out, it should reveal certain essential verbal and visual information about the story, the characters, their relationships, situations, circumstances and conflicts. The information might be subtly or boldly uncovered and build towards a resolution of some kind at the end of the movie.

Some scenes might end with some sort of climax, sub climax or story statement that leads the action and information of each scene into the other.

The way a movie scene is written, usually contains "space" for the actors to interpret the dialogue in their own way.

The writing might also include some form of descriptive "action" in the scene which might be visual, physical, verbal, emotional or psychological – or a combination of some of these elements.

Some scenes might be long, others might be short or somewhere in between, depending on the rhythm, timing and pacing of the movie.

The combined total of scenes builds to a *conclusion* of the story at the end of the movie.

The writing might contain specific directions for the actors to follow in a scene or suggest places where specific *moments* might occur which could have a profound effect on how the story develops and how the characters react to their circumstances and resolve their differences with each another.

In some scenes the "moments" that occur can be either long, brief or somewhere in between. The moment may be a subtle or obvious incident, or a reaction that states something crucial to the characters about their situation, circumstances and relationships.

For example, one of those "moments" in a scene might be when the main characters realize they love or hate each other, or when the hero in the story decides to take on the challenge that confronts him or her.

It's important for you as an actor to find those meaningful places in the story where you can create those special "moments" and work them into your performance.

Re-cap: *In a movie as in real life a moment is a point or space in time which is meaningful or profound to the characters. It can be an instant of significant realization about something important and is usually a vital place in a scene that triggers a turning point in the story.*

Summary

A personal View

What are the Qualities of a Good Actor?

- To be focused during each performance.
- To be consistent in the role you take on and to be well-prepared to perform it.
- To perform it in a professional manner and with a respectful attitude in the workplace.
- To be open to new ideas and experimentation. To be innovative and to take chances. To have the courage to try out something different. To create something original with each new acting experience.
- To have the capacity to learn from the experience of each failure and success.
- To research, study, rehearse and perform each role with passion and integrity.
- To be able to really *listen* to the information projected by the other characters and their environment - and to *interact* in each situation appropriately.
- To be able to project honest and appropriate emotions for a character, according to the requirements of the story.
- To have the ability to use your own uniqueness as a person and as an actor in the role.
- To have the skill to create an "experience" for the audience, for yourself and for the people you are working with.
- To be alert and responsive to the *moments* that may occur in a scene.
- To not be afraid of using your physical, emotional, intellectual and intuitive qualities and pushing them to their fullest potential.
- To have the capacity to separate your personal life from your professional and artistic one. To know the difference and to keep a healthy balance between the two.

What else would you add to this? What are some of the things that you personally will need to look at in yourself to become a skilful actor?

Why do you want to be an actor?

Look at the following criteria and truthfully consider how much of this applies to you.

Is it:

- Because you're passionate and have a natural, inherent feeling for acting?
- Because it's an outlet for you to express your creativity? Because you're curious by nature and have a desire to explore new things and you're open to different values and ideas?
- Because you believe in your talent?
- Because you want to get in touch with your emotions and to empathize with the feelings of others? To learn about your own psychology as well as the psychology of others?
- Because you're searching for truth, as you understand it, in different experiences?
- Because you want to develop your communication techniques?
- Because you're interested in improving your personal abilities? For example, by exploring and learning other activities such as swimming, horse riding, dancing, sports, martial arts, handling tools, mastering various vehicles, learning languages, foreign accents and other skills that will make you more interesting and versatile to watch as an actor?
- Because you enjoy keeping yourself informed about movies, TV programs and theatrical plays, and you like to read literature and appreciate different styles and cultures, and you have a love of music and works of art?

Is it because you want fame and to make a lot of money?

Does the creativity that is required to produce a movie fascinate you and inspire you to become an actor?

So, if you're really serious about all of this, as Martha Graham said, *"Keep the channel open..."*

And go for it...

Part 3

VISUALIZATION

The spirit is the master,
imagination the tool, and the
body the plastic material...

- Paracelsus

Visualization is the way we think.

Before words, images were. Visualization
is the heart of the bio-computer. The
human brain programs and self programs
through it's images. Riding a bicycle,
learning to read, baking a cake, playing
golf, acting - all skills are acquired through
the image making process. Visualization
is the ultimate consciousness tool.

- Mike Samuals, m.d. and
Nancy Samuals
Seeing With The Mind's Eye

Camera / Screen Presence

Have you ever thought about what it is?

Is it the way you:

Project yourself or the character you're playing in a truthful manner? Is it your style and about how suitable emotionally and physically you are in the part?

Is it also about the way you:

- Use your eyes, voice and body to create a presence on the screen of yourself or the character you're playing?
- Interpret the character - strong or weak, exciting or boring, comfortable or uncomfortable, confident or insecure, honest or dishonest - within the context of the story?
- Interact with other actors in a scene and how you control the situation and your workspace?
- Present yourself that you *like* who you are and *enjoy* what you do? That you are comfortable in the part, secure in yourself and that you *belong* in front of the camera? That you have a good relationship with it?
- Are versatile as an actor?

Is there is a dynamic about you that the audience will recognize? Do you radiate that "thing" which people refer to as "star" or performance quality?

Consider these questions and see what aspects you need to improve in yourself to become an accomplished actor.

Drawing the Audience In

Besides the quality of your screen presence, you pull the audience into your performance if there is a reason, intention, meaning, interest or purpose *behind* the things that your character does.

This is reflected *in the way* that your character is motivated by a situation and the circumstances of the story, and *why* they are motivated by those circumstances. Also by *what actions your character takes to resolve the situation.*

For example: Your boyfriend dumps you. Why?

Because he dumps you, that motivates you with a reason and a purpose to be angry, no matter what *his* reason was. You might now be provoked emotionally to respond with an action to get back at him.

So, depending on the psychology of the character you're playing, you react in a certain way. What is it that you do - and how do you do it - to get back at your ex-boyfriend?

There is now a meaning behind your intended action.

- Audiences are also drawn to you through the surprise elements that unfold in the story and in the manner that you *project* the personality you've created for your character.

For example: Each time she becomes attracted to a man, she has this unusual personality trait that she has to go to the toilet and urinate to relieve herself.

Why? What is the emotional or psychological cause of this?

Audiences are also drawn to you when they become interested in the way your character overcomes or fails to overcome adversary, and about *why* and *how* your character succeeds or fails in a situation.

For example: He didn't get the promotion he thinks he deserved because of his volatile personality, so he lost his temper and beat up his boss, sending him to the hospital.

He needed the extra money the promotion would have secured for him, but now he lost everything including his wife and livelihood and landed up in jail with a criminal record.

What is it about his character that made him do what he did?

How could he have handled the situation in a better way? What could he have done different to get around his predicament?

For many actors, preparing for a part is digging deeper and deeper into a character's reasons or motivations for certain actions and reactions.

Keep asking yourself:

When I'm portraying this - how, why, when, where, would I do what I do and to whom do I do it - and *what* is it that I do that makes me react as a character in the way that I do?

Caring

When you perform, the energy or vitality that you generate in the part is a direct result of how much you *care* about your character, about your place in the story, how focused you are - and about what happens around you in a scene.

If the content of a scene and what is happening in the performance is important and interesting enough to you, you would be listening carefully to the information that's generated around you physically and emotionally, and you will absorb it with sufficient intensity and energy to generate an appropriate response from the other actors in the scene.

And if the other actors are also interested and care enough about what is happening, they'll also be forced to respond to you with an appropriate intensity to lift the total performance to a higher level.

You've probably experienced this when you've watched memorable performances. It's usually difficult for an audience to not pay attention to actors who project energy and are *interested* and *caring* enough about what they're doing or saying. If you watch actors listening or watching something intently, your eyes will hold on them. This is true for both a stage and screen performance.

It's vitally important to always *care* about what's constantly moving around you in a scene, whatever that movement might be. Even the most minute energy and motivation might mean something if you're an alert actor.

And the audience will stay focused and watch you closely each time you're *connected* to every moment and opportunity in a performance.

Likewise, when you watch dynamic directors at work and see the way *they* interact with exciting actors, you'll see that the same criterion also applies to them.

Create Your Own Image and Style

The entertainment industry is filled with actors who can do a competent piece of work. Often, not much more than a basic ability to perform and remember their dialogue is required from an actor when they are contracted to play a part.

This is especially prevalent in the high pressure environment of TV production where the main purpose appears to be to turn out the product on budget and on time to meet TV Network program schedules, rather than on the quality of a performance.

How often have you observed actors who seem bland and look no different from one role to another?

• Many unexceptional parts seem to require that indifferent, conformist type of "acting" which is safe, undemanding and unchallenging. There *is a place* for that kind of "acting", but if you're entering the entertainment industry for the first time, try to keep your priorities in balance.

Play the bland roles when it's necessary. You need to gain experience wherever and whenever you can and you also need to make a living. Even a small insignificant part, if you perform it well, can open a door for you to be noticed and be cast later into more impressive roles. But keep looking for *opportunities* to step out of the unexceptional roles and *claim* something better and more fulfilling for yourself.

George Clooney is one example of an actor who did just that. He began his career in the 1980's playing a school counselor / teacher in a successful but uninspiring sitcom titled "*The Facts Of Life*". Before he re-worked his image and hit stardom on big budget movies, there was always the danger that he would be typecast as the character he played on that long running TV series, but he changed that image through perseverance and by reworking his special qualities and performing different types of dramatic roles.

Discover what's inside *you* that is special and unique. Develop *your* special qualities. That something special that's inside you is what will make *you* stand out. And if it's powerful enough, that's what people will remember.

The professional world is extremely competitive. Nurture good contacts in the right places. Someone who seems to be unimportant today may be in an important position tomorrow. It's an unfortunate truism about life, but often in the real world it's not *what* you know, but *who* you know that gets you ahead. So before you can show *what* you know begin first with *who* you know.

- Never rest on your past accomplishments. Learn to be *flexible* and *adaptable* to change. Keep *updating* your image, especially as you grow older. There can be something wonderful and mature about age which is a life wisdom that you can incorporate into a character. And this holds true for both men and women.

- Don't become comfortable and complacent - especially if you've had some success. What is catchy and unique today, soon becomes boring and outdated. Audiences are notorious for losing interest in uninspiring actors very quickly, because of the over-saturation of TV programming.

Keep learning from different sources and experiences. Use the opinions and criticisms of others in a constructive way and assess yourself periodically - and don't stop growing.

Acting Habits

We all have personal habits which are certain physical, thought and speech patterns that we tend to repeat when we communicate.

Many actors and directors have developed certain habits which stand out in their work. These are mostly subconscious and probably originated from early successes in the actor or directors career when they discovered and successfully used certain creative, physical and vocal actions in the work they were doing. They then became a sort of "security blanket" which they began to use over and over.

We consider those "habits" to be a part of a particular actor or director's style, stamp or personality.

Some actor's habits have become famous and worked well for them. There was John Wayne's special style - his trademark slouch when he walked and the slow, "cool" western drawl in his speech.

There was Marilyn Monroe's wispy body language and exaggerated sensual voice and Charlton Heston's flat, clinical, bland presence. Clint Eastwood's cold, calculating body language; Madonna's nymph-like sexuality. For some "stars" such habits have become a sort of commercial trademark which audiences accept.

However, habits appearing consistently in a performance can become annoying and predictable. You know what the actor will do, how they will say something and how they will react in a situation every time they appear on screen. After time, their habits can become monotonous and boring and lack surprise. They might even become unbelievable in certain roles.

For example, for centuries pious believers have had a specific, saintly image of the Virgin Mary, so can you ever see Madonna with her raw sexuality playing her in a movie role and giving a believable performance that will be acceptable and not offensive to devout churchgoers?

Or can you see a muscled Arnold Schwarzenegger with his Germanic trade mark accent seriously playing Jesus Christ?

Observe other actors and notice their particular habits. Become aware of your own acting habits. Some may work well - others may become predictable and look uncomfortable after a while if they become over exposed in your performance.

Versatile actors work on many levels and adapt themselves to the physical, psychological and emotional habits which are suited to the character they portray.

For example, Anthony Hopkins seemed to become Richard Nixon in *Nixon* in the way he interpreted the former president's style and mannerisms, and he "became" Hannibal Lecter in *Silence of the Lambs*. He also transformed himself into totally different characters in *The Mark of Zorro* and the *Wolfman*.

Julia Roberts empathized with Erin and "became" her in *Erin Brokovich*. In *Notting Hill, Runaway Bride* and *Charlie's War* she looked different and was appropriate as a dissimilar character in each of these roles.

Philip Seymour Hoffman "was" Capote as *Capote* and "was" the disillusioned CIA agent in *Charlie's War*. He even transformed himself verbally and physically and "became" totally diverse characters in each of these roles.

Charlize Theron also went through an intense physical and emotional character transformation from a glamour star to a psychotic killer in *Monster*.

Also look at some of the movies of Jodie Foster, Nicholas Cage, Christopher Walken or any of your favorite actors, and study the different characters they have portrayed.

Although something of these actors is the character, the character isn't them. You will always see *a part of them* that is still them in each of the roles they play.

Interpreting Subtext

Analysis

When you read a movie or TV script or a theatrical play, what do you think the most important part of it is?

- Is it the *words* or is it the *direction* and *dialogue* that is given to you in the text?

Yes, it is all of that, but it's also what's *hidden* behind the *meaning* of the words!

- It's the *INTERPRETATION* of the words.
- It's the *INTENTION* of what the author is trying to communicate to the actor's and director *through* the words.

The words indicate what the characters say, the *possible* emotional, psychological and physical states about them, the *probable* motivations for what they do and say - and *suggest* something about their personal qualities.

The words also *imply* general information about the history of each character and about the story environment. To imply means to make something understood without expressing it directly.

- What is *not* written but *implied* is what is called the *undertone* or *subtext* of the script. That subtext is what is important for the actor to understand and to interpret.

Movie and TV scripts are usually very economically written. Every word has a purpose and is usually well thought out. Much information can be implied on the screen through action or said without dialogue, because the movies are both a visual and a vocal medium.

The actor and the director's aim is to find the best possible *interpretation* of the words and to bring those words to life. Words are only words. It's what *meaning* and *interpretation* you put into them, and the way you *perform* them, that brings the story and the characters to life.

Look at the word *love,* for example. What might you mean when you say you *love* someone or something?

I love my mother? I love my brother? I really do love my wife? I love the weather? I love my friends? I love my dog because he's such a great companion? I love Greek egg and lemon soup? I love sleeping with you? I love the way you love sex?

What might the word mean or imply in each instance? Are you joking when you say it or angry, casual, serious, regretful...? It depends on why, how, when, where, what and to whom you're saying it and it will mean something quite different when each of those sentiments are expressed in different circumstances for different reasons, and with different people who have different personalities.

In each situation it might resonate with a different intention, emotion, feeling and passion.

Scene exercise:

Improvise a series of short scenes with situations and a short line of dialogue that contain each of the above "love" sentences and play out with a partner what motivates you to express them.

How would you interpret and play that line physically, emotionally and psychologically in a different way in each of those scenes that you have created?

How does your partner respond? How does their response affect you emotionally?

Then repeat the exercise improvising the same scenes and dialogue you created but change the key word *love* to *hate.*

Play the dialogue containing the word *hate* and express it with any type of emotion. Your partner reacts and responds with an *opposite* emotion using an appropriate vocal energy, emotional tonal quality and body language.

Now try it in different ways: The same line is expressed by the same two people, now using different motivations, emotions and attitudes.

Make up different scenes with action and short sentences containing a different key word.

Each time, videotape your performance and review the result.

Responding / Reacting
Performing the part - not reciting dialogue

Reminder: *In real life you respond and react emotionally to the situations and circumstances around you, which can change from moment to moment.*

You pick up on the subtleties of the information you receive - depending on why, what, where, when and how you feel or don't feel at the time.

What you give out, is what other people around you pick up - and they respond accordingly, depending on their situation and circumstances and why, what, where, when and how they feel at that moment.

Why, what, when, where, who and how are aspects that are not immediately obvious to the outside world about a person, relationship or situation. When you read a script and begin to develop a character, you need to dig underneath the surface of the words by asking such questions to find the *personality* of the character you are creating.

Exploring a character and their place in a story is partly what is meant by "Performing the part - not reciting dialogue". It's about first picking up on the *undertone* or *subtext* of what the script and dialogue *suggest* to you about a character and your understanding of what the emotional and psychological dynamics are that will give your character life and a purpose.

When an actor interprets a script from that perspective, the appropriate dialogue responses between them and the other characters in a scene will tend to flow more logically and be more true to what the author of the script intended.

When you work from this approach, the dialogue in a scene becomes much easier to learn and remember, because it follows reasonably and intuitively from the things that motivate the dialogue between the characters and causes the appropriate responses in them.

You won't be learning dialogue by rote, but rather from the emotional flow of the scene.

Verbal / Emotional Expressions

When we communicate, we might use the same word but express it with different *meanings* and *emotional intensity*, depending to whom we say it, what we really mean by it and how we feel at the time.

As a visualization exercise, look at the following words and think about how each word can be interpreted in different ways with a different meaning when you use them in different sentences or lines of dialogue:

twist	blood	tonight	care	deaf	fear	surrender
penis	rose	daybreak	bomb	piss	him	tempting
she	torso	pussy	poetry	mouse	job	pointless
poison	muscle	splendid	john	jerk	hurt	emergency

Now look at the following words which suggest different *attitudes* and *emotions* and practice the words above out loud using different sentences in the following ways:

inquiring	surprised	doubting	angry	fearful
excited	sadistic	fanatically	cruelly	lustful
heroically	shamefully	sensually	jealously	disgusted
sorrowfully	sarcastically	devastated	hurtful	erotically
triumphantly	calculating	suspiciously	lovingly	neutrally
relieved	ecstatic	vulgarly	happy	bored

Try this exercise with other words and attitudes and emotions you can think of.

Emotional Focus Exercise

Look at the words listed below. Choose any one at random.

Without speaking the word, *focus* your attention on the *feeling* of what that word triggers in you, in an incident that you can recall and *visualize* from your life experience. Stay focused on that *emotion* until you can feel it really moving through you.

With practice and concentration, you can access such different feelings at short notice:

Accepting	Adventurous	Affectionate	Aggressive
Ambitious	Angry	Anxious	Apathetic
Appreciated	Assertive	Attractive	Assisting
Bored	Carefree	Cautious	Cheerful
Competitive	Confident	Confused	Contented
Co-operative	Coquettish	Daring	Decisive
Dependant	Depressed	Disconcerted	Embarrassed
Energetic	Envious	Excited	Fit
Free	Friendly	Frightened	Grieving
Guilt-free	Guilty	Happy	Humiliated
Hurt	Indecisive	Independent	Inferior
Insecure	Interested	Involved	Irresponsible
Jealous	Joyful	Lonely	Loved
Loving	Optimistic	Out-going	Pessimistic
Powerful	Powerless	Rejected	Relaxed
Resentful	Responsible	Sad	Secure
Shy	Stressed	Strong	Superior
Supportive	Suspicious	Tense	Tired
Trusting	Un-ambitious	Unappreciated	Unassertive
Unattractive	Under-confident	Uneasy	Unfit
Un-free	Unfriendly	Unloved	Unsupportive
Unwanted	Uptight	Vulnerable	Wanted
Weak	Worried	Wanting	Wasteful

Types of Emotions / Attitudes

Think of all the *nuances* and *intensity* of energy you can explore in each of the following *emotions*:

love	fear	hope	doubt	despair
hate	envy	faith	happiness	empathy
trust	hurt	excitement	suspense	confusion
betrayal	sympathy	compassion	anticipation	
anger (volatile)	anger (suppressed)	pain (physical/psychological/emotional)		

add to this...

Think of all the *nuances* and *intensity* of energy you can explore in each of the following *attitudes*:

greed	supremacy	harmony	chaos	insecurity
shrewdness	foolishness	alertness	conceit	flimsiness
gloom	forcefulness	weakness	prejudice	arrogance
firmness	frustration	volatility	ambition	lustfulness
gratification	paranoia	cynicism	desire	intolerance
confidence	indecisiveness	misery	need	sadness
loneliness	condescension	cowardice	disgust	fear

add to this...

Now create a story situation and try performing these attitudes and emotions with a partner in a short improvisation with complimentary attitudes and emotions, and then with opposing attitudes and emotions.

Accessing an Emotion

Outside-In / Inside-Out:

There are different techniques that actors use to access an appropriate emotion for a scene. They use what works for them.

We've seen how the rhythm, timing, pacing and feeling of different types of music and sound can be used and felt by an actor to stimulate an emotion.

Another way might be for the actor to start physically with where their normal body rhythm is placed at the moment, then artificially to start creating another body rhythm that is suitable to the emotion they are trying to access.

By moving into it physically, it helps them to generate it internally. For example:

> Physically change your breathing and body rhythm with an action that is in harmony with an emotion you are trying to reach.
>
> Are you trying to reach anger? Start breathing quickly, harder, deeper and faster, and move around agitatedly to get your body rhythm to change. Begin to beat your hands on a table or bang them hard against a wall until you feel the physical pain.
>
> At the same time, express that pain verbally – yelling, crying out or perhaps even swearing. With each verbal and physical outburst, keep breathing harder and more intensely, tightening the tension and quickening the rhythm of your body physically until you start to feel and achieve the tension and rhythm of the anger you are trying to project.
>
> Panic, fear or even something sexual can also be stirred by quicker breathing and tensing your body movements.
>
> Focusing your energy on gentle breathing and tightening your body rhythm can suggest that something emotional or important is happening inside you.

This is referred to as working an emotion from *The Outside - In,* which means you start by working it physically from the outside until you can access it emotionally inside yourself.

Other actors prefer to access an emotion from inside themselves first, and then to channel it outside to the physical world.

They might do this by focusing intently on a past experience that brings up *memories* and *feelings* of an appropriate real life event which they can then connect to the emotion they want to access in the performance. That's called working from *The Inside - Out.*

A common technique for accessing an emotional memory might happen during a rehearsal for a specific scene and involve the actors sitting in a circle facing each other.

Guided by the director or one of the actors who acts as a facilitator, the actors take turns to talk about a specific emotional incident or past experience that profoundly affected their life. Depending on the theme of the session, which for example might be about fear, anger, pain, joy, good things or bad, the session can become deeply emotional,

The group listens when one person speaks and each one in the group is encouraged to respond to the person talking. Most of the actors in the group usually empathize with the experience which the speaker is expressing.

Once the appropriate emotions for the scene are accessed and the experience that triggered those emotions has been identified and released, the feelings that were accessed are used as an emotional stimulation to be played in the scene or acted out in an improvisation just before the shoot.

This is also a cathartic process and the actors in the rehearsal usually feel an emotional relief after the experience. They also learn how to use the feelings they have in a positive way, which helps them to mature into more honest actors.

Spirit

...form is emptiness, emptiness is form.

- The Heart Sutra

During a shoot one day, one of our students had trouble "finding" her character.

She told me she couldn't "control" what she wanted to create in the *personality* of the character and it was driving her crazy.

I suggested she let go and to clear her mind of any preconceived thoughts, and to let the character take hold of her. It worked. When she saw the results of the scene on tape later, it wasn't what she had envisaged. It was better, inspired and more real.

Often, when you truly let go and empty your mind of the clutter that is inside your head a magic happens. Without forcing the outcome, the idea of what you want to create seems to materialize out of nowhere. *It will tell you what it wants to become and what it wants to happen, instead of you trying to tell it what to be.*

It takes on a spirit of its own.

The same happens in writing, directing and other creative disciplines. How many times have you experienced that the harder you keep trying to force something to happen, nothing seems to come right or to connect for you. But when you let go of pushing too hard, other forces seem to take over and make everything fall into place?

The trick is to be smart enough to realize when you need to let go, and to trust that process to take over.

Summary

Short Notes

- *Act Less – Be More; Less Is More; Be Simple - Let go; Be Real - Do Nothing; Internalize; Work From The Inside; The Life Behind The Eyes; Be it; Live it; The Key Is Simplicity.*

All these statements say the same thing, and they're all accurate and correct in what they "teach" about screen acting. When you're unsure about what to do, the best thing to do is to do very little. Actors get into trouble when they try to do too much, try too hard or complicate a situation.

- Don't think logically all the time. Our emotions don't always work logically. They're spontaneous reactions to what is affecting us from moment to moment. In situations where its appropriate, just let go.

- Don't be literal or linear each time you work dialogue. Sometimes play against it.

In real life when we speak, our dialogue and emotions work in ever changing rhythms and beats. Work the same way "when you're acting".

- You are unique. You are the original. Work always from who you are, from your own special life experience. You can only perform truthfully from what *you* feel and know best.

- Passion. Passion. Passion. If you don't have enthusiasm or develop a strong liking for a subject, it becomes difficult to generate a real emotional performance around it.

Discover what is right and what works for you. Not too much, or too little, but find just the right balance of creative energy that suits your temperament and personality. Be comfortable with it.

- Most acting is reacting. You can only *react* if you're *listening* and *responding* appropriately in a situation.

Part 4

Thousands of people have talent.
I might as well congratulate you on
having eyes in your head. The one and
only thing that counts is:

Do you have staying power?

- Noel Coward

Humor in Drama

A joke is a short story with a fuse and an explosion.

- Frank McCourt

Sometimes humor can work as a positive ingredient for a writer, director and actor.

The proper use of humor in an intense story situation can be emotionally effective because it helps to enhance or endear a character's "personality" to the audience.

Humor breaks or relieves dramatic pressure in a difficult or dangerous story situation:

-   It relaxes the audience briefly and eases them into absorbing the seriousness of a "message" in the story in a more palatable way. It catches people off- guard. It doesn't strain them.

-   It might express an irony about a situation that would in other circumstances be difficult to communicate effectively.

-   It causes audiences to laugh at the absurdity and contradictions of the story characters who unexpectedly interact illogically, strangely or unreasonably in a tense dramatic situation.

-   It shows the audience in a subliminal way how to laugh at themselves if they were caught in a similar predicament.

You can probably think of other examples.

Humor can be expressed through the actor's action, body language or dialogue, or in a combination of action, body language and dialogue.

It can be played subtly or broadly. It can be brought in as a subtext in the actor's interpretation of a character.

But to be effective, it should not be overdone. Humor requires sensitivity and good taste in the way it's presented and performed. The overkill of anything diminishes its value and effectiveness.

Consider incorporating it into a character's personality if it's appropriate to do so in a scene.

The key to using humor successfully is in the actor's *feeling* for it, and in the rhythm and timing in the delivery of it.

Remember: *Sometimes when it's appropriate to do so in a scene, what the character doesn't say but feels - can make a more powerful statement than words. The screen is both a vocal and visual medium. In strong close-ups, forceful or humorous statements can be made with just nuances in a characters expression and in the way you project your feelings through body language.*

Over The Top versus Pulled In

The way to do is to be

-Tao Te Ching

In movie talk "over the top" refers to a broad, exaggerated or artificial performance.

Think about the following:

In a film or TV performance, when is it "correct" to play a performance *subtly*, *laid back* or *pulled in*? And when is playing *over the top* o.k.? Even professional actors are sometimes confused.

- On the screen things work according to certain rules. But the rules can be bent occasionally to accommodate a situation, depending on the genre or style that's chosen to tell a particular story.

"Laid back" or *"over the top"* therefore depends to a great extent on how one looks at and experiences things. For some people, certain expressive attitudes are acceptable and can even be funny. For others, those same attitudes will appear unreal, exaggerated or even insulting.

Body language and even the way people touch each other is expressed differently in different cultures and in different social / economic groups. In some places it's expressed in a broad over the top way, while elsewhere it may be played out as laid back and pulled in.

For example:

People who live in Scandinavia and other "cold" countries tend to be super "laid back" and stoic emotionally, whereas people in Mediterranean and other "warm" countries tend to be passionate with sometimes vast and exaggerated public expressions in body language, touching and speech. They tend to be "hot blooded", louder, more animated and "over the top" when they talk to each other. To these people, this kind of interaction is normal.

However, to people from other countries watching them who have a different cultural dynamic, they might appear to be hostile and volatile towards one another each time they communicate.

In North America, expressions tend to be more subtle. In Britain, expressions are even more "laid back".

Look at British royalty or the aristocracy, with its "stiff upper lip and all that" mentality. In Japan, people tend to be more reserved and secretive about letting their emotions "hang out". They are inclined to be more "polite" and "respectful" to each other, especially to the elderly. *Over the top* behavior is generally unacceptable in their culture.

In South Africa's Western Cape, people in certain ethnic communities express themselves differently in body language, rhythmic movements and verbal communication. Some people are aggressively noisy and sound harsh and guttural when they speak. Others sound pleasing and soft spoken.

There are also speech patterns and body language differences between people who are born into wealth or into poverty; a man versus a woman, or a straight person from gay. Look at the way a doctor communicates with words and body language. It's different from a banker or a lawyer's attitude, and theirs is different from a plumber or another working class person. And they're all different from a "bergie" or hobo.

Yet the way these people communicate and the way they express themselves is acceptable communication behavior in general society when people interact with them, because the way they communicate comes from a very *real* social, genetic and emotional place inside their psyche.

Much of this is the result of a person's temperament, emotional attitude, cultural conditioning and the way one is taught from childhood about how to act or react to things and circumstances.

It has to do with a person's education and economic circumstances, and whether one is encouraged or restrained by their community and society, or by their own good or bad childhood experiences, or if they've been abused or not abused; or by their social standing in a group of people, and by peer pressure to perform and react in certain "acceptable" ways.

So in a screen performance, the bottom line about whether you perform *over the top* or *laid back*, also really comes down to the cultural and social circumstances you are interpreting and how much you the actor empathizes with the characters personality.

If your performance comes from a *very real* place inside you, and is felt with *integrity* and not "acted" out, it will translate naturally and believably onto the screen.

For example, if you play a comic or comedy type character whose nature in real life really is "over the top" and you *become* the part, it should not appear false, overboard or *over the top* to the audience.

Accomplished actors give remarkable performances in some unbelievable humorous, dramatic and action situations. Yet they can *be* Batman, Spiderman, fools, heroes, villains or anything in between. They pull it off because at that moment, they are *real* and *believe* in the situation they are re-enacting and the camera captures the *truth* of their performance.

Creating Movement on Screen

They're pictures with sound that move and talk. That's why they're called *movies, motion pictures* or *talkies*.

There are a number of ways that "movement" or a "sense of movement" is created on screen:

-   Moving the camera and following the action in a scene during filming.

-   Moving the actors around physically on the set.

-   Tightening the pacing, timing and rhythm of the performance.

    For example: moving the performance at a quicker tempo during the shoot with a tighter dramatic tension in the physical *interaction* between the characters.

-   Tightening the pacing and rhythm of the dialogue when the characters speak, which gives a *feeling* of a tighter or faster movement in the action of the scene.

-   Creating interesting story action, and capturing each scene in the story from a variety of different shots that are photographed and composed from different camera angles which are then tightly edited into an *assortment of changing images*, producing an *impression* of movement in the visual action of the scene.

-   During editing to tighten or shorten the length of time in which each scene plays out. This creates an impression that the overall movie is less laborious and is moving faster.

Rhythm, Timing, Pacing

Definition: *Rhythm: A regular or measured motion; the accents, beats, tempo, pulse or heartbeat in a verse, performance or piece of music.*

Timing: The rate, pattern, or progression of movement in a performance or piece of music.

Pacing: The speed at which something or someone moves; how fast or slow someone thinks and reacts.

There's rhythm, timing and pacing in all of life - in your body, in your emotions and in your speech patterns. You and everything around you moves in this way to some extent or another.

A person's rhythm, timing and pacing reveal a lot about the state of mind of a character.

Rhythmic, timing and pacing changes happening in a character are very noticeable to an audience. Well-timed gestures, shifting verbal patterns and alternating tonal qualities are rhythmic, timing and pacing changes that can express and communicate a character's ideas, attitude, emotions and personality.

Even the most subtle type of change that happens verbally, emotionally or physically on the screen, can be clearly and immediately felt and seen. When you interact with other actors, it's essential to be responsive to their rhythmic, timing and pacing patterns.

We know how *silence* – when it's used appropriately in a performance – is a change which might communicate an attitude and information about a character. So is the raising of an eyebrow or a twitching, nervous body movement in response to a situation. Even a verbal, physical or emotional pause when properly placed is a rhythmic, timing and pacing change.

Observe people in real life. Notice how many rhythmic, timing and pacing changes happen to them from moment to moment that are caused by the changing emotions they feel.

Our emotions and feelings are affected by rhythm, timing and pacing.

For example, think about how the rhythm, timing and pacing of different types of sound or music affect you.

The intense beat of Rock music might trigger certain responses in you. Maybe you become excited, erotic, aggressive, energetic - or irritated.

Or

- The cheerless drone of funeral music might make you feel sad. Military music might arouse patriotic feelings, and certain classical music might soothe and calm you.

- Ballads might bring up romantic feelings. The sound of some styles of ethnic music might bother you, or bring up nostalgic emotions.

Different shades, nuances and qualities of rhythm, timing and pacing stimulate your feelings and moods at different times and at different moments, depending on how those dynamics are vibrating and touching you.

In a performance, the emotional fluctuations and physical energy which the actors generate are in the same way also closely connected to the rhythm, timing and pacing which they play off each other.

For instance, *when they're out of character* one actor's slow verbal and physical rhythm, timing and pacing might be in conflict with the other actor's quicker actions. *Unless it's intentionally included as part of the performance,* the result of that to the audience would be that the actors are inharmonious and completely out of sync with each other.

When an acting scene seems unintentionally uninteresting, disjointed, dull or lethargic a big part of it is usually because the actors are not giving it the appropriate rhythm, timing and pacing that draws the audience watching it, into the emotions that should be generated by the actors.

As part of their training, skillful actors have become aware of their own mood changes and the rhythmic fluctuations in their body at different moments and where it's appropriate adapt their natural rhythmic, pacing and timing qualities into a performance when they interact with other actors.

They enhance their acting skills by observing and assimilating the information they receive from the changing rhythms of their environment

When they prepare for a part they experiment with the different qualities of rhythm, timing and pacing that reverberate in the diverse styles of music and poetry and in the different styles of movement such as dance and the martial arts.

These aren't boring exercises when they're approached with the right attitude, intention and purpose.

Find out what best resonates for you and learn from that.

Footnote:

During a movie or TV shoot, a Director might say to you, "your timing in the scene is off" - or "your pacing needs to be picked up – or toned down…"

By that, they usually means it's the *rhythm,* or perhaps even the intensity of the *energy* of what you're projecting in your dialogue or action that might not be working the way it should in a scene.

The director might then suggest you try a different interpretation with different shades and nuances in the timing, rhythm and pacing of your performance.

Summary

Emotions coming from a very real place inside you reverberate with different physical body rhythms with varying intensities. For example:

- In real life when you're excited, your movements might become faster, your voice louder or high pitched.

- When you confront fear, you might break into a sweat, your pulse quickens and your heart beats louder.

- When you're calm and at peace, you relax your body and mental faculties.

- In a life threatening situation everything you experience might seem to move in slow motion.

- In love or at the height of passion, your skin color might change. You blush; flush and your breathing might become deeper and quicker.

There are probably many examples from your own life experience that you can integrate into an acting situation.

Is a character happy, confident, nervous, loving or hateful?

Any of these emotions can be detected by the rhythmic intensity of the character's voice, inflection and body language.

Recap: Everything is conditioned by rhythm. We are born into it. The seasons move in rhythmic cycles. The universe moves in rhythm. Your heart pulsates in rhythm with highs, lows and in between. Music, sound, the sea, rivers - all flow in rhythmic cycles.

It's in our nature to communicate in rhythm and in cycles of rhythm.

Integrating Rhythm, Timing, Pacing
With The Camera

In many respects the rhythm, timing and pacing of a scene, as well as that of the actors performing in it, also determines the way in which an operator will move the camera to capture a performance.

When the rhythm, timing and pacing of the actors and the action in a scene are in harmony with each other, it *motivates* an alert and sensitive camera operator to *flow* with the rhythm, timing and pacing of the actors' performance and the action. When these elements are connected, the camera captures the performance in a smooth, flawless movement, creating a balance and synchronization between the actors, the performance, the action and the camera.

It's like observing a perfect dance, and it becomes an emotional and sensual connection between what the camera sees and captures and what the actors are performing.

If the action and actor's rhythm and timing in the scene is off or disjointed, the operator's motivation for moving the camera struggles to connect with the performance and the action, which creates an unconnected dynamic between the actors, the action and the camera.

Have you noticed how some movies are difficult to watch because they seem to be disjointed technically, emotionally and rhythmically?

It's very much like what happens when you watch two people dancing and one of them is rhythmically off and their timing and pacing is erratic. You can sense right away that the dancers are unconnected; or when you listen to music and the instruments, vocalists and musicians are not harmonious and in sympathy with each other, the rhythm, timing, pacing, sound and feel of the music will be inharmonious and uncomfortable to listen to.

By the same token, the pacing, timing and rhythmic beat with which you and the other actors play the action in a scene, will also influence the way the technical aspects of the scene come together.

Part 5

Writer's deal with words and manipulate them in ways
that stir up emotions
and mind images.

They communicate concepts and give passion to ideas.

An understanding of writing and how a story is structured opens up actors to the inner dynamics of imagery and emotions. It stimulates thoughts. This in turn provides insight into the subtleties of a character and of the changing rhythms and emotional nuances in verbal, physical and emotional communication.

These aspects are an important part of acting. Without this understanding, your performance will be superficial.

The Screenplay

It's also known as a movie or TV script. It begins as a *"synopsis"*, which is a brief summary or outline that describes what the story is about. It explains who the central characters are and their relationship to each other, and indicates the conflicts and events that motivate their interactions, and how these are resolved at the end of the story.

The synopsis is usually followed by one or more in-depth outlines of the story as well as character sketches which expand the story information, and develop the characters more fully. This is followed by *"the treatment"*, which sets up the structure of the script, the order and content of the scenes, and some examples of the dialogue between the characters.

The script evolves from the treatment and usually goes through a number of versions, changes or adjustments before it's ready for shooting. These changes are also known as *"drafts"* and each new draft is numbered, dated and printed on white paper.

When the "final draft" of a script has been approved, and new scene or dialogue changes are required after that, they're typed or printed on a different colored sheet of paper which follow a specific order so that each new change can be easily identified and replaced in the script, such as yellow, blue, green, red and so on depending on how many changes follow.

Scene and dialogue changes, additions or deletions can occur right up to the time of shooting, and sometimes this can happen even while a scene is being shot.

The basic story structure of a movie/TV script is built up in a sequence of scenes and follows a precise format. The scene information and dialogue is economically written to allow space for the actors and director to interpret the story and the characters.

Also, because the movies are essentially an expansive and visual medium, there is no need for cumbersome dialogue to carry a scene because much information is absorbed by the audience visually.

It's unlike a conventional theatrical play where the production is performed in a single space and the information needs to be carried primarily through dialogue.

As a general rule, one page of movie script translates more or less into one minute of screen time - depending on how extravagant and involved the setup and staging of the action is.

For instance, a fight scene might be described in a short paragraph in the script, but when it's choreographed for a shoot, it might involve at least two or more minutes of screen time. Whereas a page of dialogue between two or more characters might take a minute or less of screen time to perform, depending on how the action is timed and paced in the scene.

Examples of movie/TV scenes are included elsewhere in this book.

The basic story structure:

A story consists of:

> *a beginning*
> *a middle*
> *an end*

The beginning establishes the setting, situation, circumstances and conflicts of the story, who the characters are, the motivations for the actions they take and their relationship to each other.

The middle takes us through the unfolding of events and the interactions between the characters. It might include elements of sharp or witty dialogue, action, intrigue, suspense and interesting twists and turns in the situations to maintain audience interest.

The end takes us through to some form of resolution of the conflicts between the characters and the relationships between them. This can be in a positive or negative way. It can be either a happy, sad or surprise ending - or anything in between.

That's the general rule.

However, like everything that's laid down in rules there are always exceptions when rules can be broken. *Once you know what the rules are, you have a base to begin with and you can bend them.*

For example, once in a while creative people appear who like to break the rules. They might start a movie with the end of the story and take the audience through the middle and back to the beginning which becomes the ending.

The opening scenes of *American Beauty* begin with visuals of a typical middle class American residential street where only the voice of the main character is heard, informing the audience that by the time the movie ends, he will be dead.

The story then takes the audience through the circumstances that led to his murder, and ends with where the movie began.

Others might experiment with the middle and go onto the beginning and follow it through to the end. Still others might make a movie more "talkie" rather than "movie" without following a specific story structure, but base it on a sequence of real life situations.

Look at the examples of the following movies where lots of well-written, natural sounding dialogue and totally absorbed performances from the actors carried a succession of events with absorbing results:

Jules et Jim (France), The Last Picture Show, Diner, Secrets and Lies, Sex, Lies and Videotape, The Darjeeling Limited, 200 Cigarettes, Thirteen Conversations about One Thing, Mindwalk or Woody Allen's *Manhattan* and *Any Which Way.*

Each captured an emotional human experience that happened in a special place at a special moment in time. The characters talked about interesting things in very human situations, and the audience could identify with the events that were unfolding in the movie.

Another reason why these movies worked was that they were directed in a very cinematic style. They were absorbing character studies which weren't ponderous to look at or to hear. They were very well photographed and edited in a way that carried the story increasingly from point to point and from scene to scene.

Some other creative movie people might structure stories as partial drama/dance/musicals. Look at: *The King and I, Cabaret, Dirty Dancing* and *All that Jazz.*

Each is set in a dramatized situation with the "dance/musical" part occurring as a natural unfolding of what is happening in the story.

Other stories might be structured as full dance/musicals that follow an operatic format where the dialogue is lyrical and the total story is told with music, song and dance, as in *Evita* and *Chicago.*

All these movies required diverse talents and exceptional performances from the actors who appeared in them.

Many approaches to structuring stories in the movies have been tried before and people keep looking for new ways to try old things. Success just depends on the vision, skills, timing and luck of the creative people involved.

The Theme

Stories usually have an objective or follow a specific theme otherwise it would be pointless to tell the story. So, what do we mean by the objective or *theme* of the story?

It means:

- The subject, topic or focus of what the story is about. It's the central statement that the story makes.

It's the story's undertone or subtext. It's the "message" that the characters are meant to communicate, and the main emotions or feelings that the story aims to arouse in the audience.

For example, it might be about the events and circumstances that influence people's encounters in:

> politics, religion, relationships, social upheavals, love, despair,
> anger, betrayal, horror, grief, compassion, evil, courage, war,

cowardice, happiness and other experiences.

Clearly focused story themes are very simply expressed, often in one word or one sentence. For instance: "It's a story about a family living in *poverty*..."

Sometimes, stories may interweave more than one central theme, incorporating various **sub themes** or minor themes, which complement the central story theme.

In story-telling and performance, it's important for the writer and actors to understand very clearly what the central theme and sub themes of the story are about.

When there's an unclear focus of what a story's theme is, it leaves the actors and the audience confused and emotionally let-down. There seems to be no purpose to the story and no appreciation of what it was intended to communicate.

Genres

In story-telling, a genre means the category, style or form in which a story is told.

The most common genres that are used to tell stories in the movies and on TV are:

> Drama / Melodrama / Tragedy
> Romance / Soapies
> Action / Adventure / Suspense / Thrillers
> Westerns
> Comedy / Sitcoms
> Science fiction / Fantasy / Horror
> Musicals
> News / Documentary / Reality / Educational
> Commercial advertising / Promotional

What do you think the unique features are that distinguish these genres from each other? How would you describe each one? What is the visual and presentation style difference between them? Why / how would a story produced in each of these genres attract you?

If one day you went to a casting and were asked to perform a part in any of the above genres, what kind of a character would you invent and how would you audition that character in each of those circumstances?

How would you approach each genre to make a good casting impression and convince the casting people that you know the difference between each one?

As a mental acting exercise to stimulate your imagination, think about that and visualize yourself as a character performing a part in each of these genres in a fantasy or story that you create.

Then improvise and videotape and assess what you have created.

Conflict

Drama is real life with the dull parts left out.

- Alfred Hitchcock

Conflict means to be opposed to something: to fight; clash; struggle.

Drama happens because of a conflict taking place somewhere.

Most stories deal with conflict. Even the news is made up of stories that happen because of a conflict happening somewhere. In your everyday life, there is conflict everywhere around you.

In the movies, conflict also motivates the encounters and relationships between the characters in stories of:

- Romance, comedy, action and adventure.
- Horror, science fiction, fantasy.
- Musicals.
- In every story genre you can imagine.

Sometimes it even motivates the content of commercials, educational, promotional and public relations presentations. For example, a TV commercial usually incorporates some kind of subliminal "story" that might make you feel insecure if you don't use a sponsor's product.

That means it's created a personal conflict in you if you don't consider buying the product. And in education, you might have a conflict in understanding the right and wrong way of a concept or answering a test question.

Conflict occurs in various circumstances and situations. It can be dramatic, intense, subtle, physical, emotional and even humorous. For example:

In comedy, a conflict might happen when one character trips another who falls into a swimming pool in an embarrassing way. We might laugh, but between the characters there is a conflict when the fallen one gets angry and has a genuine reason for being angry and looks for revenge.

Conflict can also occur between ideas, events and communities of people – or any combination of these when someone's cherished attitudes, beliefs, livelihood and relationships are challenged, threatened or opposed.

Or when one's survival is in danger; when social, cultural or physical harm happens; when the environment is damaged because of greed or carelessness; when an injustice takes place as different characters perceive it; when a person's desires and/or needs are unfulfilled.

It can also be of a spiritual, religious or psychological nature.

For example, when a person struggles to overcome the personal demons, fears and emotional battles that happen inside their conscience.

It's the never ending battle between good and evil, or right and wrong as different story characters see and understand it. Without conflict there is no drama or comedy - and in our present cultural, social and emotional circumstances, that causes most audiences to have very little interest in a story.

Where Do Ideas For Creating A Character Come From?

Ideas are everywhere around you. They can be inspired by:

- Reading about things.
- Observing ordinary people and exploring the circumstances that created their particular circumstances and situation.
- Sensitizing into the events that profoundly affected your own life and touched the lives of others.
- Focusing on the events and dynamics that have influenced the experience of your own culture, social structure and environment. Or that of others.
- Following interesting or inspiring news stories and digging into the details that created the story.

For example: Movie producers and screenwriters have always found story ideas from the real life, high drama that occurs inside the industry itself. There are many entertaining "historical" movies about the crimes, intrigues, jealousies, struggles, successes and failures of people who over the years have been seduced by the attraction of showbusiness stardom.

Some successful movie and showbusiness stories that have become classics were:

Yankee Doodle Dandy which is based on the showbusiness career and family relationships of songwriter, and song and dance man George M. Cohan who was a Broadway superstar in the early years of the 20th century. The movie is especially sizzling because of the singing and high energy tap dancing routines displayed by James Cagney, who showed that he was an incredible dancer in addition to his more recognizable star image as a movie "tough guy" in the gangster movies of the 1930's and 40's.

The Jolson Story was loosely based on the real life story of Broadway entertainer and superstar Al Jolson. It followed Jolson's career from his youth, through his rise to super stardom and into the conflicts of his personal life and the breakup of his first marriage, and the role he played in the making of the first commercially successful semi-talking movie "The Jazz Singer", which ushered in the sound era in the late 1920's.

The success of the movie continued with *Jolson Sings Again*, which followed the second part of Jolson's career and told the story of how "The Jolson Story" was made.

Both movies starred Larry Parks who empathized with the real Al Jolson's spirit and interpreted his body language and unique entertainment style to perfection.

Larry Parks was a promising star during the 1950's, but his career was wrecked because of his leftist political beliefs by the McCarthy anti-communist witch trials that were going on in the USA at that time.

Sunset Boulevard is about the murder of a screenwriter in Hollywood, and the grand illusions a faded silent screen star has of a comeback into the age of talking pictures after living for years in seclusion in an eerie grand mansion on Sunset Boulevard in 1950's Hollywood.

Directed by Billy Wilder it starred William Holden as the writer, and co-starred the real-life silent screen star Gloria Swanson as the faded silent screen star. Eric von Stroheim, who was a real-life silent screen director, played her strange butler-protector and former silent screen director in the movie.

Theatre OF Blood is a hilarious but poignant look at an actor who gets revenge on the critics who give him bad revues, and he creates unique ways to murder them off. Vincent Price is perfectly cast as the embittered classical actor with Robert Morley as one of his victims.

Singing in the Rain is probably the most popular musical to come out of MGM studios in Hollywood, which specialized in producing musicals and family entertainment.

The story is a romantic melodrama set at the time when the industry was making the transition from silent movies to sound. It's about a silent movie star who's confronted with an acting crisis and the changes in acting styles that the new technology of sound required. It's also about a talented chorus girl/movie extra who's his love interest, and who has ambitions of becoming a star herself.

In this movie Gene Kelly, Donald O'Connor and Debbie Reynolds in her first movie role, perform some marvelous song and dance routines.

The Big Knife is a powerful drama that puts an actor in direct confrontation with a Hollywood movie mogul who is the head of a "famous" Hollywood studio.

Jack Palance plays the actor whose career is destroyed because he refuses to conform to the demands of the controlling studio boss.

Day for Night made in France, is a movie about making a movie. It's a movie director's nostalgic look at the headaches and frustrations he's had when dealing with actors who can't remember their lines, animals that don't want to co-operate in a scene, stressing out about falling behind schedule, and coping with a crew and technical problems while he's making a movie.

"Day for Night" is a term used in the movies which refers to the technical process of shooting night scenes in the daytime, which might be done during a shoot because it might be more economical on the budget. A day for night shoot would require less electricity, lights and the re-scheduling of actors and crew for a night shoot.

Character Interpretation

Personal Styles

Different actors bring different qualities and different acting styles to a character.

For example:

The mystery author Agatha Christie's famous fictional detective Hercule Poirot has been interpreted many times and in different ways by a variety of actors on stage, TV and in the movies since the 1930's. And the character is still going strong today, waiting for a new generation of actors to interpret him in a fresh way.

In *Murder on the Orient Express,* Hercule Poirot has been interpreted each time with a different personality by the following actors:

In feature films, Albert Finney interpreted him expansively, almost over the top. Peter Ustinov played him more casual, almost boringly laid back. He was more British than Belgium-French.

David Suchet in the BBC TV "Poirot" series, attempted to emulate the character *in every detail* as described by Agatha Christie in a series of novels about his exploits. Although the other actors gave interesting and professional interpretations, I personally feel that David Suchet *seems* to have come closer to the author's intention and vision of the character.

If you read any of the Poirot novels and have a chance to view the above films, which actor do *you feel* was the most effective in his interpretation?

How much of their own personality do you think each actor brought into the character? To what type of audience do you think each actor was projecting? Why do you think each actor played Poirot the way he did?

As a mind experiment, *visualize* how *you* would interpret and play Poirot?

Footnotes:

In the movie *How to Rob a Bank*, David Suchet changed his image brilliantly and convincingly from the impeccable and proper "Poirot" to a ruthless gangster/villain who was also dealing with a health problem. His whole character and demeanor was a total transformation, even down to his physical presence, voice and accent.

Over the years Conan Doyle's classic detective *Sherlock Holmes* has also been interpreted in various ways by different actors. During the 1940's Sherlock Holmes was portrayed in a series of "Sherlock Holmes" feature films by the late Basil Rathbone who played him more in keeping within the morals, standards and mellow-dramatic movie style of the 1940's.

In a direct contrast to this, in 2010 Robert Downey Jr. portrayed him in an action packed movie as a somewhat violent and psychotic character that was heavily addicted to narcotics, which seemed to be closer to the image of "Holmes" that was created in the novels by Conan Doyle.

Try to view these two interpretations and see the drastic difference in the way "Holmes" was interpreted and presented by these two actors with different styles and from different generations.

Robert Downey Jr. was much younger when he played the silent screen movie star Charles Chaplin in the movie *Chaplin*. Study this movie and look at the complete change of character he achieved in this role which very closely reflected the way the real Chaplin was in real life.

Later in his career he brought a totally different acting quality and style into the *Ironman* role when he played and interpreted that comic book superhero in the movies. These roles were in total contrast to his Sherlock Holmes character.

Think about what he had to do emotionally, psychologically and physically to achieve these contrasting roles convincingly and what intense focus, versatility and concentration was needed from him to connect with these characters. It's also worthwhile looking at some of Robert Downey Jr's other movies.

Compare how Jack Nicholson interpreted *The Joker* comic book character in the first *Batman* movie in contrast to how different Heath Ledger interpreted him later in *Batman: The Dark Knight*.

Jack Nicholson portrayed *The Joker* more tongue in cheek and closer to the comic book character whereas Heath Ledger brought a stark and frightening realism into the character.

Creating a Character

You begin by *visualizing* and then *researching* the type of character you're cast to play. You might want to *observe* real-life people who might *inspire* a vision of a character for you. For example, study and research the lifestyle and conflicts of a prostitute, preacher, gangster, athlete, housewife, truck driver, lawyer or politician and so on, if you were cast to play any of those roles.

Study the actual real people. Talk to them if it's possible and use them as examples or the prototypes on which to *build* your character.

When you prepare for a part, think about the following aspects when you want to "find" the character:

• How do you personally *empathize* with the character?
• How would you portray the role? How do you *see* the character?
• Is the character serious, a comic type, casual, intense, etc..?
• How does the character behave in different situations? Why?
• How old is the character? What is the characters emotional, psychological and health state? This will determine the character's energy dynamic and how the character moves.
• How does the character relate to the other characters in the story? Why?

ROOTS: Explore the emotional, psychological, social, ethnic, cultural, educational and financial background of the character. Create their history and identify with their attitudes and the purpose of their being.

COLORIZATION: What are the character's special interests such as hobbies, sports, music, etc? What are the animated and physical things that the character does to *reveal* their personality? How good are you at incorporating these qualities into yourself as the character?

MOTIVATION: What causes the character to do and to say the things that they do, and to be who they are?

PERSONALITY: What makes the character excitable or passive? What are the character's strengths and weaknesses?

Are they:

optimistic   pessimistic   witty   intelligent
stupid   angry   painful   joyful
dishonest   honest   secretive   disillusioned...etc.

WARDROBE/GROOMING/ENVIRONMENT:

Do they fantasize? Is the character a winner, loser, defeatist, outgoing, relaxed, uptight, sexual, neat, sloppy, religious, progressive, etc.? Why?

How does the character make use of wardrobe, make-up and space at the various locations of the story?

Important information can be revealed about a character's personality by the way they are groomed and dressed.

Consider what they wear, how they wear it and the way this reflects the character's qualities, lifestyle and general life outlook. Is it flashy, high fashion, middle class or poverty stricken?

For example, during the Victorian era in Britain the style was for people to wear tight fitting clothes. Men were dressed in uncomfortable fitted suits with heavily starched collars and inhibiting ties. The women wore cumbersome clothes and asphyxiating corsets. People's hairstyles were generally stiff and formal. This reflected that culture and that time period's physical and emotionally up-tight, rigid and sometimes claustrophobic and hypocritical attitudes.

During the classical Greek and Roman eras people were generally laid back and this reflected in the way they wore their clothes. Their style was loose fitting togas and almost athletic looking sarongs or skirts.

In the South Pacific islands people wear minimal clothing which also reflects their warm natural environment and therefore their generally relaxed attitudes.

Is the role you're playing a period piece? Then consider how people would be dressed in a specific era and how this would affect their physical movement and emotional attitudes.

In what way are their clothes fitting, and how would the fit of their clothes determine their physical movements if they were loose fitting or tight fitting? The way they fit also has a bearing and meaning.

SPACE: Is the space suggestive of a slum or an up-market location? Is it a city, village, industrial or rural area?

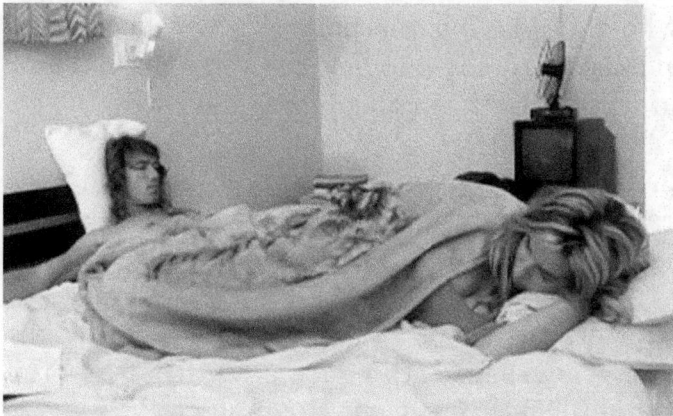

If you know the location of your scene beforehand, make a point of visiting it as part of your research and try to get a "feel" of what the space is like where you will be working. Familiarize yourself with it.

Ask yourself, "What does this space tell me?" "Does my character belong here?" How do I see myself performing in it with the other actors?

People are *unique* in the way they move, communicate and express themselves in an environment they are familiar with, whereas they might stand out of place in a space that is foreign to them.

- Think about how you can express the special features of the character you create in the way they use body language, body imagery, physical movements or hand and facial gestures to communicate, and also in the way they speak.

For instance, how does the character use their voice, language and words? Is it harsh, soft, guttural or pleasant? Is the use of language grammatically correct, or does it indicate an uneducated quality? Do they have a cultural accent when they speak? Is the character's background and dialect South African, Cockney, American, Canadian, British, French, Russian, Cape Colored, Zulu, Xhosa or something else?

PROPS: How does the character handle animals and props? If it's written into the script, would you look comfortable and knowledgeable handling things like dogs, horses, power tools or weapons like guns and knives?

Once we were preparing to shoot a horror scene in a class session which required the girl who was playing the part of a psychopath, to handle an old fashioned cutthroat razor and slit her "lovers" throat. The razor blade was blunted so that it would not injure the actor playing her "lover".

A few days before the shoot the girl was given the prop razor and was instructed to take it home and practice on it the way she would need to hold it as an experienced psychopath who was used to handling this kind of weapon.

When we rehearsed the scene just before the shoot and she was about to flick it open to use it as a "murder" weapon, she grasped it in such a way that had the real blade been in the razor she would have severely cut her fingers.

It was obvious that she had not bothered to practice with the prop, which would have given her a "feel" of it in the way she would have been required to handle such a dangerous weapon.

It's vital that you research and physically practice with the clothing, props and items you will be using, as well as getting a *feel* of the space that you will be using in a scene so that you can come off looking believable in the role you're playing.

When an actor has a bad performance, it's usually a result of a lack of confidence in not knowing how they should play the part, which is a consequence of not being well *prepared* for it.

Summary:

Like people in real life, story characters also have a background that causes them to be what they are. When you create a character, it's your responsibility to *research, interpret* and *find* the untold information about the character and to make intelligent *choices* about the character's attitudes, condition, psychology and history in bringing them to life.

Defining a Character's Purpose

When you read a script or work on a scene, consider the following:

Remember: *Whenever you prepare for a part and wherever it applies ask yourself who, what, why, when, where and how.*

- How *important* is your character to the story?

- As the story unfolds does any emotional or personality *change* come about in any of the characters? Does it happen in yours? Do any of them evolve into something bigger, better or worse than what they were before?

- Will the audience see something new or learn something interesting about you or any of the other characters? Do any of them *reveal* any unusual information about themselves throughout the story? Do we get to understand or know anyone better?

- Do any of the characters take the audience on a "journey" of some kind? Perhaps one that is personal, psychological, informative or spiritual?

- Do any of the characters make you curious or interested in wanting to watch them and listen to them? Do the relationships, actions and interactions between them touch you in any way? What thoughts or feelings do they leave you with?

- Is there sufficient pacing, rhythm and timing in the dialogue and action between the characters to keep the story and the relationships between them taut and flowing?

- What is the conflict between the characters? Does it build up into a dramatic or comic tension?

- Do the story elements end in some sort of resolution?

Interpreting the Name of a Character

Names sometimes reveal interesting information about a character. They *might* suggest something about the character's personality, nationality, social standing, cultural background and family history. For example, look at the following names. What do they *suggest* to you about a character? What *image* do you see?

Drew	Aspasia	Isabel	"Lightly"	Marshall
Karen	"Spurs"	"Chief"	George	Lance
Margaret	Orturo	Flora	Hui	Agnes
Melissa	Suzie	Sophia	Jose	Marcel
Arthur	Maria	Ingmar	"Jangles"	Stefaan
Byron	Robin	"Chokes"	Al	Alfred
Sharon	Aaron	Philippi	Akiru	Pepe
Ntene	"Terror"	Donna	Britt	"Skollie"
Emile	Pinto	Jim	Nongu	Kanji
Conte	Jessica	Paulo	Costa	"Stompie"
Baldy	Mammon	Rusty	Louie	Bunny
Jan	Morkel	Guilermo	Chrissie	Alfie
Gigolo	George	Beulah	Beauregard	
Humming Bird		False Face		

Some names have been popular for various reasons at certain times in different cultures and in different social circumstances. In what time frame / period and in which cultures and social circumstances would you place these names?

For example, names like "Sammy The Horse" or "Ham The Bookie", might bring to mind an image of an amusing Damon Runyon petty criminal type character, operating in New York during the 1930's and 40's. Or "Colette" might suggest something French. "Dimitri" could be someone with a Greek or Russian cultural connection who has an eastern orthodox religious background.

Obviously a name like "Jambo" would be unsuitable for a character set in the formal royal courts of 16 century France or some country in the Balkans. But it would most likely not be out of place somewhere in contemporary New York's Harlem for instance.

Think of other names and how they might help you to define a character.

When you *research* a character, *consider* how you would *use* a story character's "name" that's written into a script to create a personality for that character.

Summary

Working the Script

What are the vital elements *suggested* in the text that I should explore? What are the *subliminal* or unwritten features I should bear in mind so that I can better understand the story? Consider the following guidelines:

About titles:

Sometimes when a writer picks a title for a story, there "might" be some hidden suggestion behind it. Think about the titles of some movies you've seen.

Why did the title attract your attention? What did it imply? What symbolism or image do you see? For example, *The Godfather, Ironman, The Dolls House, Teenage Werewolf, Dracula, Bitter Rice, The Three Amigos, The Matrix* or *The Incredible Lightness of Being* – what kind of a movie might these titles suggest to you?

Digging further into the script, I might ask myself the following questions:

- What is my first impression of the story? Is it a drama, comedy, romance or anything else? This will determine how I approach my part.
- What is the plot or *primary* focus? Is the statement, theme or "message" clear? What is it trying to communicate? Do I understand it? Is it about murder, violence, incest, heroism, betrayal, love, hate, personal growth? Adventure? What else? Is it about one, or a combination of these elements?
- Do I identify with the text and subtext in the script?
- What is the mood of the setting? Where does it happen? Is this important to the characters? What is their relationship to it? How do the locales add texture to the story?
- What is the era or time period in which the action takes place? What information should I research about that time?
- Who are the key characters? Who are the sub characters? What are their differences? How old are they? Do they have any unusual physical, psychological or emotional traits? What are they and how does this color their personality and my relationship to them?
- What do I think is going on between the characters?

- What are their customs and beliefs? With what accent do they speak?
- What motivates their interactions and their dialogue?
- What's catchy or unusual about the *beginning*? Will it touch an audience? Moving into the *middle*, has interest in the characters and the plot been sustained up to this point? Is the *ending* conclusive? Will it leave the audience satisfied? Why? Why not?
- What is the major tension? Are there surprise twists and turns written into the script?
- Sub climaxes: How does the story progress and unfold? Does it build up scene by scene? Does each scene lead into the next – unfolding the story layer by layer?
- Is there any humor built into the story to relieve dramatic tension? What is it? Does it serve a valid purpose?
- Is the dialogue void of clichés?
- What is the story climax?
- What are the memorable qualities in the story? In the characters? In the dialogue?
- How are their conflicts resolved? What do the characters learn about themselves? About each other? What do we learn about them? About ourselves?

Conclusion: Is the story worth telling? What makes this concept original and different from what's been done before?

Is there an entertainment value in the story? What is it? If not, what do we need to do about it?

Exploring my Character

Short Notes

What will enhance my character and make my role more compelling?

As you break down and study *your part* in each scene, work from what you know about *yourself*. As you do this, look at the following *guidelines* and consider the following questions if they are appropriate for you to flush out the qualities and subtext of the character you want to create.

There is no right or wrong answer. It simply is what it is. What's important is your own *understanding* of a script that is given to you and your personal *interpretation* of how you want to *shape* the character you are being cast for and how you choose to *play* your part.

1 Who is my character in the *overall* story?

Understanding and visualizing my character:

- Where am I and how do I fit into what is going on? How did I get here? Why am I here? Why is this happening?
- When did this happen? What caused it? How did it happen? How does this affect me? What are my circumstances and what is my relationship to the other characters in the story?
- What is my character's *intention*? What is it that I want to accomplish? How do I accomplish that? What are my character's weak points? Their strong points? What is the cause of these?
- What are the emotional, psychological and physical things that impact on me and motivate me to do what I do and say what I say?
- How much of myself as a character do I give to others? Why? Why not?
- How much can I take or absorb emotionally and physically in a conflict before I'm motivated to act or react? How do I react?
- How much does my character change or evolve or not evolve in the story?
- How truthful is my interpretation of the character I created?

2 Working each scene:

- What is *each scene* that involves my character about? What is the scene setting up in terms of story / drama or moving the plot ahead? What is the *main point*, or the *bottom-line* or *thrust* in the scene that needs to be expressed verbally or visually?
- What is my objective here? What do I need to do to accomplish that?
- Does my character serve any purpose in the scene, or make some kind of impact? Where / Why / What is it?
- What happened in the scene before I appeared? How / Why does this affect me? What was I doing before that moment? What am I going to do afterwards?
- What is the most creative or effective way for me to make an appearance – or end my appearance in the scene? How can my character make an impression without upstaging the other characters or disrupting the intention of the scene?
- What is the action that I am doing? Why am I doing it?
- What props am I using? Why? How am I using them?
- How am I dressed? Why? What does my appearance and body language project about me?
- What makeup or grooming am I wearing?
- How am I feeling? What is my attitude and state of mind?
- What is the *appropriate* emotional energy that I should give out that will best play in each scene that involves my character? How should I play the rhythm, timing and pacing of the action and dialogue? Fast, slow, normal? Where are the pauses, accents and stresses? Why? How will this affect the story and the "chemistry" between me and the other characters?
- Does my feeling and attitude change or not change at any moment? If it does, where or when in the scene (or in the overall story) does this happen? What causes the change?

3 General:

- What do I need to do to *sustain* curiosity in my character throughout the places where I appear in the story? What can I do to make my character more interesting and appealing?
- Is my character's dialogue easy-flowing? Or is it boring, too wordy, rambling or preaching? Will I lose the attention of the audience because the text is

heavy handed, rather than revealing and entertaining?

- Where might I rework the dialogue, or make suggestions to make it flow better and tighter? How will my changes and choices affect the performance and energy between me and the other characters?
- What is my characters mythology, cultural history, education, social and financial status? Is it relevant to the story or to my character's personality?
- What are my desires, needs and wants? Do I or don't I achieve these and to what extent do I accomplish my dreams and aspirations?

What else can you add to this?

Part 6

*The greater the artist, the greater
the self-doubt.*

*Perfect confidence is given only to
the mediocre as a consolation prize.*

- Unknown

*The more ignorant and depraved a
person is, the more contemptuously
they treat those whom they deem
inferior.*

- Joseph Conrad

Inhibitions

Often, most of us hold back from what we really feel when we interact with others and that is largely because we feel afraid. In most instances, our feelings of fear have to do with our attitude about something.

For example, some people are afraid of the dark, others are not. Some are afraid of relationships while others are not. Some people are comfortable speaking in public, others are afraid they'll make a fool of themselves in front of a group of people they don't know. They feel afraid because of what they think others will think of them. Others are afraid of being disappointed, of being hurt, appearing weak or taking a risk. Some are afraid of exposing their emotions, physicality, sexuality or intelligence.

But attitudes such as reserve, shyness, self-consciousness, embarrassment and repression can be impediments in our personal life. Some of these we impose on ourselves because of unpleasant life experiences or because of personal traumas which we carry from childhood and our social and cultural conditioning.

If you observe interactions between people very closely, you'll notice that usually people who have trouble *receiving* an open communication from others, also have trouble *giving* of themselves.

This is quite noticeable when you see certain actors performing. You'll see an obvious restraint and a lack of energy in their performance. It fails to carry an audience through to an emotionally satisfying experience.

Perhaps in real life, there is a survival value for a person to have some inhibitions in certain circumstances and situations, but in an acting context, an over access of such a restraining attitude can become a hindrance and obstruction, and hamper any meaningful progress which is so important in the maturity and personal development of an actor.

So the question is can an actor honestly afford to be self-conscious, shy or inhibited - and especially about *feelings* of their own sensuality and sexuality?

Some years ago two actresses were cast with two actors to perform in a highly charged play. During rehearsals, the male actors were having difficulty interacting with the actresses and expressing the high level of emotional intensity that was required in the play.

The actresses were frustrated and annoyed that no emotional interaction was happening between them and the male actors, so they decided to do something about it for the opening night performance.

Unbeknown to the male actors and the audience watching the performance, the actresses decided to remove their panties, and performed the play without wearing anything under their dresses. It seemed to have had the effect they were after. For some reason, the male actors picked up on a sexual and highly charged emotional vibration from the actresses without knowing why it was happening, and began to respond with an appropriate energy to the emotional demands of the play.

Why the actresses did that, was probably an *intuitive* action from them as a reaction to what had not been happening during the rehearsals. Sexual energy when it is positively released has long been recognized as a potent *creative* force.

When they decided to do what they did, and became aware and conscious of their action, it stirred passions which somehow made the right energy happen to stimulate a response from the male actors.

Maybe knowing what they knew, which nobody else did, excited the actresses erotically. The male actors and the audience seemed to sense the undercurrent of sexual energy that was flowing and circulating on the stage and connected with it subliminally.

The very act of what the actresses did without any inhibitions and with a positive mental attitude to stimulate the performance, created a charged state of mind that translated emotionally and physically into a powerful performance on the stage.

This is not to suggest that the use of sexual energy is the only way in which an actor can stimulate a performance. It depends on the conditions, dynamics and requirements of each acting situation. But in this context it just so happened to work appropriately in the above circumstances.

We have discussed that as an actor you need to be in touch with *all* your feelings, or you cannot connect with the appropriate energy that will be required from you to generate in a performance.

Unless its part of a scene you're performing and a character you're interpreting, you cannot be closed to your feelings because that will be reflected in your attitude and body language when you perform.

Sometimes it's cathartic to allow yourself to take risks with your acting and to just let go and to accept the happening as a cleansing experience.

Confronting Fear

When changes happen in your life, or when you move into something new that you haven't tried before, it's usually a time of uncertainty and adjustment.

Sometimes the uncertainty can be painful and traumatic and makes you feel afraid because you don't know how to react, what to do, or what to expect from the new experience that's made an impact on your life.

It's usually a fear of failure and of the unknown that holds you back from fulfilling your desires.

Obviously, some experiences are good and others are bad. War, abuse and any act of terror is certainly harmful to us and others. And so is murdering somebody, even though - if you are like most people - there may have been times when you may have *felt* like doing so.

We all have a built in survival mechanism that warns us of danger when we feel afraid to confront things that will clearly harm us. And we are cautious about what is safe for us to do and what is not. In those situations it's best to keep away from the things that impact negatively on us.

However, it's inevitable that when you pursue a career as an actor, you will at some time or another be cast in an uncomfortable or unconventional challenging role that might be in conflict with your cultural, social, spiritual and moral values. You might feel afraid, shy, insecure or embarrassed because you don't know what's going to happen, or how people might criticize you when you play the part, and your fear might block you from moving on and learning from that new experience.

It's important to realize that all your feelings are for the most part good, because they are of you. And it's valuable for you to try new things, because part of your attitudes may have been formed by not experiencing things.

But that doesn't mean that if you're playing the role of a murderer you must go out and experience the real thing in order to play the part. *It's the feeling of the thing that you bring into the performance, not the reality of the act itself.*

We have seen how accomplished actors research the part they play. They *empathize* with the real life examples of the characters they are interpreting. They talk to the real people they are researching and spend time with them and try to understand their motives and hook into *their* feelings and attitudes.

Surprisingly, sometimes when you try to experience or research something new, it can be very healthy. It means you're exploring an attitude about yourself and doing something you haven't tried before. It means that once you adjust yourself to doing it and you confront your fear about the experience, that fear will most likely turn into a comfortable or acceptable feeling.

And when you interact with other actors and see them doing the same thing and that they benefit in a positive way from their experience, you'll also learn from that.

And if they can do it, so can you.

Meanwhile, if you are afraid of the things that you don't know, stay with the things that are familiar to you. It's better if you can start from a comfortable place that you already know before you attempt to move into the unknown.

From there, you can move slowly and cautiously into the things that you're afraid of.

Throughout your career as an actor you'll always have to confront something else that's new that might make you afraid - and each time you overcome your fear of it, you'll learn anew from that experience and that's the way you'll go on developing and growing all your life.

Sexuality

The sexuality that you project is energy.

It's an awesome energy that can either empower or weaken a person, depending on how it's used.

Since the beginning people have used it to manipulate each others feelings and to arouse peoples' passions to persuade them to buy what they're promoting or selling.

You see it at newsstands and at supermarkets where they sell magazines and tabloid newspapers, where week after week people never seem to get tired reading about the sex lives and scandals of the rich, the powerful and famous.

That information is so desired, it's a multi billion dollar industry world-wide.

Just observe what's happening around you in your every day life. Sexual insinuation is used all the time as a natural part of the entertainment at sporting events like football, rugby, basketball and cricket games to stimulate excitement in the spectators. Scantily dressed cheerleaders perform dance movements which are totally erotic and hide very little from a person's imagination.

It's used in the movies. It's used by rock and pop stars to promote themselves in music videos. And it's all around you in a subliminal form in your daily life, and even in places where its power is so feared that in spite of it being suppressed, it still vibrates as an intense undercurrent inside the culture. Just look at how powerful and charismatic the undertone of suppressed sexuality is that drives the emotions of congregations in conservative and puritanical religions.

Artistic and influential people have often expressed that they feel a high sexual rush when they're in the process of building, creating or promoting something. It's a part of procreation, from creating offspring to great works of art.

Become aware of your own sexual power and discover how to channel that energy constructively into your performance.

Bear in mind that sexuality isn't necessarily about how "pretty" or "good-looking" you are. If you think about it, many successful people and famous actors are really not that "pretty" or "good-looking" when you see them in person, but what they do have is vitality and a lack of fear in expressing who they really are and that is a turn-on for most people watching them.

And that's what counts. They have a vigor and exciting energy which they generate and project in their lives, performance and attitude which makes them appear "sexy".

Impotency, a lack of vitality, frustration and sexual reservations are a direct result of a lack of self-confidence, which in turn stems from a feeling of emptiness that life and the talent that you feel you have has no purpose or recognition.

Good acting automatically implies that you take a risk to perform something that is suitable to the dynamics of the scene you are playing and to the character you are interpreting each time you re-enact your inner emotions.

With the over saturation of TV and the movies, you're instantly exposed to audiences around the world. Each time you perform, audiences will compare you to what other actors in other countries and in other cultures are doing. For example, you cannot play an intense love scene without generating an appropriate emotional, sexual and physical energy.

But that is what you will be paid to do.

Remember: You are all things to all people. You reflect the world around you. And if you want to also benefit from the fame of being an actor, that's one of the things that will be required of you.

If you can't do that, another actor will. You cannot be shy or reserved about your sensuality.

Exercises to Release Inhibitions

As a group or with one of your peers, go to a nightclub or public place as different characters. Become for a period of time "someone else" - and *experience* what it would be like to be *different* in a real life situation interacting with strangers around you. Dress differently to how you normally would and move and talk differently as a character from the way you usually do.

Immerse yourselves totally in the situation. Be *spontaneous* and *listen* to each other and interact with the strangers around you. Respond and react as the characters you are at that moment. Do this exercise as often as you like, exploring the different energies, feelings and responses you pick up as the characters you're impersonating.

Or have you ever thought about what it might *feel* like if you were out of work for many months and you had to stand on a street corner poorly dressed begging for food? Think about that - and even better, try doing it as a research project. Other things you might explore are:

- Visiting a prison and talking to and interacting with different inmates, or go to a hospital and observe the action in an emergency ward, or to a police station on a Saturday night.
- Visit a mortuary or the morgue. Watch an autopsy.
- Interact with people from a different ethnic group and culture. Try and immerse yourself in it.
- Interview people on the street while you hold a dead fish and observe people's reactions.
- Model underwear in a public place.
- Visit a nudist colony and experience being naked in front of people you don't know.
- Kiss and caress someone you're not attracted to.
- Think of other "experiences" you can research ...

This type of experimentation into "characters" and different "energies" and "experiences" will sharpen your understanding, and develop your emotional integrity as well as broadening your acting and interpretive skills.

Playing Love Scenes

This type of scene is probably one of the most difficult things for an actor to perform and not everyone can do it convincingly.

How intimately would you allow yourself to be caressed in a scene? How passionately would you allow yourself to be aroused? How would you feel performing this with an actor you don't like or don't sense anything for? How would you feel to perform a gay or lesbian love scene, or even to interpret dialogue that implies a sexual undertone?

How would you feel performing such intimate and private scenes in front of an audience or surrounded by a film crew watching you during a shoot? How would you feel exposing yourself naked with another actor in front of strangers?

How would you respond to all of this and hold the scene within the bounds of an artistic expression and not come across as vulgar or depraved while still maintaining your integrity and self worth?

How far an actor decides to go in a situation like this depends on a person's temperament and courage, and social and cultural upbringing.

In our acting classes students seem to perform scenes of anger and violence fairly readily and they even do it enthusiastically when they act it out with play guns and other types of prop "weapons". They play out their emotions of anger and violence. And most of this has to do with the way they've been primed by our culture, the news and the general media to accept situations of anger and violence as a somewhat "normal" occurrence in their everyday lives.

However, when it comes to doing a love scene, you immediately see their embarrassment and defensive mechanism kick in, even when the scene calls for a simple action like touching or kissing another person. And most of this also has to do with the way they've been conditioned to suppress their emotions and any public expression of intimacy.

And there may well be some valid purpose in real life in this type of defensive attitude to protect a person from undesirable experiences.

However, we have already discussed that as an actor you need to allow yourself a greater emotional freedom in order to play a part better.

When it comes to playing love scenes, remember that you can *choose* to play the scene with the actor you're performing with as intimately or as boldly as it is comfortable for you to do under the guidance of the director.

You have a choice to do or not to do such a scene when you're cast in a particular role that requires you to do this.

Scenes like this and how intimate they are, are usually written into the script and you would be informed by the director about what you'll be required to do in a love scene. If it's not for you, you can refuse to do it before you are cast in the role.

But once you are cast in the role and you have accepted it, the conditions of what will be expected of you in the scene will be outlined in the performance contract between you and the producers of the movie.

And any reputable production company would take the utmost care and consideration to make you feel focused and comfortable performing that role.

Some brilliant movies have been made that have explored different aspects of love and intimacy. Creative movie people keep exploring further and further into ways to connect audiences emotionally with the passions, desires and realism of the characters being portrayed.

However, for a study about performing intimate love scenes, it would be worth your time to review the following five movie examples from different countries:

> *The Reader* a British/German co-production released in 2007,
> *When a Man loves a Woman* made in the USA, released in 1994,
> *The Secret Diaries of Miss Anne Lister* a BBC production made in 1996.
> *How to make an American Quilt* made in 1995 and
> *Betty Blue* made in France in 1984.

See how sensitively the actors exposed the drama that was unfolding between the characters in these movies, and how far and how deep *intimately, emotionally, psychologically, physically, erotically and truthfully* these actors went in performing those parts and how they still kept their performance within the boundaries of realism and good taste.

These movies were also visually powerful and thoughtfully written and directed, and that high-level combination of acting and production talent seems to be the difference between something that is blatantly pornographic and something that is a slice of life expressed through art.

Being in the moment:

An improv or a scene is like a living organism. It's like a creature that feeds off the *energy* that surrounds it. The more energy it gets from the parts that surround it, the more *alive* it becomes.

Each actor who performs a role is a part of that creature and the more energy each actor gives out in the improv or scene that they are performing from moment to moment, the more that creature grows and the stronger it becomes.

When you hold back from *allowing* yourself to be in the moment and block yourself from *moving* with each moment as it is happening, the weaker you become as an actor.

To be in each moment means that you have to let go of your inhibitions and of everything else of unimportance that surrounds your work space. It means that your energy should be *focused* on really living the requirements of what is unfolding around you in the circumstances of each performance situation.

It means that you must allow yourself to become lost in the actions, reactions and emotions that happen from moment to moment and that you should be truly *living the experience* of what is *occurring* in the improv or scene.

An exercise in intimacy:

Acting can be an overpowering and wonderful emotional and physical experience. It can also be a painful one. These are different aspects of one's SELF that every actor will always move through when they perform different roles, because each acting experience is different.

During this exercise try to connect with your real, true feelings whatever they might be and allow yourself to flow and react freely with the emotions and physical responses that are happening to you.

Fear, passion, anger, embarrassment, eroticism, arousal, disgust, playfulness - whatever the feeling is that is happening to you during the exercise it's ok, and even if you are unable to allow yourself to respond, to feel anything that's also ok.

Recognize that a non response is also a *reaction* and *feeling* about something.

Release your intuition and trust your instincts. LISTEN and TRUST the voice or feeling inside you. Interact spontaneously and try to focus consciously on the experience and absorb it.

Personalize your experience. Find your unique YOU-NESS and do it with someone you are comfortable with and who you trust. Or, play it out in an acting class which is facilitated by an experienced acting coach.

The exercise involves TWO PEOPLE: – Male / female   or   male / male or female / female.

Explore each other intimately, emotionally and physically using all your senses – touch, taste, smell, sound and sight and as you do this express verbally what you are each sensing and honestly feeling, whatever your emotions and reactions might be.

Interact with each others' thoughts and vibrations and go to wherever your emotions and your bodies lead you and only as far as it is comfortable for you to go. Change partners to experience different sensations.

Remember: This is an acting exercise. Afterwards breathe deeply and let go of the feelings that may have affected you.

For any exercise to be effective it should be practiced many times.

Using Performance Energy Constructively

It's emotionally and physically draining when you have to keep up a high level of energy throughout a performance. And this becomes magnified if you have to do it day after day and week after week during a long movie shoot or extended theatrical run.

How well an actor generates and retains that high level of energy depends on many things. For instance:

• The actor and director's *attitude* and state of mind. This has to do with the daily *interaction* between the actor, director, production crew and the other actors in the cast. Is the *"vibe"* they produce on the set each day *harmonious*?

If it is, your energy becomes replenished because your enthusiasm and good feelings about what you are creating inspires you to keep pushing for more in your performance. You feel there's a *purpose* to what you are doing.

This is the result of:

The actor and director's intense *focus* on the story and performance. When this is connected, it projects positive creative exchanges to the rest of the cast and crew and encourages a satisfying working environment during the run of a production.

• When the actor and director are *prepared* for the production mentally, emotionally and physically it generates confidence on the set in what they are trying to accomplish.

The actor and director's *imaginative interpretation* of the story and their belief in what they are creating also inspires excitement when they collaborate well together and uncover new and interesting ways to reveal what motivates, transpires and resolves the interaction and situations between the characters.

• This might be in the *colorful* or unusual way in which the action is presented and how the characters are *seen* and how they talk and interact.

As the visual, artistic and technical *aesthetics* of the production begin to take shape in a positive way, it makes it a *stimulating* "experience" for the people working on it and lifts everyone's enthusiasm to a higher level.

- If the actor has the ability to *release* themselves and become the part, and become a *channel* for creative energy, it motivates the director to draw out of the actor a more satisfying performance.

When the performance and technical requirements of the production are running smoothly and its *completion* is on schedule, it relieves the pressure on everybody and gives them space to *concentrate* on the job they have to do.

You can feel the tension on a set when things are not going well, just as you can feel the excitement when things are going right. And this has a direct bearing on how everybody's energy plays out on the set.

Criticism

Let the stumbling blocks
be your stepping stones.

- Paul Roos

The broad definition of a critic is: *any person who gives an opinion about literature, a movie, a performance or a work of art; one who finds fault with something; one who is fond of judging someone or something.*

One of the most difficult things for an actor to cope with is criticism. You become an easy target to be criticized by the audience, the media and your peers, because you expose yourself emotionally, physically and psychologically each time you perform.

When you receive positive comments, they inspire you and make you feel good about yourself, but that's only a passing instant that might last until the next time you perform.

Often the criticism that many actors experience is harsh and in some instances it can be damaging. This is especially true when your performance is reviewed by a professional critic who gives a scathing assessment about your work and whose remarks might reach millions of people through the media.

You need to realize that there are good critics and bad critics. A good critic is a *discerning* and *objective* observer. Most people consider good criticism to be a constructive / positive process.

• Good or bad criticism really comes down to what is a matter of someone's personal opinion. And opinions vary from one culture to another and from person to person, depending on the critic's level of education, sophistication, observation, understanding and cultural and life experience, and how they personally feel from moment to moment.

Obviously if the person who is doing a critique of something has had a bad day, or is concerned with personal problems, they won't be fully receptive to what's going on in what they're critiquing.

You can't please all people all of the time. Different genres of movies and different styles of acting appeal to different types of audiences and to different levels of discernment in people.

Even in a group of people watching the same performance, some in the audience might be drawn in totally by an actor, while others might find the performance boring or find fault with whatever the actor does.

It's been known that when some critics at first reviewed something in a negative way, those same people looking at the same thing months later changed their opinion about it when they evaluated it again.

They now saw it in a positive way, because their attitude, circumstances and perspective had changed.

For many creative people, the bottom line of what really matters is not what a professional critic thinks, but what the audience you are playing to feels about your performance.

If the audience enjoys what you do, they'll support you. If they don't, they won't.

- You need to develop an inner strength to deal with criticism if you want to be respected as an actor. You need to rise above what you might perceive as a put down when people comment insensitively on certain aspects of your performance. You have to learn about criticism and how to look at yourself truthfully and positively.

When you lack self-confidence, *you* are your own worst critic. It's easy to pull yourself down. That's self criticism. It's negative. It's self defeating. It doesn't help you grow or to develop.

It's also easy to put others down. People who criticize in a negative way just for the sake of appearing important don't offer anything of value. They don't offer positive *solutions* that can make things better.

- Harmful criticism reflects a person's narrow-mindedness, immaturity, jealousy, arrogance and a lack of understanding. It exposes a *poor* critic.

- Poor critics are usually people who themselves don't have the talent or courage to perform and expose themselves the way you do.

Constructive criticism attempts to look at an acting situation in an encouraging way when it's performed with sincerity. It looks to find the positive qualities in the performance and to offer *observations* for improvement.

However, there is a big difference between something that's *obviously bad and lacks a performer's ability* and something that's presented with at least some *understanding, integrity* and *talent*.

What is important then, is for you to know the difference.

Summary

Self Assessment

Evaluate yourself and your peers in an encouraging way. Absorb the criticism or comments about your performance and change what you need to change. You also improve poor performance skills by releasing bad technique through practice, experience and conscious awareness.

Guidelines: When I look at a playback of my work on the screen, what do I need to consider?

- What were the positive features of my performance?
- Where did it fall flat? Why / Where did it work for me or the audience? Why didn't it?
- Was there any depth in my performance? Was I properly focused in the part? Was I *listening*? Did I project an appropriate energy, rhythm, pacing and timing in the scenes that involved me?
- Was my performance consistent emotionally and technically?
- Did I play for the subtext in the scene? How? How not?
- How did others watching me feel? Did I miss something they didn't? What was it?
- Did the script, director, the production or other problems fault the performance? How might these have been resolved? How did I cope under such conditions?
- Did I look natural and comfortable in the setting and with my use of props and wardrobe?
- What are the weak areas of my performance that I need to improve? What would I do different and better next time?
- How did I feel after the performance?

  - On a high?
  - Happy?
  - Disappointed?
  - Neutral?
  - Depressed?

What is the most valuable lesson I learnt from the experience?

Part 7

*An artist is a dreamer consenting
to dream of the actual world.*

- George Santayana
  The Actual World

Interpreting a Movie / TV Script

The following is an example of a movie or TV scene that may be given to you to interpret at an acting audition.

Excerpt from *Honour Thy Father*
CBC TV Canada

INT.   BILL'S APARTMENT   BEDROOM   MORNING

The bed is ruffled - unmade. He sits on it. He wears track suit pants and a T-shirt.

She's by the window - contemplative. **She** wears one of his heavy sweaters and nothing else. **She** stares out the window.

He moves to her.

BILL
So what happens now...?

Silence. **She** looks at him.

Do you want me to tell him...?

She shakes her head.

Do you want to stay...?

She nods. Looks outside again.

End

How would you approach this scene? How do you break it down? How do you begin to understand what the characters are all about?

Look at it.

Some obvious things stand out about the scene at first glance:

- The scene appears to be extremely short with hardly any dialogue spoken.
- The text is sparse and economically written.
- **He** is the only one who speaks.
- **She** remains silent.

Study the scene and consider the following story background that sets up the situation and relationship between the two characters.

The story background:

She's from a conservative Middle Eastern family, perhaps Muslim. Eighteen years old, she lives a sheltered life at home and has never been allowed to go out with men.

The family are immigrants, now settled in a liberal Western country. She's fallen under the influence of the different morals and values which are customary in the family's adopted country.

He's 23, born and bred in the liberal Western country. It's his homeland. He's financially independent and lives in a high-rise apartment overlooking the city. Middle Eastern culture is unfamiliar to him.

They met recently by chance at the place where he works and were attracted to each other for different reasons. He chased her romantically and convinced her to spend the night with him against her better judgment.

She had never dared before this to spend a night away from home without her family. She lost her virginity. This is likely to cause a backlash and major crisis with her family, especially with her father who has already arranged a marriage for her with a man of his choosing.

Read the scene again.

Now you'll see that it's potentially loaded with subtext that can be flushed out and made to play longer by the unspoken action between **He** and **She** that is set up at the beginning of the scene, which was designed to establish a mood and the *feelings* that are going on between the two characters even before a word is spoken.

It's about gripping the audiences' attention by playing the "moments" that are happening between the two characters and how they move and respond to each other without words.

Analysis / Making Performance Choices:

By their attitude and the setting, does the scene suggest something about what Bill and She did in that bedroom? Considering her cultural history and the consequences of what she did, what is it that she might now be thinking? Why?

What is her "vibe"? Might it be Guilt? Fear? Regret? Resolve? Acceptance?

What is his attitude? What is he feeling? Why?

What is he implying by saying "So what happens now?" Is he perhaps suggesting that they need to find some sort of solution to their situation? What might that be?

"Do you want me to tell him?" What is he talking about? Who does he mean by "him"?

Might the subtext be implying that things are better here with him rather than with her circumstances at home? Is he offering her a space and a relationship? If so, might it imply that he was satisfied with the sex they had, suggested in the visual opening of the scene?

When she nods, does that imply she's made a life-changing decision to stay with him and not worry about the consequences of her father's reaction? Does she think that things really are better here with him, or was her decision motivated by an emotional, anti-cultural or psychological dynamic?

What might that dynamic be?

What is his attitude at the end of the scene? What is hers? What do they "read" off each other and how might they end the scene emotionally or physically?

What motivates their thoughts and actions? Are there any possible attitude and emotional beats and changes between the characters in the scene? Where, How and What might they be?

How would you approach the rhythm, timing and pacing of the scene?

Changing dynamics:

When the background information and circumstances of a scene change, it will affect and change the dynamic of a performance, even though the dialogue remains the same.

Dialogue is just dialogue. It's what you do with it, how you interpret it and how you play it that changes the intention, energy and outlook of the scene.

So experiment with different dynamics. Change the setting, and your action, interpretation, wardrobe, props and make-up.

Play it dramatically – then with the same dialogue play it humorously or in a light manner.

Now, think about how the same dialogue can be interpreted in alternative ways in the following circumstances:

- Bill feels guilty. Her attitude has disturbed him.
- He's apprehensive about the future, is not keen on a permanent relationship and is only saying what he says to pacify her.
- She feels used. The sex was not what she anticipated. She regrets losing her virginity.
- She feels guilty about the night she spent with him. She's apprehensive and fearful about the future. Her cultural upbringing is creating an emotional and psychological turmoil within her. She has realized there will be a traumatic or perhaps violent confrontation with her family.
- Change the subtext and meaning of the dialogue to something *you* create.

Think about what would happen to the emotional dynamic of the scene and the performance if you changed the *relationship* of the characters and their *motivation* for being together? For example, if the "him" referred to in the dialogue was:

-   *She's* husband.
-   *She's* boyfriend and Bill's best friend.
-   *She* is older and is also having an affair with Bill's father.
-   *Him* is their child, they're married - but are now getting a divorce.
-   *Bill* is married. He's in love with *She*. His wife, *her,* is away. *She* spent the night with Bill at his house and slept in his bridal bed which excited *She* very much. "Do you want me to tell "<u>her</u>"...?"
-   "Bill" is a woman who has seduced *She* into her first lesbian encounter. "Him" is *She's* husband or boyfriend.
-   *She* is his *stepmother*, much younger than his father and closer to Bills age.

Try performing the scene now with each of these changed dynamics.

A Mental Acting Exercise

Exploring changing performance dynamics and emotional responses.

Even a very short scene can have a profound impact on the emotions and relationship between different characters.

Look at the following dialogue. Again, it's dynamic depends on what you do with it and how you play it:

TWO PEOPLE ON A TIGHTROPE

A
I've had enough. I can't take this
anymore...!
B
I like balmy weather... Do you like my
new shirt...?

The scene can be played by a man and a woman, two women or two men.

Visualize yourself performing one of the characters.

The first thing you'll notice is that the dialogue between the two characters seems totally unrelated. But look closer. B's response *appears* to be unsympathetic.

Or, is this perhaps some sort of defensive response by B to avoid a confrontation in a strange way, about what B might have done that's bothering A.

The dialogue and emotional rhythmic change could *imply* there's a tension about something that occurred between them.

What does the title of the scene suggest about a relationship and a situation that has occurred? What might the subtext be indicating? What might A be talking about? What might have happened to motivate A's dialogue and B's response?

What could B be hiding and feeling by not responding directly to A? How would you play the transitional "moments" and emotional beats of the scene?

As an exercise, create a set of fictitious circumstances in your own mind that might have triggered what is going on between the characters.

Establish an action and subtext at the opening of the scene that builds up into some sort of dramatic tension between the two characters even before the dialogue begins. Then see how that might make an emotional and performance sense out of the dialogue.

Now perform the scene. How would you end it to bring each characters response to a conclusion?

Continue to explore how the scene would play if for some reason there was an attitude of indifference between the characters.

Exploring dialogue with the energy of the setting and action in a scene:

The dialogue in a scene can be played in a more interesting way if the characters are placed in an unexpected location and are seen to be doing something unusual.

For example, look at the above two scenes again and see how the dynamic of the same dialogue might change, as well as the energy between the characters when you alter the location and action.

How different would the scene play if they were exchanging the dialogue somewhere in the country horse-riding? Or repairing a punctured car tire off a busy highway? Perhaps sitting at a coffee shop? Or maybe confronting each other in the street? Or trying to avoid each other above the noise while shopping frantically at a busy supermarket? Or maybe they are sopping wet while trying to stop a burst water pipe flooding the basement of one characters house?

Consider creating your own scenario and place the characters somewhere else doing some other action but working with the same dialogue.

Creating a Situation

You can create a variety of different situations and relationships between two
or more characters with just about any piece of dialogue. For example, look at
the dialogue exchange between the three characters, A, B and C in the
following short scene:

CHUMS

INT. OR EXT. A PLACE   ANYTIME

A

You do it.

B

Why does it always have to be me?

C

C'mon.

B

 No.

A

Just do it. You always ask too many
questions.

C

Yeah, you ask too may questions.

A

Do it! Just do it...!

.......continue.......

Keep on building the argument between them by repeating the dialogue or
improvising your own until you feel an appropriate pacing, timing, rhythm and
energy happening in the scene.

Keep it clean and simple and when you feel that the argument has reached enough of a peak, B hesitates a moment and finally gives in to do "it".

Who do you think these three characters are? What is their connection to each other? How friendly are they, and what is "it" that they are *doing* that motivates this verbal exchange between them?

Visualize that this is a scene in a movie.

- Are they planning to enter and rob a house? Is it their first time?
- Are they dismantling a bomb?
- Are they doctors performing an operation on someone?
- Is it the first time they're trying out drugs?
- Are they living together and is the toilet in their apartment blocked and stinking, and is one of them being pressured to do the dirty work to unplug it with a plunger?
- Has this to do with some kind of sexual or love triangle experiment between them?
- Are they planning to pick up dog poo in the garden?
- Invent your own situation.

You can play the scene as a comedy or a drama or interpret it in any other genre you wish.

What is your choice of action and the use of props in the scene? How would you build up the intrigue and suspense that is implied at the beginning? How would you begin the scene by not revealing what it is they are doing? How would you end it by *revealing in a surprising way the punchline* of what it is that they are doing?

Experience the scene in different ways with different rhythms, pacing and timing, and with different energy dynamics and subtext and explore how different the dialogue and the performances will play under different interpretations and in different circumstances.

Videotape the scene and review the results.

Summary

Performance Energy

Keep something happening with your energy all the time. Keep it *connected* to the real moments happening in a scene.

The process of *feeling*, *listening* and *thinking* is energy in transition. It's energy in motion even when no physical action is taking place. So take the time to *feel* and allow your energy to *move* from one transition to another.

As long as you're intense, focused and interested in what is happening between you and the characters and the situation in the scene, people watching you will also be.

How you move, what you wear, how you wear it and how you use clothes and props is a necessary part of how you create an image of your character.

It's energy that you use to communicate information.

Part 8

You American actors wait to
catch the truth before you
start running.

I prefer to run first and let
the truth find me...

- Lawrence Olivier

Professionalism

To be a professional means:

- You're earning money for your acting. It can be a full time or part time career.

- You're building a reputation and gaining screen credits as an actor.

  "Credits" in movie talk means that your name is acknowledged in the title sequence of a production. It's recognition of your contribution. The more screen credits you accumulate, the more "professional" your status becomes in the industry. You gain knowledge and skills each time you work on a project.

Even the smallest part is significant. Give it all you can and treat it with the consideration it deserves. If it's in the script, it usually means it had a purpose for being there and is important to the story. Some "stars" became famous because they stood out in very minor roles early in their careers. John Wayne, Marilyn Monroe and Gene Wilder are three examples.

- Each time you take on a part, you'll be expected to deliver at the very least a competent piece of work that satisfies a director or producer. Your self-esteem and sense of professionalism will also require you to do this.

- You'll be expected to deliver the work you were assigned to do on time. Often, this happens under very tight shooting and scheduling conditions.

- You'll be expected to adjust and adapt to production changes, cope with production problems and conform to other circumstances that may affect the technical and creative aspects of a production. It's important that you learn to be patient, co-operative and responsible.

- Never be late for a shoot. Check your shooting times and anything else that might be required of you on the call sheet. The "call sheet" is the daily schedule handed out to everyone involved in a production.

There's a saying in movie circles that the only time you don't show up for a shoot is if you're dead. It's a bit far-fetched, but it makes a point of what is expected of you in a professional work environment.

- Know your dialogue for the days shoot. Not knowing your lines is disastrous for productions, especially those operating under tight shooting schedules. It causes frustration and a bad working atmosphere on the set while everyone waits for you to get your act together.

- Know you dialogue! Know your dialogue! Know your dialogue! If you don't, it will reflect badly on your reputation.

- Arguments on set waste time and money. Producers, directors and crews are always uptight about that.

- Discuss *acting, technique* or *approach* matters with the director. Though there are good and bad directors, they are the ones who should steer you through to a good performance. The director is your main link to the audience who will eventually see you on the screen.

- *The crew on a movie set is also an audience to an alert actor.* He/she would be sensitive to the crew's response and use it to gauge their performance in a scene. If your performance is riveting, you'll sense the attention of the crew. If it's not, you'll know that too.

- Crews cannot stand irresponsible or egotistical actors. If a crew has a good opinion of you, they'll energize your performance. If they lose respect for you, they can disrupt it. Crews have been known to find ways to sabotage some difficult actors technically and to make them look bad on screen. Good actors always have the crews' respect.

- You'll be expected to contribute in a positive way to the public relations, promotion and general success of the production. It will be in your best interest to do so.

- Sometimes you might have to work with someone you don't like. A professional rises above that and makes sure that the job gets done, even if it's difficult to do.

Rehearsal / Setup Time

On a film, TV or commercial production, you'll probably be required to go through a number of rehearsals to get a scene working just right. Full rehearsals are generally a luxury limited to well financed feature films.

Often, under the intense pressure, tight scheduling and rigid budget conditions of TV shoots, rehearsal time is very limited. Sometimes your "rehearsal" might consist only of the director blocking the scene with the cast and running a technical walk through of what everyone will be required to do on the set just before the shoot.

After the director has rehearsed the actors and blocked their action, the camera, lighting and sound crews need time to block, place and rehearse their physical and technical moves because it's crucial that all the information that will be photographed and recorded in the scene is properly lit, framed and composed.

In TV and particularly on a series, this often becomes more important than the actors rehearsals because it's assumed the actors will already have been prepared for their roles.

- ***Prepare your part properly for the rehearsal and the shoot.*** Pass on any sound, props, wardrobe and action *requirements* you might need to the assistant director first, then to the camera, sound, wardrobe, make-up and props persons if it's about anything technical.

Usually the director is too pre-occupied with the crucial details of the shoot to be concerned with an actor's *minor* problems. Many don't like to be distracted from what they're focused on, unless your requirements specifically affect the dynamics of the scene.

Setting up to shoot a scene usually takes time. Sometimes you might have to wait a long while for the crew to work out the technical details of the scene after you've rehearsed it.

You also might have to wait while other scenes - or a part of the scene that doesn't involve you - are being shot.

Waiting can be very tiring and emotionally frustrating, especially when you're primed and ready to get on with the shoot, but that's the nature of the industry. Be patient and co-operate with the people on set while they're working hard, doing their job, to make you look good on camera, and don't complain about the waiting.

While you're waiting, it's important to stay quiet and remain focused on what you need to do when you're called on set.

Any disruption can distract you, and throw your energy and focus off and leave you emotionally depleted by the time you're needed to perform. That's why the main actors are supplied with trailers or dressing rooms near the set where they can relax and stay prepared for the moment when they're called to play their part.

It's also the reason why the lead actors or "stars" of a production will have a "stand-in" to work with the crew during the technical set-up. A "stand-in" is usually someone who resembles the main actor physically. The crew rehearses their camera, sound and lighting moves with the stand-in who replaces the main actor on the set while they are resting.

The stand-in is also matched in wardrobe with what the main actor is wearing in the scene, and is required to mimic the actual moves and action that the main actor will be performing during the shoot.

To be a stand-in is specialized work and it's not something everybody can do well. To be a good quality stand-in you have to be alert and attentive to what the main actor is doing during their rehearsal and you need to have some idea of what the actor is performing.

Prepare yourself before you appear on set. Just as athletes take time to "warm up" physically and mentally before attempting something difficult, it'll also benefit you to warm up with body and voice exercises discreetly out of everybody's way.

When you're called on set, don't rush to play out the scene. Concentrate on the moment, feel your energy moving, become comfortable with your own rhythm and allow the character to take over.

Technical

When you perform for the screen, it's useful to have some understanding of the technical details of a shoot and how this will affect your performance.

For example, are you aware of:

- What your relationship is with the camera? Are you knowledgeable of the way in which the camera "sees" you, and how sound equipment picks up the sounds you make?

- How far or how close the camera is to you in the scene and how this will shape your performance?

As a general rule, acting for the screen should be more laid back than performing on stage. We know that doing less is best, because on the screen you don't have far to project the intimacy of your performance to an audience.

- Camera lenses have different magnification qualities. The farther away the camera is from you - or the wider the lens, such as in a *wide shot* – then as a general rule, your acting can be slightly more expressive.

- When the camera is closer to you – or when the lens is more telescopic, such as in a *close-up* – as a general rule, your acting should be more subtle and downplayed because every move you make becomes more magnified. Any facial expression or body movement will become larger than life on the screen, making you to appear to be overacting.

- In *big close-ups,* your actions and movements are magnified on screen so you'll need to play your action slightly *slower*, otherwise each move you make will appear to move too quickly for the camera operator to follow and to keep properly framed and focused during the shoot. If you move too fast, it will look like you're bobbing in and out of frame.

In wider shots, your actions and movements can be normal. Overacting on the screen is usually the result of a performance not happening from a real emotional place.

If your performance is truthful and focused the camera will pick that up - or the lack of it - in your eyes - especially in *close-ups.*

Unless it's part of the character you're playing, any exaggerated, dishonest eye movement, like shifty eyes, translates very badly on the screen.

- TV monitors are smaller than theatre screens, so generally *close-ups* and *mid shots* are used more often on TV shoots than on feature films.

Wide panoramic shots that contain a large cast of actors and spectacular *staged* action are expensive and time consuming to set-up and shoot because of the larger amount of detail that needs to be positioned, rehearsed and covered in a scene, so as a general rule these are used less frequently on TV because the nature of TV is to produce programs economically.

Therefore shooting a scene in less elaborate Masters and closer shots is more economical and quicker to do than in expansive wide shots. It's a more practical way of shooting TV programs and low budget movies.

The general pattern in the way movies are shot:

Movie and TV scenes are normally shot from a number of different camera angles with different photographic compositions that capture different visual qualities in a scene. The most common procedure is:

The scene is played out in it's entirety in a *Wide* or *Mid-Wide* shot, which lays out the location and geography of the scene. It also establishes the mood and 'blocking' of the action. This is referred to as *The Master Shot*. The *Master Shot* is usually the first camera set-up. It may be static or incorporate camera movement. This is followed by a selection of tighter shots such as:

- *Medium Shots, Medium Close-ups* Or
- *Close-up Shots* or *Extreme Close-ups*

These shots are taken from a number of different camera angles and capture the heart and finer details of the scene.

Every detail of the scene that was played out and photographed in the *Master Shot*, is played out again *in continuity* in every shot that follows after this.

Camera Angles:

The camera angles and shots that are selected for a scene depend on the creative style of the director.

An adequate selection of well-placed camera angles and shots are crucial for the editing process. When they are properly edited into a final component they give rhythm, dimension, variety and focus to a scene. They can make the scene more exciting and more powerful to look at because of the changing visual perspectives that are happening on the screen.

They can also enhance and highlight the subtleties of an actor's performance.

With a variety of good camera angles to choose from, even an ordinary performance in the hands of a creative editor can be artificially manipulated and turned into a fairly good one. But don't always count on an inspirational editor to salvage a poor performance. It still comes down to you playing your part well.

Out of Sequence Continuity:

Most movie and TV stories are shot *out of sequence*. This means that the beginning of the story may be shot on the last day, the middle another day and the end of the story on the first day of production, or anywhere else in between.

This is done mainly for financial considerations:

To keep the budget of the production cost effective and within a reasonable shooting schedule, scheduling and shooting all the different scenes involving the same location at the same time makes economic sense. It saves unnecessary repetitive traveling costs and set-up time.

And to accommodate the availability and organization of shooting locations, sets, props and the key actors contracted to the production.

Working *out of sequence*:

You'll need to stay focused and recall physically and emotionally the flow of your part and how it's connected to the overall story.

Throughout the tenure of your role, you'll need to hold onto the story in your head, in terms of what happened before and what will come after the scene you are acting at the present time.

A follow-up scene of what you shoot today may not be shot for days or perhaps weeks later in a different location, representing a different story time and different characters you will be interacting with.

This means that you are responsible for maintaining a sense of emotional, physical and visual *continuity* for the character you are playing. It means you need to be aware of sustaining your characters physical changes, psychology, motivations, timing, feelings, actions, dress, props, make-up and so on, not only throughout your time on the production, but also within each specific scene that you appear in - and how that is connected to the overall story.

Scene Continuity:

When a camera angle is set-up to photograph a scene, it's referred to as a "shot" in movie talk. Because a movie or TV scene is usually photographed from various camera angles, it will require many "shots" to record the scene.

That means the same scene has to be repeated a number of times and performed in continuity exactly the same way each time to accommodate the set-up of the various camera angles.

Within the same camera angle, a number of "takes" may be required, which means that once again the performance has to be repeated a number of times, but now for various other reasons.

For example:

• The director may not have been satisfied with your performance, or the camera, sound and lighting crews may have encountered a technical hitch, or wardrobe, makeup, props and set-dressing may have encountered a continuity fault.

Repeating a scene over and over and *maintaining continuity* requires tremendous concentration and a generous amount of physical fitness from the actors, because each time the scene is re-shot:

- The actors again have to perform it the same way, with the same emotional intensity and nuances.

- Your body language, actions and movements also have to remain consistent for each take.

We've discussed how the dialogue in a script has a meaning, intention and interpretation. Once this has been locked into the scene in the Master Shot, it's the actor's responsibility to match the delivery, nuances and emotional qualities of the dialogue the same way during each take of the scene for the purposes of continuity.

Exceptions may occur in *multiple camera shoots* where more than one camera is recording or filming the scene at the same time. For example: on TV soapies and sitcoms - or on action and high budget movies that can afford the cost of multiple cameras and the technicians to operate them where shoots are scheduled over a long period of time.

Usually a *continuity person* on the set keeps an overall track of the various actions, dialogue and physical and technical details of the shoot, but the actors are also expected to be aware of their own specific continuity details in these situations.

Sound awareness:

Recording equipment today is extremely sophisticated and hi tech. A sigh, a breath and the tonal quality of a sound and its emotion can be picked up by extremely sensitive microphones and recorded.

So dialogue needn't be belted out to be heard, but must be felt and delivered creatively, with an understanding of the emotional intention behind the line.

- Sometimes it might happen that for some technical or recording reason the sound of your dialogue may not be picked up. You may then be asked to *project* your dialogue louder. This doesn't mean you have to shout the dialogue. It means that you have to *raise the volume of your delivery without losing the appropriate emotional energy and dynamic* of the scene.

- Many actors often rush to start a scene. As soon as the director calls "action" they are already speaking their lines and overlapping the director's voice on the take. Don't rush. It creates a sound problem and with your voice overlapping the director's, there's no room to edit out their voice.

   Rushing to speak your dialogue also creates a false rhythm for the start of the scene and is usually an indication to the director that the actor is not properly focused.

Upstaging / scene stealing:

There's a right way to do this, and a wrong way. Unless it's intended as part of the action in a scene, blocking another actor from view when they are speaking a crucial piece of dialogue – when the camera is focused on them – shows a total lack of camera and sound awareness. It steals the scene away from "the character" that should be the primary centre of attention at that moment.

Often actors are unaware how they upstage someone. The most common occurrence is when one actor steps in front of another while the other actor is speaking dialogue and blocks that actor from the cameras view, even after the scene has been blocked for camera.

A good technique to remember about camera awareness is that if you can see the camera, the camera can see you.

Another scene stealing blunder occurs when actors use props and make a noise, banging something down while they or another character is speaking. Or slam a door during an entrance when dialogue is going on.

Incidents like this distract the other cast members and spoil the scene, which will just have to be shot over again.

Blocking a Scene / Hitting your Marks:

Blocking a scene means working out the technical moves, action and performance details on the set just prior to shooting. It happens during rehearsals.

Once a scene has been blocked, the camera crew will lay out tape or chalk marks, usually on the floor of the set, to indicate *specific positions* where the actors can move to or from one spot to another during the shoot. The spot, or spots to where the actors have been blocked to move, is referred to as *hitting your marks.*

The reason for hitting your marks is to maintain *technical continuity*. For example:

- To keep the actors movements consistent from take to take each time they move from one position to another in the scene.
- To ensure that the actors' movements remain photographically sharp and are kept within the boundaries of the camera's movie or TV frame each time they move to a different position in a scene.
- To ensure that any sound recording can be picked up crisp and clear at the specific points where the actors move to and from their "marks".
- For lighting purposes: to ensure that the actors do not move into unlit areas once the scene has been set up for shooting, and that no unwanted shadows are cast from technical equipment or the actors movements during each take or after a camera angle change.

Never look down at those marks during the performance. Stay focused on the scene. "Hit" those spots intuitively. With experience, actors learn to sense those positions naturally.

Conclusion:

All this sounds much harder than it actually is, with most actors finding that the process becomes second nature. They usually don't even think about it. It's amazing what happens on a set during a shoot. When an actors' focus is intense – body, voice, dialogue and action seem to program intuitively and rhythmically into the whole technical process.

Besides, if an actor sometimes fluffs something on a take, there'll always be someone on a crew of thirty people or more on the set who'll remind the actor to correct it for the next "take".

Distractions: It's important for you to realize that there are always bound to be interruptions on a movie set, from the crew doing their job, to people visiting the set, to uncontrollable circumstances on a location shoot and sometimes, beside the normal distractions that occur, even from the director who may interrupt your performance at some appropriate moment in a scene to give you a directing note because they may have picked up a slight fault in your performance, or a small interruption from the set that affects the scene.

For instance:

While you're still playing the scene as its being shot, a director may interrupt you and ask you to repeat a portion of the dialogue because you may have flubbed a line or a word. Or while the camera is still running, you may be instructed to pick up your pacing and energy, or to bring it down a bit, or to redo your action with a minor adjustment because the way you're doing it is not quite connected.

Don't let such interruptions throw you. Rather than stopping and re-shooting the entire scene again, the director might have a technical or creative reason for intruding into your performance in this *particular* way.

So when you're rehearsing off camera or performing on camera, don't break your rhythm, energy and focus if you hear a disruption or distraction *outside* of what you should be doing in the scene.

Your responsibility is to *stay focused*. But at the same time, you should also *hear* the instructions that the director gives you, then take a beat or a moment to absorb the new information that's been directed at you, and then you adjust your performance and delivery to correct it, staying *inside* the scene at all times.

Most inexperienced actors don't do that. They immediately loose their concentration or turn to look at the director when they hear them giving a directing note off camera, or they may break into some sort of unrelated grimacing expression to show they realized their mistake or they become upset, or say they're "sorry" when the director interrupts the scene to point out their error.

It's a natural reaction for a person to do that when someone is talking to you. You normally turn to look at them to respond to what you hear.

However, you *don't do that* on a shoot. If you do, it's one indication to a director that you may not be focused in the scene. And on the set, people don't have time to see you get upset or to hear you say sorry each time you make a mistake. They just want you to get on with the job of doing what you have to do so that they can get on doing with what they have to do.

Once you break your concentration away from the scene even for an instant, it's difficult to get back into it and to pick up the energy, focus and rhythm of the performance from the place where you left it off.

And your loss of focus will also affect and disrupt the energy, concentration and rhythm of the other actors who are performing with you in the scene.

Learn to LISTEN to the director's notes off camera, while still staying focused and concentrated inside the scene.

Also refer to the section on PICKUPS.

Re-cap

Continuity

After each "take", remember:

- How you interacted with other characters in the scene.
- Your relationship with them in the scene you are performing as well as in the overall story.
- The energy you projected.
- At what point in the scene you did what you did.
- How you moved physically.
- When you said and did what you said.
- How you said it.
- The subtext you were projecting.
- How you felt emotionally.
- Your rhythm, pacing, and timing in the scene.
- How you used props, wardrobe, make-up, your hairstyle and other character details.
- Your purpose and objective in the scene and how that fits into the rest of the story.

Reminder: *After you have performed in "each" scene that involved you in the movie, and before you perform in the next one, you will need to remember:*

That because the movie is shot out of sequence during the time that you are working on it, you will need to keep in your head the **linear** *feel, shape, structure and progression of your character and how your character changes and evolves emotionally and physically in a linear progression throughout the story.*

Pickups

Even the most experienced actors fluff their lines. And often technical mess-ups occur during a shoot.

If that happens – or when a director is not satisfied with the way an actor delivers *a fragment* of action and dialogue in a scene, or when something unwanted intrudes on the flow of the performance – the director might call for a "pickup" of the particular action and dialogue where the fluff occurred.

The director does this rather than waste time by re-doing a complete "take" of the scene again from beginning to end if most of it was overall satisfactory.

So when a "pick up" is called:

- The actors have to repeat or "pickup" only that portion of the action and dialogue in *the part* of the scene where the fluff or error occurred.

When a "pickup" is called, always re-do the *complete text* of your dialogue and action in *the part* of the scene where the error occurred.

Do not repeat just the error of the single line and/or action and begin the "pickup" at the exact spot where the fluff occurred, or just at any random point in your text.

Always start from the beginning of the complete section of dialogue and action where the fluff occurred and carry your action and dialogue through to the end, or until the director calls "cut".

- If the piece of the scene that needs to be "picked up" also involves another actor, begin with the other actor feeding you their dialogue or action first, to *lead* you into your action or speech.

This will help you to get back into the rhythm, timing, pacing and subtext of what you were doing before the interruption occurred. It keeps your performance in harmony with the whole scene for continuity and editing.

Technical

Crossing the Line

One day, one of our students came to class upset and confused. She had just completed her first professional part in a TV drama. It was a small role and she thought her performance had gone well.

Then someone in the crew said, "She crossed the line", and they had to re-shoot that part of the scene over again. She felt intimidated and confused because she didn't know what she had done wrong by "crossing the line", and no one seemed able to explain it clearly to her.

"Crossing the line" is not the actors' problem. It's the director and the crew's responsibility. It's about where they place the camera to shoot additional camera angles of a scene once the master shot has been established.

However, as a film actor it's probably to your advantage to be aware of what that technicality means, so that you can adjust accordingly and not be thrown off rhythm in terms of your performance in the scene.

Explanation:

Each time you look into a mirror, your image inside the mirror looking back at you is reversed. For example, your right hand outside the mirror becomes your left hand inside the mirror as it faces back at you. And your left hand becomes your right.

If you were able to move and cross over past the physical point, or *line* of the mirror in front of you, you would have "crossed the line". You would have crossed over to the other side, and your image would become reversed to what it was where you stood on the original side of the mirror.

The same sort of thing happens when the camera is placed facing the actors to establish the master shot of a scene.

Look at the following illustrations:

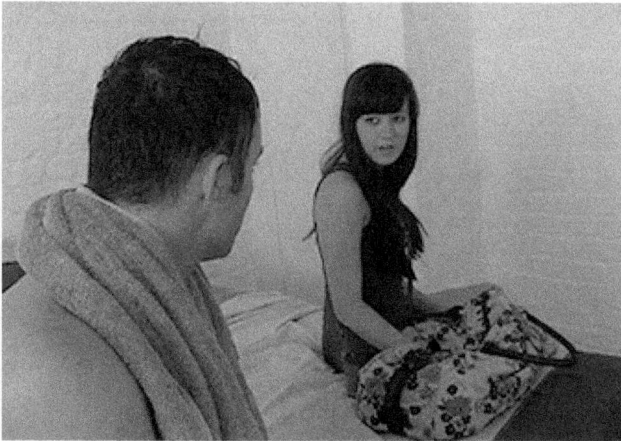

From the master shot position of where the camera has been placed, there is an imaginary 180 degree line that cuts across the actors facing each other. Like the mirror example, that *imaginary line* separates the actors playing to the camera, from their opposite or reverse side.

Once the camera has established a master shot on one side of that imaginary line, all the camera angles for the scene that will be required after that must remain on the same side of that line, otherwise if the camera has crossed that line aimlessly and the scene is put together for editing, some of the camera angles will look reversed and out of harmony with what has been established in the master shot.

Sometimes crossing the line intentionally can be used effectively by a director as a dramatic ploy. Commercials and music videos do it all the time, and you see it quite often in fast paced action movies and sports programs where suddenly the action in a scene looks momentarily reversed and the actors are facing each other in opposite positions.

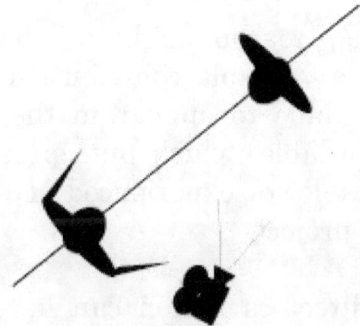

However, if crossing the line is done indiscriminately in drama, it does disrupt the smooth flow of a movie once it's been edited, especially in close-ups. Because close-ups are so overpowering, the actor's eye-lines will look different when they're talking and looking at each other from opposite sides of the line.

Recap:

As a general rule, so long as the camera remains on one side of the 180 degree line that's been originally established in the master shot, then every new camera angle that's incorporated into the scene after that must be shot from the same side that line.

Shooting Compromises

Many movie and television projects begin with wonderful ideas. But often creative people are forced to compromise their original vision of a project and to re-adjust their thinking to fit a more practical reality when the time comes to produce it.

This can happen for many reasons:

Unanticipated script and production problems, location losses, weather delays and so on can impede the shooting schedule of a production. Any such impediment that compromises the shooting schedule of a project, also adversely affects the budget of the project and any restraints that affect the budget can cause monetary cuts that deny the production the affordability of a more extravagant look.

Another reason might be that "Name" actors whose drawing power might make a valuable contribution to the financial success of the project may be unavailable to appear in the production or their salary demands might be unaffordable, which puts pressure on the director to work with less known "bankable" or experienced actors which might further compromise the budget of the project.

The directors' vision can be even more compromised because they may be forced to economize on the "look" of the project by using less complicated and time consuming camera angle set-ups, and to shoot fewer takes which means using less film which is expensive to purchase and process; or to cut down on lavish camera moves and special effects which are expensive to set-up and shoot, and to readjust to simpler and more affordable locations, props and wardrobe and to use fewer actors in scenes.

The end result of all of this is that the outcome of the shoot now becomes more important – which diminishes the grand vision of the production at all costs, and does not accommodate the director's original objective.

This is especially true on TV shoots where schedules, budgets and the cost of turning out a production is particularly tight and the product has to be completed on time to meet TV broadcasting schedules.

The pressures of production are enormous because money and time are involved so frustrations and tensions can become severe.

However, there can also be a plus side to this when a production team works under tight budget conditions.

Occasionally, the pressure of compromising forces people to become more creative and to compensate for the limited funds they have in other ways.

Some wonderful movies have been made with fewer resources because of the enthusiasm and passion of the people involved in creating the project. And sometimes enthusiasm and passion is more potent in creating something memorable than having too much money to play around with.

High budgets and working with a comfortable shooting schedule is a luxury that's mostly limited to big screen movies. But the down side to this is that the people working with an over inflated production budget sometimes tend to become lax, wasteful and over confident about what they're doing, and the truth is that most of those high budget movies have been financial disasters.

It's important for actors to realize that there are many things production people have to cope with to make something work. Just focus on what is expected of you and don't complain or criticize those things that you are not aware of.

Professional Courtesy / Respect

It happens often. Some actors are seduced by an illusion of "fame and fortune", and it usually happens after they've "landed" their first important "starring" role.

You see them working on TV and movie sets. They've lost perspective of who they are and where they've come from. They strut around and look down on their *co-workers* with a sense of self-importance.

They're disrespectful, demanding and impatient with people who they assume are "unimportant" crew members who work hard and long hours to get a job done. They treat *supporting* players in minor roles with a lack of consideration, and especially *elder* actors who sometimes move slower and struggle to meet the pace and pressures of difficult and demanding parts.

Arrogance is a sign of immaturity, insecurity and a lack of knowledge about the bigger picture of things. You owe it to the *experience* of the people you work with, especially if they've "been there" before you, to be courteous and respectful.

The entertainment business is exceptionally fickle. You're only as good and as popular as the last successful role you played. One day you too might go through a difficult period, or find that your popularity is slumping or your energy is moving at a slower pace. Then, how will *you* want to be treated by your co-workers?

A number of years ago in Los Angeles, a young actor got a "break" and became *one* of the "stars" of a TV action series. He was in a perfect position to become a successful movie star, but he threw away his chance to really hit the big time because of his inflated ego.

As the series became popular with TV viewers, he began making unreasonable demands from the producers. His attitude on the set also became more impossible to deal with, and that reverberated negatively onto the crew and other actors in the series. He created a lot of resentment and people were unhappy doing their job, which reflected badly on the quality of the production.

The ratings of the series began to drop and it ended quickly after that. He tried to get work elsewhere, but only a few minor roles came his way where he appeared as "a guest" in one or two episodes on other actors' series.

He made many enemies with people who remembered his attitude. Eventually the parts stopped coming and he faded into obscurity.

This story is not unique.

There's a saying in Hollywood: "Be careful how you treat me. I'll meet you on your way down, on my way up!"

Tread cautiously in your relationships. Your co-workers deserve your consideration.

Part 9

Charisma

*The degree of self-confidence and
passion you project.*

*If you have doubts and insecurities,
don't show them.*

*Success represents 1% of your work which
results from the 99% that is called failure.*

- Unknown

Performing in Theatre versus the Movies

Performance Adjustments

There are different styles and techniques of acting.

The broader type of acting which is more clinical and technically focused is more commonly observed in theatrical performances, and to some extent in soapies and sitcoms which are basically more theatrical in style rather than having the look, feel and flair of a movie.

The type of acting that is common in a theatrical play is more dialogue oriented and is usually over written because much of the story information in this genre has to be presented verbally.

In many cases, this makes it more difficult for the actors to perform realistically. It has to do with the way the dialogue is written and the way the performance is staged in an artificial setting, because it needs to compensate for information that cannot be included visually within the confines of the theatre.

In a theatrical setting, the actor's image and size on the stage is seen normally, and the actor has to project outwards vocally and usually in broader body language to reach the audience sitting in the theatre space.

Because of the visual nature of the movies, and the fact that a movie has the power to draw the audience *directly* into the action on the screen, much subtle and detailed information is subliminally projected visually.

Less is required to be explained through dialogue and a more "real" or "internalized" type of acting is best suited to perform in the movies.

Another major difference between a theatrical and a screen performance is in the linear direction in which a story is acted out in theatre, versus a non linear shooting and performance progression for the screen.

Each time an actor performs a theatrical play, they act the part in an uninterrupted *linear* direction from beginning to end within a set time frame that can be anywhere from a few minutes to two hours or more, and performed over and over again through a number of showings.

Due to this linear direction which a theatrical play follows when its performed on the stage, it allows an actor flexibility to make changes and to experiment with emotional, dialogue, blocking and technical variations to the character they are playing from one performance to the next.

The very nature of theatre also allows the actors to play with energy and dialogue variations in a performance from one showing to the next if they feel that an adjustment to the dialogue or the action indicated in the script will benefit the overall quality of the play.

However, when actors are involved in a theatrical performance, they don't make any unnecessary adjustment to their performance unless they've first talked it through with the director and their co-actors in the play. Their co-actors are also crucial to what is happening on stage, and any adjustments they make will also affect what the other actors are doing.

In screen acting, because of the *non-linear* way in which a movie is shot the actors emotional, technical and character dynamics must be maintained and sustained for continuity in a non-linear manner from scene to scene and from take to take over a period of time that can last for days, weeks or even months once the performance have been established and committed onto camera.

Performance energy must also be maintained and sustained over days, weeks or even months, and be consistent from take to take within the circumstances of the story and what is unfolding between the characters from scene to scene.

Over such a lengthy time frame the actor's performance energy must be made to feel natural, spontaneous and appropriate to the situation each time the actor appears on the screen.

So for a screen performance, once you've established the details of your character, you cannot keep making major adjustments to those dynamics from take to take or from scene to scene each time you appear on camera. If you do, your continuity will be inconsistent and your performance will come across as disjointed in the completed film.

Of course, minor adjustments and changes also *do* occur during a movie shoot, but each time a change is made, it needs to be a controlled dynamic, which requires the actor to be aware of what's been shot and established before in the movie, and what still needs to be shot after the place where the adjustment is to be made.

When adjustments and changes are necessary, they must also be made in harmony with what everyone else is doing who is involved in each scene and in the overall creative process of making the movie.

Auditions

How the system works

First of all, you need an agent to represent you in the industry. So try to connect with a reputable actors' agent to speak for you.

Find someone you feel comfortable with, who believes in your potential and who will *promote* you. Without credible representation, most producers and directors won't take you seriously and if some do there's a good chance that they'll use your talent, make a lot of promises and just neglect to compensate you financially.

There are good agents with integrity who genuinely would like to see you succeed. There are also bad one's who are basically just "bookers", who "book" you to go to an audition and who do the least amount of work for you. They might have a large roster of "clients" listed in their business that they "represent" who they send to general auditions. If one of their clients gets a part so be it, and such agents survive by collecting a generous percentage from their clients' payments.

 A good agent should be well-informed about what is going on in the industry. They should work for you, not against you. For the percentage that they receive of your payment an agent should:

- Negotiate good financial and comfort terms for you with the producers of a production.
- Advise you and keep you informed about the needs of the industry and about upcoming parts that might be suitable for you.
- Send you to *appropriate* auditions that are suitable for you and not waste your time.
- Inform you about the dynamics of the part and what is required of you at the audition.
- Promote you in the appropriate circles in the industry, as well as in the media and make you known to the general public.
- Treat you with consideration and respect once they decide to represent you.

In short, a good agent should look after your interests and see that you're treated properly and fairly by the people involved in a production.

Ask around for the kind of agent you think could best represent you and get opinions from other actors who are already linked with one to refer you.

Some agents are notoriously slack, especially in promoting newcomers. So when you're starting out in the industry continue to follow your own leads about what auditions are taking place, what productions are scheduled to be happening and who is doing what. Don't always rely on your agent to keep you informed, so stay on top of whoever is representing you.

• Follow any leads you hear about through rumors in the industry "grapevine". Read the trade papers to see what projects are up for casting in theatre, film, TV, voice over and commercial work. No part is too small - go for it if you believe its right for you! Whether you get the part or not, don't be disheartened. It adds to your experience.

• Do some basic research on what the audition requires. Is it a play? Movie? TV show? Commercial? A voice over? What will the part involve? Prepare yourself emotionally, psychologically and physically to audition for it.

Why should *you* be chosen? Why do you *feel* right for it? Be clear about that in your mind and focus on the part to convince your agent and the producer/director of the project that they should cast you.

Appear at the audition on time. You'll be given a number and usually you'll have to wait to be seen 'til your number is called, but it's a good professional discipline for you to be there even if it's a long wait, and to be ready when they call you.

Casting sessions can be upsetting, especially when you arrive at a place and find thirty people or more holding numbers and waiting for their turn to audition, and all of them competing for the same part. That type of audition is known in the industry as a "cattle call" because many actors have said that they really do feel like they've been herded and treated like cattle waiting around like that at those sessions.

This kind of audition can be particularly tiresome and humiliating even for some well-known actors who already have an impressive performance reputation and a number of significant screen credits behind them. It's unfortunate, but this is the way the system works at this time. Unless you're a really big international star or a well-known "personality", very few people are able to avoid being treated in such an indifferent way.

The important thing is, to not to let that put you off. Keep focused on what *you* need to do to get the part.

Be co-operative. Doing a production is stressful and people don't need the headache of dealing with un-cooperative or aggressive actors. Remember, you can always be replaced. At this stage of your career, you need them more than they need you. If you have to talk to someone about something, be courteous about it.

- Make a good appearance. Be well groomed, unless the audition calls for a specific type of character or cultural image. Be prepared for any unexpected instructions that might be thrown at you. Be flexible. *Listen* to any directions if any are given to you. How you take direction is also a good indicator to an alert casting person that there's a professional quality about you.

- Psyche up your energy and confidence. You might be expected to learn lines and *interpret* a scene with short notice. It's not uncommon for a scene to be handed to you as you arrive at the venue. You'll be expected to audition for it within a few minutes while you wait your turn outside the venue. It impresses people if you can learn a few lines and *interpret* a scene relatively quickly.

- If you're in doubt about what to do in terms of a performance, it's better to underplay a scene rather than to overdo it. *Internalize* your energy. The casting people can always tell you to do more if your internal energy is vibrating convincingly.

Create something memorable for the *casting people* to look at. If you do, they'll remember you. Very often the people holding an audition might not have "locked into" what they're looking for when they're *casting* a particular part.

This could be an opportunity for you to *create* a character's image for them.

- If it's appropriate for the audition, you might even add something visual to your character with a touch of wardrobe or props. See what you can use that's available in the casting room. It could swing the role in your favor.

When you do a "reading", don't keep looking down at the script. That's a turn-off for casting people. They expect you to at least *try* and do something interesting. If it's appropriate, include some physicality and movement in the audition.

If there's another actor involved, use *eye contact* and try to make an emotional connection with them as a character. This also applies to first rehearsal readings after you've landed the part.

If you have questions, ask. The answers you get will help you to focus more clearly onto what the *director* and *producer* might be looking for.

- Rejection and criticism is always painful, but realize that the people who do castings have specific reasons for *choosing* the actor who is cast. That doesn't necessarily mean you were bad, just *different* from what they were looking for at that time, at that specific casting session.

Each time you go to an audition, you'll get to know the right people. The more they see you, the more they'll get used to you and they'll get to know you. And sooner or later, you'll make that important connection.

Producers, writers and directors are generally sensitive about the written material of the production they're casting. Don't look down on the quality of the material that's handed to you and don't diminish it, even if you can't connect with it.

Many years ago I was directing a movie for the CBC TV Network in Toronto, Canada and we were holding auditions for a major role that had not been cast yet. I took a break from the casting, left the room and walked to the vending machine at the end of the hallway to get refreshment.

The hallway was packed with young male actors studying the scene that was handed to them, waiting for their turn to audition. No one was aware that I was the director.

That particular audition scene consisted of three short but very important lines from the movie. As I walked by I overheard one of the "actors" comment loudly, "What shit is this!" I said nothing, continued to the vending machine and returned to the casting room.

Later, that "actor" appeared in front of us to audition.

After his comment in the hallway, I wondered why he bothered to stay for the session. I looked at him and said, "Thanks, but you already had your audition in the hallway". He was offended that I had stopped him from continuing.

However, he had already indicated to me that his acting skills were probably minimal and that he had no concept of how to interpret the subtext of the scene, and probably much less how to perform it. So I wasn't prepared to waste anymore time with him.

That movie went on to win an international drama award and introduced a newcomer to television who became a leading Canadian actress.

Respect the objective of the people who hold casting sessions. If you don't understand the material that's handed to you, ask someone who does.

Actors who are really good at their job can take even the most mundane dialogue and make it sound brilliant.

It's in the way they *interpret* it and how they play it.

Preparing for the Audition

Guidelines
Commercials, movies and television

- What is the product? Who is my character?   What am I selling?
- What is the history or "story" of the product?   What is my character's history?
- What is my feeling about the product? Of my character?
- What is the "feel" of the script or the scene? What does it suggest?
- What is the theme, subtext or statement of the story-board? Where / what is the setting? What is the "look" of the environment / setting?
- What attitude am I required to project / what body language - dialogue - voice or psychology?
- How should I be dressed to make a personal impression, or as a character?
- What is my relationship to the other characters in the "story"?
- What is the action? What is the right rhythm, timing and pacing for the scene? Where are the moments of impact?
- What can I do to make the selling of the product or the role unique or memorable?
- What can I do to bring "life" to the role and/or the product? How should I interpret the scene, product and the character?
- What is the "look" and feel of the other characters, their body make-up, wardrobe and the set and props that will be used?
- What is my approach and body language? How can I work with props and my space in the setting? If other actors are involved in the scene, how do I work with them?
- How do I begin the scene and how do I end it with some sort of impact.
- What is the presentation style of the production? Is it a comedy, drama, romance, an action piece, musical or anything else...?
- Do I perform this: laid back, broad, subtle or neutral? Or in any other way...?
- What is there in the audition room that I can use to complement my audition as a character?

Casting Sessions

What happens behind closed doors?

Casting is just another word for auditions.

Casting sessions are handled indifferent ways. The two most common are:

[1] Auditions that are overseen by a *casting director* and [2] Auditions that are overseen personally by the *director* and *producer*.

[1] The casting director is a person who is usually contracted by a production company throughout the period of a production to audition actors to play different parts that will be required in the making of a movie or television program.

The casting director will send a script, scene or brief to all the actors agencies in your area, with information about the project they're casting. If your agent feels you might be suitable for the part, your agent will pass on that information to you and other actors represented by your agency.

• You'll be given the date, time and venue of the audition.

Alternatively, you might be handed a script or a scene containing the part you are auditioning when you arrive at the venue.

- You might have a few minutes to look the scene over to consider what you think you'll have to do.

- Realistically, you won't be expected to learn the dialogue at such short notice, although it will help to make a favorable impact if you can give an impression of remembering some of it.

- Make use of your "waiting" time to develop an *interpretation* of the scene. Do the same with another actor if one is involved in the scene with you.

- During the audition you can refer to your script. But don't just "read" the lines. Try and give the casting people some *sense* of a performance. What's more important is to give an indication that you *understand* how to *interpret* a scene.

An interpretation is your personal understanding of the scene and how you would play it. It *validates* your audition, even if your interpretation does not agree with what the casting people are looking for.

- Ask questions that might clarify the character and concept for you. Suggest things if you want.

• Your audition will most likely be video recorded by the casting people to capture your *look*. If the *casting director* is impressed with your audition, the video will then be forwarded to the director and producer of the project.

If the director and/or producer are interested in your *look* and interpretation of the scene, you'll get a *call back* for another audition, probably to be seen personally by the director.

That's a good sign, but not a guarantee that you've landed the part. However, it does mean you're in the running for it and are at least on the shortlist of the top five candidates.

Whether you get the part or not, either way you should be informed about it within a reasonable time by your agent.

However, agents sometimes neglect to inform their clients when a casting decision has been reached, especially when they represent a large roster of talent. So, make sure your agent keeps track of your audition and notifies you about any *feedback*.

Constructive feedback of what you're doing, right or wrong, will help you improve for your next audition.

[2] The director and producer might both be involved in the casting session right from the beginning, and this usually happens when the actors already have an "established reputation" in the industry.

This session will probably also be video recorded for later reference.

You need to understand that when a director or casting person look at thirty or more people during a daylong casting session, it becomes tiring and difficult for them to remember what each actor looked like or how they performed.

So the recording of your audition is very important. The director can review the recording and compare the best auditions later in less tiring and less stressful surroundings.

What prompts the decision?

You're chosen or not chosen for a part for various reasons. Generally, none of them are personal nor do they imply an acceptance or rejection of your talent.

Some reasons may be:

What was the first impression you made to the casting people when you entered the audition space? Were you nervous? Were you uncertain about yourself or unprepared for the part?

Sometimes you can be *intimidated* by people you don't know. Don't allow that to unsettle you. Maintain your composure. Be pleasant but not over friendly, because that gives the impression that you're trying too hard and that's a turn-off for some people.

> Just *be* your *real* self! Trying to find the actor's *real self* is what many directors often look for in a casting session.

Do you or don't you *fit* into the *image* of the role the way the director, producers, investors and casting people *interpret* it?

You get the part because you performed something interesting in the audition. Perhaps you were innovative, special and exciting to watch, or you had the right *energy* and *feel* for the part. It *suited* you!

- Your *look* and talent was new, refreshing, unusual and exceptional. It's *different* from what's been seen before. You made people auditioning you sit up and notice your presence. You took *control* of your space.

- Perhaps you got the part because a *specific role* was being cast. You have an *average* quality that the director and producers thought viewers could identify with. You projected something, especially for sitcoms and soapies, that would *appeal* to the largest common sector of the viewing public.

- You have an *established reputation* as an actor. You have a recognizable name that the people at the audition are comfortable with. They know you'll *deliver* what is expected of you in a performance.

- But you might *not* get the part if you've been *overexposed* in the movies, commercials or on TV. Then you'll need to "disappear" for a while until you've created a new image and re-appear fresh and rejuvenated.

- You get the part because you're a *famous* and *timely PERSONALITY in* sports, fashion, politics, trade, showbusiness, the arts and other such things. In this case, your acting ability is not what matters. It's your *celebrity* that is important. Your *name* is "bankable" and the programme or commercial will be made to work around you.

- You might get, or not get the part because of an *agreement* or *disagreement* about your audition between the director, producers, casting people or investors of the project.

  Then choosing *you* becomes a matter of different opinions and arguments between these people. And opinions between them will vary. The final decision then rests with the person who has the most creative or financial control over the project.

Sometimes, it also depends on how the people who are involved in the casting decision are feeling on a particular day. If they're feeling good, they'll probably be more responsive to your audition. If not, they'll always look for the easiest way out.

Personal notes:

I never liked holding casting sessions, especially the "cattle call" kind. Those sessions often made me feel uncomfortable and uninspired, but I had to sit through them many times, because that was the formal way of doing things, especially when I was working on a TV series.

That type of casting session didn't give me a true sense of who the *person* in the actor was.

Then from personal experience I realized that some truly remarkable actors are not very good at auditions. However they were terrific when by chance or intuition, I decided to cast them in a movie anyway because I sensed there was something interesting about them. It became obvious to me, that some people are just not good at formal casting sessions.

Conversely, I've also been bitterly disappointed by other actors who came across very strong in auditions and presented me with an impressive display of diplomas in dramatic art accredited by some pretty high powered international universities, but who completely fell apart once they were cast and on the set performing in a movie.

I learnt that when I'm interested in an actor, the *first* thing that draws me to them before they even talk is what I see in the "look" and "feeling" of that particular person, whether they have diplomas or not.

Before I cast someone in an important role, I chat to them privately about various things before even discussing the part, because I'm more interested at this stage in getting to know *who* the person is and to sense *if* I can work with them.

I look to see how well the actor *listens* to the information I give them. How did they respond to it and how well did they absorb it and understand it?

I look to see how creative they are and try to sense if they will be able to build on what I transmit to them and to deliver what will be required of them if I cast them in the part.

Once the communication barriers are broken down and we feel comfortable with each other, it gives me a better sense about the actor and how they feel and how they would treat the role.

Although this is only my personal opinion, I've talked to other directors who agree.

When I audition an actor I've not seen before, I prefer to look at film or video footage of them if they have something available, to give me an idea of how they look, move and perform on camera.

I usually do this before I meet them because I want to know how the camera sees them and how they relate to the camera. If they have nothing available but their look and personality feels right to me, I'm even prepared to videotape a screen test of them if the budget and circumstances on the production will allow me to do that.

Once I've done that and if they interest me further, it's easier for me to concentrate on script readings and to *work* with them in a formal session before I commit them to the production.

Recap

Audition phobia or jittery nerves during a casting session is usually a consequence of:

- Not understanding and analyzing what the part is *about*.
- Insecurity and a lack of proper focus on what you should be doing at the audition, which is a result of not properly listening to the instructions you are given about the requirements of the part. If you lack information about the part you will not be fully prepared for it.
- If you are *excessively* trying to memorize the dialogue in the scene in a technical manner rather than performing your interpretation of it, the result of this will be that it will block the free flow of your creativity and performance energy which will consequently make you nervous.
- Not trusting the *value* of your interpretation of the part.
- Your *over-eagerness* on wanting the part with too much energy concentrated on your anxiety which is applied in the wrong direction.
- *Over compensating* your integrity as an actor by trying to please the casting people with what you *think* they are looking for.
- Projecting your performance outwards and trying to "act" it rather than internalizing it and *experiencing* being inside it.

Tips to overcome performance anxiety and stress:

From a qualified teacher learn to do breathing exercises to release performance tension and also voice drills to loosen the power of your voice.

To help you relax before you enter the audition or start a performance, you might consider doing some physical movement from disciplines such as yoga, Tai Chi or different forms of dance. Different types of meditation are also useful for calming you down.

- Turn your energy to *enjoy the experience* of the audition and *trust* your intuition about how *you* should interpret the part.

- Re-channel your focus from anxiety to the *spirit* of a performance and don't worry about getting or not getting the part.

You and the Audience

What is it about *you* or the character you're playing that will make an audience sit up and take notice? Why should someone pay money to look at you on the screen?

Place yourself in the audience's position:

Is it the way you look because you're beautiful or handsome? Then think about this: What's beauty? The idea of beauty changes from culture to culture and even from time to time. An advertising label and hyped-up "image" that's "in" now, will be "out" tomorrow and something new will replace it until people get bored with that.

If you look at it objectively, some of the most remarkable actors from different times and in different places have never really been "beautiful" in the way that "beauty" is promoted in our culture at present.

Looking at her movies now, Marilyn Monroe would be considered plump, overweight and over-dressed in her wardrobe and make up by many audiences today. She is seen as not really that "pretty" or sexy. But she was a great sex symbol during the 1950's and in some way still remains a "legend", even though she's a fading one.

In the 1930's and 40's, Bette Davis was a "bad, tough girl" on the screen, but she was not "beautiful" by today's standards. Humphrey Bogart wasn't even "handsome" and he even had a bad lip and lisp when he talked. Edward G. Robinson was short, plump and not "good looking". Gary Cooper was tall, lanky, moved slowly and spoke lazily. James Cagney was small, skinny and over-compensated his performances with fast talking and high energy. But they were big stars in their time and audiences loved them.

Conversely, some extremely "beautiful" looking people look stilted and come across blandly on screen. There seems to be nothing there under the façade of their "beauty". We've seen how each person has an energy and quality that's unique to them, which they project to others.

But what about you?

Do you attract people to watch you because of the way *you* talk or the way you sound to others? Is it the power of your physical presence? Is it the way you move or dress? Or the way you claim your space? Are you relaxed or stressed? Do you project any kind of "image"?

Are you intriguing, mysterious or passionate? Is it your mouth? Is it your sensuality and sexuality? Are you serious, cool, funny or zany? Do you have personality, charm, appeal, allure? Is it because you're relaxed and comfortable with yourself? Is it your confidence, intellect, focus and concentration? Is it about the way you *feel* about yourself?

The bottom line then about what seems to make you "attractive" to other people, is the *degree of life that glows within you.* It's when you are *being alive and totally involved* in a given situation that stimulates an audience to watch you. That appears to be a vital quality which legendary movie stars have.

Don't force an authenticity. If it's not happening for real at that moment, it's best to perform with simplicity and impartiality.

Use the special quality in yourself, whatever it is, to make you stand out in an audition, on the screen and in your personal life.

Relaxation / sensory exercises:

Fill your lungs with the smell of fresh-cut grass; feel the earth, caress the contours of a rock, run sand through your fingers and *sense* these textures moving through your fingers and on your skin; feel rain falling through your hair and on your body; hug a tree and stay rooted to it for a while until you feel yourself becoming revitalized by its energy. In some parts of North America that's what the Indians do to realign their emotional energy.

It really does work when you are unhurried, fully conscious and focused inside the experience.

Summary

Auditions

When you go to an audition or work with other actors for the first time, you need to *sass out* the "vibe" of the place and of each other. You need to *tune into* the "vibe" that will *set the tone* of your audition or working relationship. You need to *connect* with those *new* energies and *tune into* energy interactions you can use in your performance.

One way you do this is to *study* those other peoples' actions, moods, physical characteristics and vocal qualities while you're waiting for your turn to audition.

Don't just sit there being bored or nervous. Be alert to what is happening and *Listen* for any information that might be projecting back to you. See what you can use during the audition. What sort of feelings or emotions are those other actors – who are also waiting for their turn to audition – *giving* to you and how are they *interacting* with you emotionally and physically?

When your turn comes up, try and give a "performance" instead of reading lines. *Interpret* the scene or the information that is given to you, as you understand it.

Keep eye contact and interact with the other actor if the scene includes another character.

It will make a good impression if you can memorize at least *some* of the dialogue in the scene. Refer to your script if you have to, but what is more important is to *interpret* the scene and the character you are auditioning for.

If it's appropriate at that moment and helpful to you, ask if you can use any objects that you see in the room, which you can use as props when you audition.

Every part is important in a script. No role is too small. Often, actors who are famous today were discovered because of the way they interpreted and performed the small roles they played at the start of their careers.

Part 10

.

...the artist appeals to that part of our being which is not dependent on wisdom; to that in us which is a gift and not an acquisition – and, therefore, more permanently enduring.

He speaks to our capacity for delight and wonder, to the sense of mystery surrounding our lives: to our sense of pity, and beauty and pain.

- Josef Conrad

To Thine own Self Be True...

- Proverbs

Performance Choices

When an actor takes on a part, they make *choices* about *how* to play a character.

The *choices* you make are determined by how *you* interpret the information that is given in the script and by the director's guidelines.

Some of the *choices* you can make about how you perform your character are:

- Your physical appearance: How you look, how you are groomed and what you wear.
- Your attitude and how intensely you relate emotionally to the other characters in a scene. Are you loud, soft, casual, overbearing, cowering or something else?
- How your character evolves and progresses - or doesn't - in the context of the story and in the overall continuity of the movie or television production.
- How your character responds in conflicts.
- How you perform the scene: dramatically, tragically, humorously, over the top or laid back and so on.
- The energy and passion you give the part.
- The rhythm, timing and pacing of your performance. For example: Fast, slow, neutral, etc.
- The emotional mood swings that happen and the rhythmic changes that affect you in your interactions with the other characters.
- The way you make the dialogue flow. For example: How you speak and use pauses, accents, stresses and project your voice.
- How you perform the physical action required in the scene.
- What you *choose* to be your *objective*. For example, what your character needs to accomplish in the scene.
- How you begin and end the scene.
- How far and how deep you push yourself. What performance risks you're willing to take to excite the people watching you.

Each *choice* you make will affect the energy, story dynamics and chemistry between you and the other characters in the scene.

The following scenes could be audition pieces. What performance *choices* would you make when you play each scene?

[1]   LOOK AT ME

The following dialogue between two characters, A and B, is very simple.

The exercise is intended to stimulate your creativity, so there is no story or character background information given. *You* create the situation, circumstances and the setting.

You can *choose* to perform it either dramatically or humorously. Fast paced or slow.

Based on the background you've created:

- Who are A and B? What is their relationship to each other?
- Where are they? What could they be talking about? What are the emotional exchanges that are happening between them? Why?
- What props are they using and what physical action might they be doing at the beginning of the scene?
- What is it that might have happened between A and B just before the scene began that motivated the dialogue?
- How do they end the scene? What do you think is going to happen?
- Do you sense any rhythmic changes and pauses happening verbally or physically anywhere in the scene? If so, where would you place them? How would you perform them?

A

Look at me.

B

What do you want me to say?

A

Don't you understand? I want to
hear it from you.

B

There's nothing to say.

A
You're not honest with yourself.

B
Why do you keep putting me down?
Does it excite you, or something?

A
Why won't you open up to me?

B
Do you know something I don't?

A
Look. Just forget the past. Where do
we go from here?

B
I don't know. You tell me.

A
Alright. If that's the way you want it,
there's nothing more to say.

B
O.K.

A
O.K...!

END

Experiment further with the scene: Perform it with one type of rhythm, timing and pacing – and then with another – and with different moods and energy.

[2]   THINGS YOU CANNOT TELL JUST BY LOOKING AT HER
by Samantha Gray

EXT. HOUSE GARDEN NIGHT

SHE enters - doesn't see HIM concealed in the shadows. He wears shorts, no top. On his chest is a tattoo of a naked woman.

HE watches her then approaches.

> HIM
> Your mother hates me.

SHE looks at HIM.

> SHE
> Do me a favor. Keep yourself covered.
> I don't want my parents to think you're
> cheap.

> HE
> When are they leaving?

> SHE
> Why?

> HIM
> Why are you so awful? This afternoon you
> were so wonderful. You took care of me and
> I really loved you.

> SHE
> You pathetic little man.

SHE lights a cigarette.

                                HIM
When did you start smoking?

                                SHE
I don't know...

                                HIM
Those are my cigarettes.

                                SHE
What's wrong with you...?

SHE coughs then chokes. HE tries to help - snatches the cigarette. The lit end drops into his pants. It burns him.

SHE tries to help. One mishap leads into another. They struggle until they drop exhausted onto the ground.

Silence.

                                SHE
Why do we do this to each other?

                                HIM
I don't know...Are there anymore...?

SHE looks at him, shakes her head.

                                                        END

At first glance, the dialogue in this scene probably suggests a dramatic interpretation.

But think of a *different* or alternative way to *re-interpret* the *obvious*.

What would happen if you performed the scene with a humorous, lighter dynamic to make the drama and relationship between HIM and HER emotionally more poignant?

Might the dialogue suggest some sort of neurotic co-dependency relationship between these two characters?

What might he be doing before she enters? How would you approach the ending?

[3]   Excerpt from: HONOUR THY FATHER
CBC-TV, Canada

Cultural/social interpretations

To a large extent, people in real life are "products" of their culture. Their actions and reactions are motivated by the beliefs and manner of their conditioning.

Their attitude and personal temperament will also determine how they'll act and react – and with how much intensity - in a situation or in a relationship.

In the same way, story characters are also conditioned and motivated by *their* cultural background and "history" and by the nature and quality of their relationships with other story characters which is implied in the script.

When you work on the interpretation of a character, consider their social, cultural and ethnic background and the status of their relationship with others in the story.

How do they express themselves through body language? Observe the emotional and physical attitudes of people from another culture as it applies to the role you are playing. What is the significance of the body language that they might project under certain circumstances? For example:

A handshake or a kiss or even the way you greet someone might mean one thing in your culture, but might mean something totally different or even be offensive in another one.

Explore the difference and nuances of peoples' attitudes and how they communicate in different cultures.

This will help you to find **your** character in a more complete way.

The social and cultural circumstances of the other story characters should also influence *the way* you play the part.

For example, if the story circumstances are appropriate to the personality of the character you are creating, how might any of the following conditions affect your actions and reactions?

religious	fanaticism	violence	crime	totalitarianism
decadence	greed	poverty	intolerance	ignorance
addiction	war	deceit	labor unrest	illness
patriotism	famine	corruption	discord	
over population		social/family unrest	physical/psychological	

Or

education /enlightenment	healing/health	consideration/respect	
personal and social freedom	prosperity and opportunity		
integrity	social harmony	caring	leisure
abundance	wealth	tolerance	peace
creativity	co-operation	harmony	optimism

In the scene below create a background and a set of circumstances that you feel might have motivated the following dialogue, and a cultural, ethnic and social history for the two characters as you interpret them.

The Scene

EXT.   A PARK   DAY

Silence. She looks at him and walks away. He follows.

[What do you think could have happened just before the beginning of the scene? What might ANASTASIA have said to BILL to trigger his opening dialogue? Why is there silence when the scene begins? Why does she walk away? Why does he follow her? What is the emotional energy transmitted between them? That information is implied next in BILL'S opening dialogue.]

BILL
...But you can't marry him just because
your father tells you to.

[Is he telling her she's responsible for her own life?]

ANASTASIA
For my father there is no other way...

[What is she implying?]

BILL
You really believe that, don't you?

[What does he mean by this?]

ANASTASIA
I just don't want to hurt my father...

[Is she in turmoil about something? What might it be?]

BILL
Then why did you come and see me
today...?

[Is she really interested in him - and does he suspect it?]

She stops.

ANASTASIA
Oh, I only wanted to...

She looks at him. He kisses her.

[What motivated him to kiss her? What is her reaction? Why?]

End

How would you end the scene after they kiss? You make the choice.

Look at the same scene again, but now interpret it in alternative ways.

Experiment with different performance choices, with different rhythms, timing and pacing and with the different story information outlined below.

Depending on the *choices* you make, see how it influences the emotional dynamics of your performance each time you change the background information about the story and the characters.

- Is her family "history" conservative, fanatical, moderate...?

- What is his?

- Anastasia *doubts* his love for her?

- She's *testing* him? Wants reassurance or a commitment?

- Bill really *loves* her?   Or,

- For him she's more a *sexual* attraction? He wants to sleep with her. Or,

- She's *torn* between her sexual feelings for him and her upbringing. What might it be?

- She's focused and manipulative and is playing a game. She's extremely sexual and wants to sleep with him.

- He's never been with a woman before, is nervous and over eager.

[4] FEUD

Interpreting conscience: The psychology of good and evil.

How would you describe evil - or someone who is evil?

Is it what a person does, how a person looks or talks, or is it the "vibe" of a person that makes them evil?

Is anyone good or evil all the time? Or is there something of both these aspects in each of us?

How does an evil person perceive themself?

Is "good" or "evil" an attitude in the mind of the beholder?

How would you react to someone who is "good" or "evil"?

Is "our" culture "good" and "theirs" "evil"? Are our wars "good" and theirs "evil"? Is our religion better and theirs worse? Why?

- Very often when we first make contact with people, the good or evil about them is hidden from us. A first impression of a good or evil person is often misleading as whether a person is good or evil is not always obvious.

- We each handle aspects of good and evil differently, relative to our history and psychology.

- Think about your own feelings. Have you ever felt like harming someone, getting even or perhaps desired to get rid of them?

- In a "normal" society, if you got rid someone, it might be considered that you did an evil thing. But you might feel justified in what you did.

In SILENCE OF THE LAMBS, Hannibal Lecter perceived himself as "normal". He saw nothing wrong about killing people and eating them. The way he perceived things, he didn't feel there was anything wrong about what he did.

To the outside world, he gave the impression that he was a normal, polite and intelligent person.

In THE BAD SEED a sweet, angelic, very neat ten year old appeared as the perfect little girl to her parents and neighbors. She was always polite and well-mannered.

But she could murder someone viciously and coldly if she was offended for the most mundane reason.

Look at your own culture.

Or remember the real life characters that appeared before the Truth and Reconciliation Commission in South Africa or at the World Court in The Hague to justify the various horrendous crimes they committed for apartheid or their own ethnic, social and cultural principles?

How did they look? What did they believe? How did they perceive themselves and about what they did?

- Think of the times throughout history of the "devout" and "good" people who've been responsible for the most inhumane crimes and the most horrifying evil?

  The Spanish Inquisition? The Crusades? The Nazis? Vietnam? Al-Qa'ida? Iraq? Israel/Palestine? How did the "good" people rationalize what they did?

- Look at the "good people", who control financial institutions and corporate conglomerates that manipulate peoples' minds and extort billions keeping the poor, poor and the downtrodden down.

What is good?

First impressions can also be misleading. How often have we seen rough, tough looking people whose looks scare us, but who turn out to have soft hearts and real compassion and social tolerance.

- What is "having a conscience"? How would you communicate this when you play a character?

Perhaps evil makes a more powerful impression when we see that "evildoers" perceive themselves as "good people" and that they consider the things that they do to be "normal".

All of us probably know some of them and watching them portrayed on the screen doing something "evil" disturbs us because that challenges our perceptions of "normal".

Two interesting books worth looking at which explore the personality and psychology of evil are: *Dark Nature* by Lyall Watson, and *People of the Lie* by M. Scott Peck M.D.

Now look at the following scene:

Interpret it in any way you like, bearing in mind that it's an exploration about "good" and "evil". Choose one of the characters and play the role *against* the obvious. It can be played by a male/female, two males or two females.

- What qualities of good or evil in yourself can you bring into the role?
- Take a chance when you develop a character. Explore attitudes, mannerisms, physical actions and speech patterns that might reveal something interesting and unexpected about the character's psychology.

Go where your feelings and imagination take you. And *listen* to each other.

Create a situation and the circumstances that prompt the dialogue between the two characters A and B. The most obvious situation on first reading the scene probably suggests some kind of interrogation set-up. However*, try a different approach that is not as obvious and plays totally opposite from that and see where that takes you.*

- Set up a beginning for the scene and bring it to a climax. How would you end it emotionally and physically?
- Establish a relationship between A and B? What is their history and social/cultural conditioning?
- How old are they?
- Who is the "good" guy? Who is the "evil" one? Why?
- What *attitude* do you think you can project to make the "good guy" also come across with a touch of evil? Perhaps it has to do with the *intention* behind the "good guys" dialogue?
- How do they "look" physically and culturally? What is each character's emotional and physical focus in the scene?
- What wardrobe and makeup are A and B wearing? What is the setting/location? Would you be using any props? Why? How?
- In what time period would you place the scene?
- Do you visualize movement or physical action in the scene? If so, what is it?
- Perform the scene in different ways. Explore differences in rhythm, timing and pacing each time you play it out.
- Motivated by the dialogue as you interpret it, explore emotional, physical and attitude changes in your portrayal of the character in the body of the scene.

The Scene

INT. A PLACE NIGHT

A

Did you want to kill him, Sam?

B

I don't know.

A

What did he do to you?

B

Nothing. He did nothing to me.

A

Well then, why did you kill him?

B

I don't know.

A

How can you not know?

B

Well, it was something I had to do.

A

It was something you had to do?

B

Well...it was on account of the quarrel.

A

What quarrel?

B

Didn't you know?

A

No. Tell me about it.

B

Well, one of my cousins had a quarrel
with another man and killed him. Then
that man's brother killed my cousin...
Then my cousin's brother killed that
other man's brother. Then all the brothers
and sisters and cousins on both sides got
involved and started killing each other.
Then it became a matter of us killing them
before they killed us...

A

How long has this been going on?

B

I don't know...forty years, maybe...?

A

You weren't even born then... What was the
quarrel about?

B

There was some trouble about something.
Then there was a lawsuit, and the lawsuit
went against my cousin, so he shot the man
who won the lawsuit.

A

Was it about money? Or land?

B

I don't know. I think there was a
woman involved.

A

How did it start?

B

I don't know. It was a long time ago.

A

Does anybody know?

B

I think maybe my dad or my mom and
maybe some of the older people. But I
don't think they really know what the
quarrel was about.

A

And you killed a man for that?

B

It was something I had to do. Wouldn't
you have done the same...?

END

We have seen how story characters like people in real life have a psychology
and how that psychology exists for different reasons.

To an actor, an *awareness* of a person's psychology reveals a lot about a person
or a character's true state of being. Their feelings motivate the way they act,
react and project information in certain situations.

Psychological attitudes are usually not written into a script. They're left open
for the actor and director to draw out and interpret when they develop a
character.

If it's appropriate, various psychological nuances can be subtly incorporated into a performance. It makes the character more interesting to watch, more alive and truer to real life.

However, one should be cautious not to get too hung up on the psychology of each character they play. More than being consciously analyzed, a character's psychology should be intuitively felt, understood and played on a subconscious level in a performance.

A character's psychology is noticeable in subtle ways. It's expressed in attitudes, habits, tonal qualities and body language which reflect their true emotions no matter what words are used to communicate something different to the outside world.

They leave an *impression* about the person or character and are often clues into a person's history and early life experience – which are the conditions that molded the character today.

In psychological terms:

- Your exterior reflects your interior. What you project outside, reflects what's going on inside.

- If you can't give - you can't receive (emotionally / psychologically / physically).

Personal psychology is very complex. However, certain psychological attitudes, habits, tonal qualities and body language in a character *might* suggest - in a general way - the state of mind of the character.

For example:

Attitude	Symbolism
Personal and environmental untidiness/disarray Confusion/disorganization/ compulsive untidiness	Inner confusion /irresponsibility / laziness Poverty thinking/low self worth/anger/resentment
Excessive charm/chronic politeness/over-eagerness/chronic niceness	Insincerity/deviousness/insecurity /deceitfulness

Psychotic hoarding of things and/or other people's space	Fear of loss/insecurity/need to control/bloodsucking/power lust
Alcoholism/drug addiction/work-aholic/uncontrolled anger/violence	Unresolved hurt/resentment/low self worth/personal fears
Self denial/martyrdom/chronic humility	Self pity/spiritual weakness/love/denial/submissive ness/sense of worthlessness
Religious and/or political fanaticism	Sadism-masochism /intolerance /manipulation /power lust /narrow-mindedness
Chronic aggressiveness /arrogance /cockiness/ looking for trouble/male-female machismo/cool	Immaturity/insecurity/low self-worth/unresolved hurt-abuse/peer pressure/fear of commitment
Chronic shyness/timidity	Lack of self-worth /insecurity /hidden volatile anger/unfulfilled longings-desires/controlled passion/fear of loss
Insatiable greed	Not having enough materially, emotionally, spiritually/fear of commitment, of living/insecurity
Physical/emotional/verbal armor	Insecurity/fear of giving/fear of honest communication/fear of exposure/fear of commitment
Arrogance	Illusions of grandeur, of superiority/insecurity/self-centeredness/stupidity
Compulsive lying	Lack of self-worth/insecurity/low self-esteem /insecurity /deceitfulness/disrespect

In many ways attitudes such as these are the cause of conflict when people of different temperaments and backgrounds establish different kinds of relationships (social/commercial/personal). This is the kind of stuff which creates drama when temperaments clash.

What symbolism would you observe in a person/character that has the following attitudes:

HYPOCRISY	Guilt / deceit?
IRRESPONSIBILITY	Laziness / resentment / anger / fear of failure?
COMPULSIVE DEFENSIVENESS	Guilt / insecurity?
COMPULSIVE CRIMINALITY	Anger / violence /social maladjustment?
SEXUAL GREED/CHRONIC LUST	Possessiveness / control / manipulation?
SEXUAL BLOCKAGE/DENIAL	Low self-worth / social anger / life trauma / fear of relationships / cultural conditioning?

[5]   THIS PLACE

Interpreting a character's psychology:

Make a choice of how you want to explore the two characters A and B suggested by the dialogue in the following scene:

Create a situation and the circumstances that motivate their interaction.

The scene can be played dramatically, humorously or unemotionally. It's how you play the subtext, and the way you express the communication between them that will give the scene substance and life.

- Who are these characters? What is their relationship? Are they friends, enemies or relatives or are they connected in some other way?

- What is each character's cultural, ethnic and social "history"?

- What is the setting / location where we find them? Is it a jail, rehab centre, mental institution?

- Anything else...? Try performing it in different situations.

Why is one of them "in this place"? Why is the other character visiting? Is one a male, the other a female? Are they two women or two men? Or is the scene reflecting some psychological confusion happening in one character's mind where both of them are "in this place...?"

- How are they dressed? Are they using props? What is each one doing?

- What is the attitude between them? What could they be talking about?

- Consider that in real life people don't always make linear or logical sense.

- What will your body language project?

What is the subtext and the psychology that might be suggested in your character's attitude, habits and tonal qualities?

What might the emotional moments, rhythmic changes or pauses that you choose to play in your dialogue suggest about your character's attitude and state of mind?

- How would you project, imply or suggest some of the attitudes and symbolism outlined above emotionally and/or physically? Just focus into the *feeling* of this and see what happens when you perform the scene.

- How would you begin the scene? How would you end it?

Interpret it from your own life experience, incidents you might remember, or observations you've made about people, situations and things.

The Scene

INT.   A PLACE   DAY

A

Hey...

B

Why are you here?

A

I'm here. That's all.

B

So you're here. Have you nothing
to say...?

A

This place isn't too bad. How are
they treating you...?

B

It's a place. It gets cold in here.

A

It gets cold in other places.

B

Yes. But I'd rather be in my own place.
One can't always choose what one
wants. Can they...?

A

That's true. But sometimes unavoidable,
hey...

B

Yeah. Unavoidable... Sit down...

A

No. I want to stand.

B

Why? Is something bothering you?

A

Do you have something on your mind?

B

If you say so...

A

What do you mean if I say so? Do you
think I wanted it this way?

B

You could have made yourself more available.

A

You could have called back when I
phoned.

B

You know, sometimes I think you're
getting too big for your own good.

A

What?

B

We could not be talking at all.

A
We have to talk. We must talk.

B
Alright. I'm here. I might as well listen...

End

[6] LABIDO

From: *People in Trenchcoats*
By Ryan Sheraton

Working in Real Life Locations:

Most movies and TV series today are shot in real life locations where distractions can be frustrating to the actors performing a scene, as well as to the crew working on it.

Although well budgeted productions can control a real life shooting environment to a certain extent, it still takes an enormous amount of concentration for an actor to stay focused on a scene when the locations involve busy street set-ups, crowds, noise or working in a moving vehicle.

The following scene, *LABIDO*, is about two characters having an argument in a vehicle moving through heavy traffic. It was shot in an uncontrolled environment on a busy real life highway and involved a number of takes.

The original interpretation of the argument taking place between the two characters was played with a light, humorous high energy. It can also be played in an intense, dramatic way.

In whatever way you might choose to play the scene, think about how you would need to be aware of not only the safety and technical concerns of shooting it, but also about staying focused on your character if you were performing the scene in an *uncontrollable* environment.

What makes the scene potentially humorous and poignant, is that the argument between BOB and his brother in the car is played *against* the background of a radio CELEBRITY discussing "happiness" as a clown, balloons and laughter, contrasted by the tension between them in a car speeding through heavy traffic.

The radio celebrity's commentary was edited into the scene later during post production.

The Scene

EXT.   BROTHER'S HOUSE   DAY

His BROTHER waits, impatient. He's casual, but well dressed. A suitcase and traveling bag are by him, tagged with different airline stickers.

BOB drives up, screeches to a stop, keeps the motor running, and gets out.

> BOB
>
> I'm late...I'm late...

> BROTHER
>
> Just shut up and put them in the car...

BOB dumps the luggage onto the back seat.

> ...I told you to be here at 8, not 8:30...

> BOB
>
> Yeah...yeah...

They enter the car and speed off.

INT.   CAR   HIGHWAY   DAY

Over the radio, a talk show CELEBRITY discusses happiness: "It's a clown, balloons and laughter..."

                        BROTHER
Can't you go faster...

                          BOB
Look at the traffic...I'm doing my best...

The CELEBRITY continues her discourse as they continue through the traffic.
BROTHER becomes irritated and impatient. He turns the radio off, which
annoys BOB who turns it back on again.

                        BROTHER
        You should've taken the N1. It's quicker
        than the N2. Go into the fast...

                          BOB
        I can't. There's traffic passing me.
        Didn't you see that car...!

                        BROTHER
        Well, you should've taken the quarry road.
        You just missed it...You should've taken it...

                          BOB
        Look, do you want me to cause an accident?

                        BROTHER
        You could've gone that way...

                          BOB
        Will you lay off, will you...I'm trying to
        drive...

                        BROTHER
        Well, you should've taken it...

                          BOB
        Look! Do you want to drive...!

BROTHER
What crawled up your arse this morning...

BOB
Wow! That's it! This is my car and my way of
driving! I'm doing you a favor! If you don't
like it, get a taxi! Do you think I'm taxi? Oh,
look, I'm in Africa and I don't have a gun under
my seat! Oh, how about that! So I'm not a taxi...
          (looks in mirror)
And I have all my front teeth...
          (smiles)
Oh, and I'm not British Airways, SAA,
Nationwide or Khulula.com...'cause I don't
have any fuckin' wings...Do you think I'm
Mr. Delivery with my cap and bowtie, with
a bumper sticker that says, "How's my driving..."

BROTHER
Yaadaa, yaadaa, yaadaa...will you just shut up...

BOB
Amsterdam, London, New York... Where do you
go all the time? What do you do in all your label
clothes... Do you check into five star hotels?

BROTHER
Just fuck off! That's enough already...

BOB
Are you a drug courier? Are you in the diamond
business? Are you a special government agent?

BROTHER
Why don't you shut up and go out and get a job!

BOB
Does mom know! Does dad know? I do have
a job, delivering things for you!

BROTHER
Just get me to the airport. I'm late already...

BOB
(calmer)
Look...why don't you just cut me in on whatever
it is you're doing...? I'm tired of just working
for petrol money...

BROTHER
Shut up and keep driving...

BOB
Nuts to you too...

Over the radio, the CELEBRITY concludes her discourse on "Happiness".
                                        - End -

INTERPRETATION NOTE:

To understand what BOB is talking about when he says, "Do you think I'm a taxi", that comment in the movie came out of a current South African cultural and social experience. The dialogue that followed was also interpreted out of that experience.

"Taxi" is a misnomer. Although everyone calls them "taxis", they should be more correctly referred to as mini busses. They're mini vans with three or four rows of seats closely spaced that can cram in 8 and up to 10 passengers packed intimately together. With strangers touching each other in such close proximity, smells and body heat can sometimes be overwhelming and uncomfortable.

The "taxis" speed along designated routes to pick up passengers who hail them to stop at wherever they're standing and to drop them off anywhere along a set route. It's a relatively economical and fast method of transport for the masses, but it's not always safe.

Wealthy rival owners called "taxi kings" control fleets of mini vans and employ low paid and sometimes unlicensed drivers to compete ferociously to pick up passengers along the most lucrative routes. Often fights and gang warfare break out when one faction's interests to pick up passengers is undermined and another rival faction moves into its territory. Incidents can become violent and many drivers, who work for the "taxi king" mini van owners, carry guns and clubs for protection.

The cultural climate of this business can be compared to what was happening in places like Chicago, Detroit and New York during the era of prohibition during the 1930's.

However, if you want to play with a different dynamic in the argument between Bob and his brother and experiment with a different cultural and social setting, adjust the phrasing of the dialogue with colorful cultural and social sayings that are appropriate to your own interpretation of the scene.

Release exercise: The focus of the following activity is not the dialogue – but to free your energy emotionally and physically. With your partner choose any scene in this book.

First perform the dialogue as you normally would in a setting of your own choosing.

Now: without hurting each other perform the scene again while doing some *vigorous* physical activity like having an intense pillow fight, wrestling, jogging, playing handball, tennis or some other demanding physical activity you can think of.

Be sure that the setting of the exercise is cleared of items that could cause damage or block your movements or injure you.

Yell and shout if you like. if that is a natural expression of your physical activity.

You don't have to be word perfect with the dialogue. Concentrate on the *tension* of the physical activity you are doing while saying the words.

If you forget the lines don't try to remember them – just continue repeating the same one line over and over without breaking the rhythm of your physical activity. Don't stop until you feel exhausted or when you have reached a peak.

Now: Slow down. Become quiet. Be still. Don't hurry. Repeat the dialogue again, *whispering* to each other. At the same time – without losing your concentration – sense what is happening around you and *listen* to any sounds that you hear.

Now stop. Breathe slowly. Relax. You probably would have experienced emotional energy shifts each time you played the scene.

Try the exercise with any other scenes you wish.

Part 11

Monologue

Scene in a drama in which one person speaks by him/herself; dramatic composition for single performance; long speech by one person in a company; soliloquy.

- Concise Oxford Dictionary

About Monologues

A monologue can be either a long or short speech, or a long or short piece of dialogue.

Many actors find monologues one of the most difficult things to do because they find themselves completely alone performing a scene without the feedback, energy and physical presence of another person to interact with.

A lot of people make the mistake of treating a monologue like a recitation learning the text by rote, probably because they've been conditioned from early schooling to learn and recite lines from classical texts for examination purposes, where memorizing the information was considered more important than understanding, expressing and performing it.

Some casting agents and directors like to have actors do a monologue in auditions because their reasoning is, if an actor can perform something alone and sustain a character, then they can probably perform something well in a scene with other actors.

But this is not necessarily true.

Exactly what is a monologue, besides the dictionary definition of it?

One viewpoint is that there are different *types* of "monologues". There is:

- The "dramatic" kind, where the story character is serious and intense about their inner thoughts and is speaking them intimately to themselves, as Hamlet does in "To be, or not to be…"

- The humorous type where a stand-up comic or actor makes poignant and emotional observations directly to an audience about important issues such as relationships, culture, politics, society and/or their personal experiences.

- A telephone dialogue where an actor has to set up specific story information, talking to an unseen character off-screen without the other characters feedback or response.

On the screen a monologue can be performed as a character's *voice only*, speaking over visuals, as in a situation where only the character's voice is heard expressing inner thoughts that compliment or re-enforce the visual information playing on the screen. This would also be referred to as a narration.

Or it can be articulated physically on the screen by a character projecting their thoughts – *talking and listening to themselves* – without the benefit of other characters or actors listening and responding back.

Some monologues work. Some don't. When they don't, it's because they're not *felt* as a normal or emotional *conversation*. When the actor is not "real" or just being theatrical in the role, they fall into the trap of "acting" or "performing" the words.

Treat a "monologue" as you would any other role. For example:

- What is it about?
- What is the objective, subtext or statement of the "monologue"?
- Why are you using a monologue, other than the fact that it's in the script?
- To whom are you saying it, even though another character is not present?
- Why are you saying it?
- What are the circumstances and the situation that *motivated* it?
- What is it *emotionally* and *physically* that you're trying to communicate? How are you dressed? What are you doing? Are you using props or doing some kind of physical activity while you're delivering it?
- Are you expressing the character's thoughts and emotions in a humorous or intense way?

Remember: *Be wary that you don't become melodramatic. Don't "act" it. Just feel it like you would if you were interacting with another character.*

Look at the following monologues. How would you perform them?

[1] Pearly's Monologue

Adapted from the play: TIME OF FOOTSTEPS
by Aletta Bezuidenhout

This monologue is an indictment against the wealthy 'first world's' exploitation of the working class in Africa.

The punctuation in the text has been deliberately left out. If you were performing the piece, how would you interpret the pauses, rhythm, timing, pacing and play of emotions that is implied in the text?

How would you describe and interpret Pearly's character, culture and social status? What is the conflict suggested here? What is Pearly's emotional, psychological and physical state? Is Pearly justified in how he/she perceives things? Is Pearly talking about struggle, hardship, survival or anything else? Is there anger, jealousy, resentment, disdain, greed or a subliminal admiration and awe of the entities he/she is attacking?

What is the setting, what activity or what is the action you are doing and how are you groomed and dressed?

How will you be using the props written into the text? How would you begin your monologue and how would you end it?

What is your focus and bottom line as you understand the text and what performance choices would *you* make?

The Text

'Your kind the commissioners of the world with your rose gardens and english tea and porcelain skins your kind come and inspect a job after it's all been finished and make speeches…

[Wheezes – searches for his/her asthma pump – breathes]

The commissioners who are handed a golden shovel to dig one teaspoon of earth so you can say 'see I'm also a laborer and a worker at heart' you're just ceremony man planting rubber plants when we are the ones, me and Gogga and Dirk and Jacob and Thambo who built one hell of a road where nothing existed before where's my jacket where's my jacket did you hide my jacket...

[Finds misplaced jacket – puts it on]

you never had to finish a job we felt the heat the sweat the asthma your only dream is giving orders and drinking a cool gin and tonic what are you destroying things for progress we're like...what did Mr. Baker-Jones say –'the jugular vein of progress...' yes you know that Mr. Baker-Jones we are the one's we make it happen

your kind you're the kind of people who come out here and collect african masks to hang on your walls to show your friends that you've also been here you don't even know what those masks are for i don't even have walls man not even a rose garden ok I do have a gypsy caravan talk of broken rhythms you ask me man inside it's all broken

[wheezes again – breathes into the asthma pump}

once someone told me of a tortoise that was buried under a dam he survived by slowing down his pulse years later when they uncovered him he was still alive sometimes I feel like that I just want to breathe man'

Performance notes:

In places where it's appropriate in your delivery and where you want to make a dramatic impact, consider incorporating the following techniques into your performance:

- Stress a key word in the text of the monologue. For example, *I, you your, we, yes, sweat, heat*...etc.
- Use an intentional pause where it feels right.
- Use a timely and well-placed sigh or an intake of breath to create an emotional or dramatic impact.
- Play against the normal. For example: accent an action or feeling opposite to what it's supposed to be.
- Use body language. Stress a point in the way you use your hands. Throw

in a vocal gesture such as perhaps doing something with your mouth. For example, some sort of suitable sound, or a click with your tongue, etc. if it suits your delivery.

- Adjust the energy and sound of your voice in a way that highlights your character and makes your performance more interesting for the audience to listen to. For example, over pronounced – too high – too low – pitched up – pitched down ...

- Highlight the importance and meaning of certain words if they are significant in your interpretation of the dialogue. For example, look at the following key words in Pearly's Monologue again: *ceremony, man, progress, that, broken, breathe,* etc.

- Consciously change the emotion and quality in your voice to draw attention to what you are saying. For example: from high to low, soft, fast or vice versa...

- Deliberately manipulate the pacing of a particular phrase, such as adjusting the pace and/or the rhythm of a passage from slow to fast or vice versa.

- Keep the pacing and rhythm of your performance tight, keep it real and be careful that you do not mellow dramatise your delivery.

[2] Natalie's Monologue
by Natalie Lasker

From: *PEOPLE IN TRENCHCOATS*

There was a touch of humor in the way this monologue was originally performed in the movie. It made the anger and loneliness of Natalie's character even more poignant.

INT.   NATALIE'S APARTMENT   NIGHT

NATALIE is in THE KITCHEN dishing an elegant meal onto two dinner plates on a tray. She speaks to herself.

NATALIE
Well, I can be if I wanted to be, but I choose
not to...Philosophy, monogamy, controversy...

NATALIE (cont.)
What's my purpose in life? About living...?
Inner peace...? Inner beauty...? Bullshit...!
Is that all I can think about right now?

She moves with the tray to THE LIVING ROOM, places it on a table uncorks a bottle of wine, pours two glasses.

...I'm stuck! Drawn between two lines! Red and red.
Where do I go from here? What am I going to do
with myself? This is a no-go sign. I mean, no one has
faith in others anymore... Money, status, finance...
I keep asking myself, is this who I really am? Is this
really what I want? Is comfort the only thing that
will make me happy? I feel contaminated. Where's
my source...? My link? My connection to something
better? I bloody well pay my dues...I know what
you're thinking... She's at it again...

She places one plate of food in front of a TERRIER-COLLIE PUPPY. Lifts her wine glass, sighs and sips the wine.

So, to who are we toasting this one tonight...?

[3] Phone Talk

There will be a time in every actor's movie or TV career when the script will call for them to have a conversation with some unseen character over the telephone.

This kind of conversation is basically a monologue because the actor will be required to deliver to the unseen character the intention and dynamics of the scene through a solo piece of dialogue.

When such a scene is shot, the actor will often not have the other actor's physical presence on the set available to interact with which might be because of various production or scheduling reasons. So the other actors *interaction* on the other side of the telephone may not be shot for days or even weeks later.

Sometimes, the other characters dialogue *response* might also not be included as part of the scene and not be written into the script.

The challenge for the actor then is for them to carry the rhythm, timing, pacing and essence of what the telephone scene is about and the state of their relationship to the unseen character single handedly.

The trick is to make the whole scene sound like a real conversation with appropriate responses and reactions happening between the actor and the unseen "other person".

The actor will therefore need to establish emotionally what their purpose is in making the phone call and play the *subtext* of the conversation.

The actor will need to *Listen* in their mind to the unseen character and *hear* the unseen character talking back, even though no dialogue is heard from the other side of the phone.

The actor will have to create an "impression" of the unseen character's responses and respond back appropriately to the unseen characters emotional dynamics which they "hear" over the phone - and create appropriate rhythmic and emotional exchanges in their own performance.

Consider also that during those moments of silence while the actor is "listening", what might their eyes and body language be communicating emotionally and physically if it's appropriate to the moment?

Think about these points and create your own story circumstances and the situation that motivated your dialogue in the following telephone conversation:

The Scene

The setting can be anywhere, anytime of day.

Something has been bothering you. YOU decide to make a phone call. YOU dial, listen to the dial tone and wait. The unseen person, HE/SHE answers.

YOU

...Hi. It was Jo. She did it...

...Sam. Your friend from Giorgio's. We
worked together, remember...

Are you still angry with me...? No. No.
Don't hang up. Just listen...But I'm telling
you, it was Jo. It makes sense. It's been
bothering me. I thought about it. She was
the only one who had access to the code...

You thought it was me...?

Yes. I know I blamed you...

Yes. I know...How have you been coping?

Mmmm...I'm sorry about that...What can
we do about it...?

Yeah...That sounds right...Tell me more...
Yes...yes...I think it'll work...

End

Working the scene:

The scene can be interpreted in different ways. To play it, what performance
choices would you make?

Consider the following guidelines:

- What do you think this scene is about? Who/what is GIORGIO'S?
- What type of character are you interpreting? What motivates you to make
  the phone call and to use the specific dialogue that's written in the scene?
- What activity were you doing before you decided to make the phone call?
- How do you look visually? Tired, energetic, nervous, excited, calm, angry,
  enthusiastic...? Why?
- How does your character speak? How does your voice resonate? From the

chest, solar plexus, through the nose...? Why?
- How are you dressed?
- Do you hesitate or not, before you make the phone call? Why?
  What is your attitude or state of mind? Are you anxious, patient, friendly, sarcastic, guilty, cautious, anything else...? Why?
- What do you think happened between YOU and the unseen him/her before you made the phone call? How long ago was it? What is the subtext here?
- What was your relationship with him/her at that time? What is it now?
- Do you *listen* to him/her before you answer? Do you take *time* to *hear* and *react* to what he/she is saying?
- What is the unheard dialogue that only *you* can *hear* over the phone that might make you respond the way you do?

What do you think the unwritten dialogue *might be* that he/she is saying to you?

To help you connect with it, *make up your own dialogue for the unseen characters response and place it in the blank spaces between the pauses in your conversation.*

Now use what you have written as the dialogue for the unseen person to be the *"dialogue"* that only you *"hear"* over the phone that you respond to.

To try and get a *feel* for an appropriate rhythm, timing and pacing in the scene, rehearse it first if you can with another actor who can "perform" the appropriate "responses" to your dialogue by "playing" the unseen character you are conversing with.

Once you get a feeling of how the scene might work, re-enact it again without the support and "dialogue exchanges" of the other actor.

- Motivated by what you *"hear"* on the other side of the phone, will your emotional and rhythmic dynamics change as the scene develops?

  If so, from what to what? How? Why? Where in the text do you feel that might happen?

- With what action and attitude would you end the scene?

Connect your emotional and physical responses in the scene to something that is familiar to you out of your own life experience.

Experiment with different performance textures. For example, play the scene in one way dramatically, and then try to perform it again humorously.

[4] Tania's Monologue
by Jennifer Waltner

Some of the most interesting dialogue in story telling is often inspired by peoples' real life experiences.

In this monologue, what do you think the subtext or statement is? Can you identify emotionally with the feeling of the words and what this character is saying?

How would you perform this monologue? What is the setting of the scene? What is her state of mind? How is she *feeling*? What is she doing? Might she be expressing these thoughts to an unseen someone off camera?

Are there clues in the text that might suggest her psychological and social history, or her experience with relationships? How old do you think she is? Why?

To whom is she referring? Is it a man or a woman? How would the scene play in each situation? Where do you think that person might be now?

Was it a recent or long-standing relationship that she's referring to? Why did it break up? What do you think happened between them?

What is she implying about the personality, qualities and connection she had with that person?

What do you think the powerful emotional, psychological and physical events in that relationship were that still make her feel for it?

What do you think triggered her thoughts at this particular time and motivated her to express them this way?

How *far* do you think she was willing to explore the "experience" that she's talking about?

There is no right or wrong answer. Just personal interpretation choices you might make to perform this piece.

TANIA

"The erotic is a journey which can take you into heaven or hell. For most people, it's hell.

Sex just for the sake of sex alone is a shallow and empty experience.

It made me feel bad about myself. I felt ugly. Guilty! Betrayed and lied to. I took on your insecurities and hooked mine into yours. It went downhill after that.

The way to heaven is a commitment. It's a bond between two people. You have to be body and soul present in the experience and give all of yourself to another person. If you can connect with that, your spirit rejoices.

For me, sex without that bond is meaningless. I can do it better on my own and it saves all the hang-ups.

But I must be honest. I miss your touch very much. It was my reason for going beyond the boundaries of the ordinary, into a healing experience. I was hoping to explore that road more intensely with you. But our insecurities and hang-ups prevented us from going further.

A feeling of what could have been has haunted me for many months. I will most likely not find it in this lifetime. I miss you in many ways. But I know where I want to travel.

People play games to attract someone. They hang onto illusions like beauty, youth, money and power - only to possess it and drop it when it's convenient.

TANIA (cont.)

Such a world isn't mine anymore.

I hope you can rebuild your sexuality after the damage that's been done to you.

But you can do it, better than anybody else I know.

You and I are not pushy people. But really, that's a quality which exists only when people look up to each other as equals".

Performance notes:

In places where it's appropriate in your delivery and where you want to make a dramatic impact, consider incorporating the following vocal techniques into your performance:

- Stress a key word in the text of the monologue. For example, *I, you, we, yes, wooonderfuuul*...etc.
- Use an intentional pause where it feels right.
- Use a timely and well-placed sigh or an intake of breath to create an emotional or dramatic impact.
- Play against the normal. For example, accent a feeling or something emotional opposite to what it's supposed to be.
- Use body language. Stress a point in the way you use your hands. Throw in a vocal gesture such as perhaps doing something with your mouth. For example, sigh or make some sort of suitable sound, or a click with your tongue, etc. if it suits your delivery.
- Adjust the energy and sound of your voice in a way that highlights your character and makes your performance more interesting for the audience to listen to. For example, over pronounced – too high – too low – pitched up – pitched down …
- Highlight the importance and meaning of certain words by stressing the word. For example, *massacres, holocausts, impunity, mad, noble,* etc.
- Consciously change the emotion and quality in your voice to draw attention to what you are saying. For example, from high to low, soft, fast or visa versa...
- Deliberately manipulate the pacing of a particular phrase, such as adjusting the pace and/or the rhythm of a passage from slow to

extremely fast or visa versa.

Poetry

I am the poet of the body,
And I am the poet of the soul.

The pleasures of heaven are
with me,

The first I graft and increase
upon myself...the latter I
translate into a new tongue.

- Walt Whitman
Leaves of Grass

Many actors have difficulty understanding and interpreting poetry. When they read some styles of poetry, the cold words looking up at them seem bland, disjointed and usually don't seem to make any sense.

Poetry is about story-telling. It's about someone who expresses his or her thoughts and feelings, or relates a story that's told in verse.

The lyrics or words of songs are poetry. When you read the lyrics of many operas or classical, popular and rock songs they also seem bland, cold and empty on paper when you first look at them.

But when you hear them *performed* with passion and emotion and insight, they come alive and might touch your feelings. They might take you into an emotional, spiritual or philosophical experience of some kind.

Poetry is about connecting you with the poet or songwriter's meaning, intention and *feeling* behind the words.

The words of the poet are about trying to touch a *feeling* inside you.

People feel about things in different ways at different times and through different phases of their lives, and how *you feel* about something is also a very personal experience.

For example:

> *I hear thunder*
> *The abyss is deep*
> *No way out. No way in.*
> *Starlight twilight*
> *Dawn is breaking*
> *New day dawning*
> *New day dawning*

If anything, what might these words *suggest* to *you*? How would you interpret them? Are they telling a "story"? What "feelings" and passions are they intended to express? What do you feel the *emotion* is behind the words? Is it about anger? Hope? Despair? Could it be something humorous or even something tongue in cheek or something else that the poet was trying to express?

Do they touch any sort of feeling inside you? Even if the words leave you emotionless and cold, that's also ok. And whatever your understanding of it is, it's ok because that is also a feeling that it stirred in you.

Understanding and interpreting different types of poetry in a personal way is a valuable discipline for an actor to develop. It trains your senses to interpret text and to understand and explore the different rhythms, timing and pacing of dialogue.

Poetry is not about reciting it. It's about *experiencing* and *performing* it. It's like a monologue.

So approach poetry as you would a monologue. And apply the same criteria in the way you analyze, understand and interpret it.

Part 12

For good or for bad, this is the age
of entertainment. Audiences are sick
of lectures, even though there are good
one's.

- Darryl F. Zanuck
  Co-Founder / President
  20ᵗʰ Century-Fox

Entertainment

Entertainment means: *"to keep people agreeably preoccupied or amused by performing for them, showing them something that's enjoyable to watch or to take them through an emotional experience of some sort".*

Keeping people emotionally engaged depends in varying degrees on different peoples' perceptions, sophistication, interests, state of mind and taste.

Entertainment is basically the way the action and information, for example in a movie, is presented. It's also about how a story character communicates something and how the other characters in the story relate and interact with each other in different situations and how those situations are resolved, which keeps the audience who are watching, attentive and involved in the circumstances of the characters.

Are the characters and their situations funny or painful - do they make you laugh or cry? Do they keep you in suspense? Does the action in the situations excite you and keep you spellbound? Do the circumstances touch you with pathos, or make you feel romantic and in love? Do they strike you in a way that makes you experience something meaningful or to recall different emotions?

Some forms of entertainment are subtle and you're hardly aware of them. Others are obvious and literally hit you over the head in the stark way the information is presented. Think about this the next time you watch a movie, TV program or live performance.

Entertainment also includes a certain amount of *production value*, which is in the way the story *looks* on the screen and in the way it's *told* and *brought* across to the audience. Production value is an integral part of entertainment. It includes features such as:

The Visual Things:
How action, photography, lighting, sets, props, sensuality, costumes, fashions, wardrobe and the environment are used to tell the story. Sometimes it incorporates spectacular stunts and special effects to excite the audience.

The Setup:
This is about establishing the circumstances, situations and mood of the story and unfolding it in an appealing way that creates curiosity in the audience about why things are about to happen.

The Characters: Outlining the relationship, motivations and causes for the interaction that happens between them. How their different personalities affect and play off each other.

The Connections:
How the physical, psychological and emotional elements of the story are directed and manipulated in unexpected ways to arouse the audience to a level of excitement that makes them want to feel and experience more.

The Buildup: How suspense, surprise, intrigue, and twists and turns are used in the movie to keep the audience watching it engaged until its conclusion.

The Performance:
How the energy and focus of the actors brings the characters to life.

The Dialogue: As the characters interact and talk with each other, how comfortable, natural and genuine does this sound to the audience?

The Resolution: The emotional or dynamic way in which the story elements are resolved and concluded.

Production value helps to satisfy the entertainment needs of the audience. It's about giving them value for the time and money they put out to experience a *happening* on the screen.

Production value needn't be an expensive aspect in the making of a movie. It can be built-in quite economically in the way it's made. It's about how *innovatively* creative people use these features and integrate them into a movie within the budget limitations of the production.

In many ways the majority of modern audiences are a contradiction. They have a notoriously low attention span and a childlike mentality – while at the same time they also have a certain level of sophistication because of the way they're swamped with programs on TV, and with movies on videos, DVD's and the internet. There are thousands upon thousands of different programs to look at - and different types of entertainment to choose from.

The incredible amount of entertainment that's available today is really mind boggling and nerve wracking for producers, writers, directors and actors who have to compete vigorously for the attention of the audience.

But this sort of challenge opens up creative possibilities for even old things to be presented and performed in new ways.

Looking at Comedy

There are different genres, categories and styles of comedy. Each caters to different types of audiences and to different cultural, social and educational backgrounds.

Some examples are:

Stylish or sophisticated comedy: this type of humor is subtle and performed realistically around tasteful story lines with sharp dialogue that communicates the foibles of the human condition. Look at Jack Nicholson and Helen Hunt in the romantic comedy *As Good As It Gets*, Robin Williams and Nathan Lane in *The Birdcage,* Neil Simon's *The Odd Couple* series or any of Woody Allen's movies.

Or the TV sitcom *Sex and the City* which deals with adult, real life themes that play on contemporary relationships and social issues in a light, amusing and thought provoking manner.

The humor lies in the sincerity of the performance. It's in the way clever dialogue is written by witty writers and delivered by skillful actors. It's how the characters interact with each other in sometimes absurd situations, and how they respond to them and eventually resolve their differences in amusing, yet poignant, circumstances.

Cartoon Comedy: Look at *Men in Black, Blazing Saddles, Young Frankenstein* and the *Pink Panther* series.

The characters and situations are larger than life and sometimes even far-fetched. There's a comic book flavor about them. Yet we accept that there is a certain "reality" happening at the moment we are watching them because the dialogue and exchanges between the characters is clever and amusing, and the actors are playing their roles in those situations very believably.

They entertain us and make us feel comfortable. So we accept the roles they're playing as well as their circumstances, situations and the humor they project.

Perhaps it's also partly because there's something surprising in the characters and the comedy they're playing which we haven't seen or heard before. Or it may even be that they're doing something old which is performed in a *different* way that comes across as being sort of fresh and "real" - but funny.

Indirectly, clever comedy might even teach us something, like Jamie Uys did about African versus Western social and cultural issues in his classic movie *The Gods Must Be Crazy*.

Satirical comedy: Satire means *"the use of wit to criticize behavior; especially irony, sarcasm and ridicule to criticize faults"*. It usually deals with political, social or cultural issues, and sometimes even religion.

Probably the masters of satirical comedy are the British, with their laid back, dry sense of humor. Look at some of the early Peter Sellers and Alec Guinness movies of the 1940's and 50's as well as the *Yes Minister* and *Absolutely Fabulous* TV series of a few years ago.

Only a few episodes of *Fawlty Towers* with John Cleese and a supporting cast of wonderful character actors was produced in the mid 1970's and it's still hilarious when you look at it today. Rowan Atkinson's *Blackadder, Father Ted* and the *'Allo 'Allo* series are well over the top and the characters are broad and larger than life, but somehow they also work quite well.

Through their characters and sharp dialogue these comedies confront various issues and make fun of the class divisions in British society. The humor comes in the super seriousness of the characters and the dialogue which cuts straight through the façade and sometimes folly of political, social, cultural and even religious double standards.

Farce or Black comedy: Sometimes this is also referred to as **Dark comedy**. This type of humor deals with unpleasant subjects, and often contains bitter jokes about the more unpleasant aspects of life. It also looks irreverently at cherished institutions and cuts into peoples' belief systems.

This type of humor usually relies on its shock appeal at the expense of the people, organizations or a culture that is the brunt of the jokes. Many people find this type of comedy offensive, especially when it mocks their personal circumstances and values.

An example of this humor is the movie *The Life of Brian*, which re-enacted the story of the life of Christ, through a Christ-like but comical character named Brian. It tried to make a social commentary about religion through the use of irreverent humor. Other examples are *Monty Python and the Holy Grail* and *The Rocky Horror Picture Show*.

The TV series *Six Feet Under* is a sort of "darkish humor", dealing with real looking characters living their lives in sometimes amusing situations in the setting of a funeral parlor and surrounded by death.

Slapstick comedy: This type of comedy evolved naturally from vaudeville into the movies. The physical action that is so much a part of this humor was tailor made for the movies, and the slapstick formula was established right from the beginning in the days of the silent era.

It's a boisterous type of comedy, with the emphasis on fast physical action, farcical situations, and obvious jokes that are visual and do not depend primarily on language.

Its' basic ingredient is the chase, with characters trying to get to someone or something before someone else does, and involves actions like pie throwing, slapping and hitting, various mishaps, misfortunes and other forms of violence and abuse that never seem to actually harm the leading characters.

The humor relies on the actions of characters that appear larger than life, interacting in over the top situations.

It's best expressed in a series of highly popular movie shorts which began in the silent era and starred Mac Sennett's *The Keystone Cops*, and in the 1930's and 40's movie shorts of *The Three Stooges*. It's a childish type of humor, depending on laughs from characters bashing and hurting each other.

Slapstick has also been built around stupid, stoned characters with the humor revolving around the contemporary drug culture. During the 1980's, the movies of *Cheech and Chong* characterized this style of humor.

Sometimes the action can be just plain crude, catering to the lowest common denominator in audience intelligence. What's funny to one person may be insulting to someone with a different life experience. When it's done in bad taste, it can come across as something offensive.

For example, a few years ago there were perhaps some people who found something funny about an elephant farting and releasing a vile bathtub load of elephant shit on a character representing a different cultural group. However, this was in fact offensive to many people regardless of their cultural background. Despite this, the movie made a small fortune at the box office just like many movies made in this genre.

Sitcoms: This type of comedy is basically a development of TV programming. The humor relies on the same leading characters interacting with each other in a familiar setting in sometimes predictable situations week in and week out. It depends on quick pacing, tightly written dialogue, sometimes exaggerated performances and a higher energy projection and delivery than in drama.

It's difficult for writers competing with hundreds of other sitcoms to keep coming up with something "funny" week after week and year after year. The humor can become cliché; the plots are usually artificial and look imitated from other shows. And they are because different series cannibalize plots, ideas and even dialogue from each other with only the characters changing.

The gags are often not even funny. Canned laughter is edited into the final product to cue the audience where to laugh and to make the humor sound like it's supposed to be funny. Try watching and listening to a sitcom sometime without the "cues" of canned laughter.

The drawing power of most sitcoms relies on actors who've become popular because of the special "characters" they've created in the role. And when this is combined with good writing, a fresh approach, original and really humorous characters, good performances and presented with integrity, it can make even an ordinary sitcom genuinely funny and unique.

Look at the stylish situation comedy in shows like *Cheers, Frasier, Seinfeld* and even *Everyone Loves Raymond*.

The Clown-hero: has always been around. Usually a loner, the clown-hero seems to come from nowhere and ends up going to nowhere. In spite of their desperate circumstances, the clown-hero enters peoples' lives and touches them in poignant and sympathetic ways. The crisis in other peoples' lives is always much more important and painful than their own. Often sacrificing their own needs, they are helpful to the helpless.

They're clowns because they make people laugh in the way they handle the mishaps that happened to themselves and to the characters in a story. They're heroes because of the comic way in which they confront the world on their own terms and because of how they stand up against evil and the bad guys.

They may look like fools performing their antics, but they're sharply perceptive and observant about what goes on around them. There's a practical wisdom and common sense approach in everything they do. They have compassion for the down-trodden in a difficult, non-caring world.

In the end the clown-hero wins. Even if they don't win in their own situations, they still win in different and unexpected ways. Their stories are modern fables, and in a subliminal way, their comedy always has some kind of moral or social statement to make.

Three classic examples of the clown-hero in the movies is the comedy of Charlie Chaplin, Harold Lloyd and Buster Keaton. Starting in the silent era before the movies could talk, their comedy, combined with pathos, was brilliantly communicated through action, simple stories and the personalities of the characters they created.

In the 1940's and 50's the image of clown-heroes like Danny Kaye and Red Skelton was more sophisticated. The basic premise of the clown-hero didn't changed much, but the material and the style of presenting it did, which catered to the tastes of more modern movie audiences. And closer to our time starting in the 1980's and 90's it would be worthwhile to compare some of the movies of clown-heroes like Peter Sellers, Gene Wilder, Bill Murray, Eddie Murphy and Steve Martin to see how the image, technique and story material of the clown-hero has evolved and changed in the movies over the years.

The Comedy Team: consists of a straight man and the fall guy, who is the buffoon or clown of the team. The clown takes the brunt of the jokes and performs the crazy antics, while the straight man takes on the role of the "authority figure" and is the "level-headed" of the team. The straight man gives the "feed", or sets up the gag or comic action, and the fall guy delivers the "punch line", or completion of the situation.

Many successful comedy teams acknowledge that it takes an exceptional straight man with perfect rhythm, pacing and timing to make the team work. They say that a good straight man is difficult to find. He or she can make or break the success of the team. When the wacky antics of the fall guy bounce off the "feed" of a good straight man, they become much easier to carry off.

In the movies, a great deal of a comedy team's humor consists of action chases and slapstick. Sometimes it involves snappy dialogue. The basic premise of the comedy team follows the standard action/comedy formula where they always find themselves in a series of situations or trouble involving authority and bad guys, then finding their way out of it. And the trouble usually starts with the fall guy.

The famous movie comedy teams of the 1930's, 40's, 50's and later in TV, also evolved naturally out of vaudeville and the nightclub circuit. Each comedy team was known for its special running gags or trade mark routines which were recycled in different skits and in different ways in most of their movies.

In the 1930' the most well-known were arguably Laurel and Hardy. Thin, small and funny looking, Stan Laurel was the fall guy and big, overweight Oliver Hardy was the straight man. They wore bowler hats and wore suits that always looked too tight-fitting on them. Their running gag was that each time Stan Laurel got into trouble, Oliver Hardy would fume angrily with the running line, "This is another fine mess you've gotten me into".

In the 40's there was thin Bud Abbot, the straight man, who was considered by many comedians at that time to be the best in the business – and short, chubby, baby-faced and cuddly Lou Costello, the fall guy. Lou Costello's running gag in their movies was crying like a baby when he got "scared" in a creepy situation, and saying the often repeated line, "I've been a naughty boy", when he did something "wrong" and was reprimanded by Bud Abbot.

In the 1950's Dean Martin and Jerry Lewis became the most successful box office comedy team in the movies. Their appeal lasted a few years 'til their partnership ended due to incompatible differences. Dean Martin was the straight man, playing against Jerry Lewis' fall guy.

Dean Martin was good-looking with an Italian romantic flare that was popular with audiences during the late 50's and early 60's. He always played the love interest in their movies and he was the one who ended up getting the girl. He was different to the type of straight man that came before, and played as an ideal contrast to skinny, tall, crazy, funny looking and "immature" Jerry Lewis.

Dean Martin's trade mark routine was to sing at least one new romantic song in each movie which then became popular on the music hit parade, while Jerry Lewis' running gag was to pull funny faces and make weird body contortions each time he ran confused or out of control in a scene.

Around this time one of the most popular comedy teams in the early days of American TV was the husband and wife team of George Burns and Gracie Allen who were originally stars in vaudeville. In their routine, he played the straight man to Gracie Allen's "dumb blond", constantly chattering "fall guy".

As part of his image, he wore black thick-rimmed glasses with heavy lenses, and held a cigar as a prop in his hand.

As he threw the feed lines to Gracie, he would look like he was about to light it up and smoke it, but never did. And to stop Gracie from continually chattering, he would say to her, "Say Goodnight, Gracie", and end each show.

Probably the most famous and longest running comedy team on TV was the husband and wife team of Lucille Ball and Dezi Arnaz. Their comedy was focused around a sitcom in the series *I Love Lucy*. This series hit the airwaves when TV was still in its infancy and established the style, setup and basic story structure of many sitcoms that we see today.

She played a housewife to his Latin American band leader image, which is also what he was in real life. What's remarkable about the series is that during the 1950's when American prejudice against foreigners was at a peak, she played a typical All American housewife and mother, but with the switch that *she* was married to a Cuban "foreigner" who could hardly speak proper English.

It's interesting that she was made the fall guy, played against the "foreigner's" relatively straight man approach. Part of the charm and success of this comedy team was that their humor sometimes played subliminally on their cultural differences and the misunderstandings that occur and are compounded in a mixed relationship.

It also endeared them to the American TV public because their TV baby son was also their son in real life, whose growth over the years into a drum playing teenager on TV was followed by millions of viewers.

They pulled it off, because they emerged out of their mishaps each time stronger and more committed together as a family.

The Stand-up Comic: Is basically a one man or one woman show. It's predominantly played on the nightclub circuit and in some late night coffee houses that also provide entertainment for the customers. This circuit offers new comedians a venue to showcase and work their talent. Stand-up comics are also a recurring feature on late night TV Talk Shows and variety programs.

Stand-up comedy is basically a series of sharp, witty and sometimes satirical monologues that cut through contemporary issues. The monologues might reflect the current state of a country's politics, culture, the world condition, human foibles and relationships – as seen from the personal perspective of the stand-up comedian.

The stand-up comic plays both the straight man setting up the feed of the comedy, and the fall guy delivering the punch line, sometimes at their own expense.

They look at the humor or irony of various issues that might be serious or sacred to somebody else. But in the rhythm, timing, pacing, delivery and personality of a good comedian, there always seems to be some truth in the humor of what they observe about life and the state of the world. And sometimes that resonates with audiences on a far deeper level than a serious dialogue might.

There have been many brilliant stand-up comedians on TV, and anyone interested in this genre of comedy should look at the style, material and delivery of American comedians from the 1950's and early 60's. Among them there are people like Jack Benny, Milton Berle, Sid Caesar, Bob Newhart and Lenny Bruce. And closer to our time, Robin Williams and the remarkable stand-up comedy of Jerry Seinfeld who can make the most everyday mundane occurrences in life sound poignant and funny.

And from South Africa, explore the humor of Pieter Dirk Uys and the politically oriented stand-up comedy he gets away with, through the amusing characters he has created.

The Marx Brothers: Their movies were popular during the 1930's and 40's. Their humor was high energy and a cross between slap-stick and a sort of "sophisticated" style that suited the level of refinement that existed in audiences at that time.

They were unique as a comedy team. There were four of them. There was Groucho, Chico, Harpo and Zeppo, and each had a specialty comedy talent that always played something to someone who watched them.

Groucho wore round glasses and had a thick, wet-looking moustache painted across his upper lip and was the zaniest and the most irreverent member of the team. He was the cunning prankster and his trick was to make wise-cracks and sometimes cheeky remarks to pompous types of story characters who appeared in their movies.

Chico's character was a cross between a straight man and a clown. He spoke with a sort of Italian accent and wore a cone hat and a jacket that seemed to fit about one size too short on him. He was a brilliant piano player and performed at least one fast paced piece of music with clownish acrobatics on the keyboard in each of their movies.

Harpo looked like a doll. He had a circus clown quality about him, with large round eyes, a mop of curly blond hair and wore baggy clothes, a long coat and a funny top hat. He played a mute and never spoke, and communicated with sound effects and an old fashioned car horn that he carried around with him which made a squeaky noise each time he squeezed it to say something. He played classical music on the harp and performed on it at least once in each of their movies.

Zeppo was the straight man, and he was so straight he seemed to be non existent. There appeared to be no reason to have him around other than the fact that he was sort of handsome and that he sort of carried the romantic interest in each movie. He was the one who would get the girl at the end when all the humor had been played out. His character was eventually written out of the team.

Playing Comedy

It's true that not everyone can play comedy. Not everyone is good at it. Not everyone has a genuine *feel* for it. Some people are naturally funny. Others are not. But what is it about some people that make them funny? Is it in the way they look, the way they talk, the way they move?

Or is it in the way they *time* and *feel* the humor they're projecting? Without even *trying* to be funny, they are truly funny people. They even *think* funny. The truly great comedians have an inherent talent and feeling for comedy. It's in their personality.

Many actors say that comedy is more difficult to play than drama. When actors don't have a feel for comedy, they come across on the screen that they're trying too hard to be funny and it just doesn't work.

They feel comedy less than drama. Perhaps that's because in real life, like most of us, they're more conditioned through experience, the media and the news every day to tragedy and struggle, rather than to the light-hearted and funny side of life.

I'm not so sure that a *feel* for comedy can be taught, although some *techniques* can be passed along to a humorless actor to perhaps help them generate some sense of comedy in a performance. But the technique alone will not necessarily turn a humorless actor into a good comedian.

Look at some of the following techniques and situations that might make comedy work or fall flat for an actor:

- Vocal energy is usually played up in certain types of comedy. For example, as it is in sitcoms. It's obvious that when you look at a sitcom, you'll see that the actor's vocal deliveries are usually performed on a higher vibration or more over the top than in drama.

As a general rule, the pacing, rhythm and timing of the dialogue and action between the actors is quicker than it is in drama. The transitions and responses are much tighter and the humor is closely written, which makes an allowance for quicker responses. A good example is the sophisticated feature film comedy of Woody Allen.

However, not all comedy is required to be fast-paced and high energy as in sitcoms and some other genres where the energy is projected outwards. In some styles of British comedy, the energy that's projected is an *internalized* kind of energy.

When you look at the wry, dry humor in the 1950's feature film comedies of Alec Guinness and Peter Sellers, the comedy relied not so much on quick tempo, fast pacing and rhythm - but on the interesting characters they created, and on the *energy* and *perfect timing* of the *delayed* reaction and response.

They were masters at it.

- In comedy, the actors play their part in all seriousness. Their character is based on reality and they play the reality and truthfulness of the situation. They *live* it from a very real place. The humor happens because the characters look so serious reacting to and resolving in all earnestness, the sometimes preposterous situations they find themselves in.

- Some types of humor which are meaningful and funny in some places may not be in others. Living inside a particular culture and having an insight into its conditions and values, as well as the different social and cultural levels of sophistication of its inhabitants also play a role in determining what's funny to some people, and what's not to others.

- Some actors try to be funny by relying solely on slapstick comedy. It isn't funny because they rely on the action for laughs instead of on the personality of the comic performing the action. They push for the laughs and it just doesn't work.

- What's funny also depends on the maturity level of the audience watching the comedy.

When the same comedy routines are seen over and over again but played out in different situations, they just don't look funny anymore. It takes an exceptional comic to make an old routine appear fresh and funny.

- It also happens that sometimes comedy is produced by directors who really don't have a feel for it, or don't understand the rhythm, timing, pacing and the delivery of comedy - or how to direct the actors to perform it.

It's hard to pinpoint what the dynamic is that makes something work and something else not. When you try comedy, only practice and experience will teach you what works for *you* and what doesn't.

One thing is certain. The world needs to smile more and we need funny people in our lives to make us laugh more.

.

Soapies / Sitcoms

What is it about soapies and sitcoms that attract people? People even become addicted to them. Some even live their lives through the story "experiences" of the characters they see on TV. Why are soapies and sitcoms so popular?

Psychologists have speculated that many peoples' lives are uninteresting and rigid because of their social, cultural and religious conditioning. Because of that, they need to "experience" their own lives through fictional characters that become familiar to them and exciting to watch. And perhaps it's also because there's a little bit of "voyeurism" in each of us that makes us want to look at actors performing uninhibitedly on a TV screen.

The truth is that most soapies and sitcoms are boring. They're not really that great to look at. With few exceptions, the stories and characters are usually predictable and the situations look false. The dialogue is generally over-written and the characters talk too much with very little real action happening between them.

In most instances the acting is formulaic. It's a type of acting that's done by rote which is – as a general rule – not as psychologically demanding on the actors as might be required of them in a feature movie. It's usually acceptable for the actors in a soapie or sitcom to perform their roles in whatever way they wish as long as they're prepared for the shoot, say their lines competently and are sometimes even able to "fake" a performance.

And yet, audiences become so attached to particular actors playing specific roles in a series that they live their everyday lives by following the real-life intrigues and gossip of those actors they see on their TV screens in tabloid magazines and news reports.

TV Networks also love soapies and sitcoms. They're relatively economical to produce with the major expense going to the principal "stars" salaries. And because they're popular with audiences, it's easier for the networks to get sponsors to purchase commercial broadcasting time and to profit from that.

However, it is extremely *stressful* and *physically* draining for an actor to work on a soapie or sitcom. The hours are long and tiring, especially on the key actors who are committed to perform the same character continuously week after week or day after day over a prolonged period of time. Sometimes this can amount to many years in a long running series.

The actors and crew function under enormous pressure to complete each episode on schedule, to meet precise broadcast programming times and they are required to complete it under tight budget conditions.

The production time per episode of most half hour sitcoms can be anywhere from three to five days, which includes prepping the episode, and blocking and rehearsing the actors moves, with a final on set rehearsal on the shoot day.

Different episodes are assigned to alternating directors who are familiar with the series and are specialists in sitcom and soapie production.

On some "daily" running soapies an entire rehearsal and shooting schedule for an episode might involve only one day. The actors might come in for a rehearsal starting in the early hours of the morning and shoot the episode on set later in the day or in the same evening.

There's little leeway to make mistakes. The actors who are committed in running roles have to memorize the complete text of their dialogue for each days shoot day after day. The pace is unforgiving on those who can't cope with the difficult production demands of acting on a soapie or sitcom and actor's who can't deal with these conditions are soon replaced by an actor who can.

For beginners, the pay on soapies and sitcoms is usually not that rewarding, but they provide a wonderful training ground for a newcomer to gain professional experience and the exposure in a sitcom or soapie can provide an opportunity for new actors to become established and known in the industry.

The shows are mostly videotaped or filmed on a standard studio set or on a series of sets which are specially designed for the program. They are recorded by three or more cameras whose movements are pre-planned and blocked on the studio floor.

With few exceptions, each show is recorded and performed in a linear sequence as opposed to out of sequence continuity, usually in front of a live studio audience. It's very much like a theatre performance, where the lighting and sets look obviously theatrical and artificial. The camera set-ups are pre-blocked on the studio floor and the sets are pre-lit and pre-dressed and used over and over again till the end run of the series. Each show may even be video edited simultaneously as it's happening.

If the budget permits, extra sets might be added for a special episode. To give the look of the show additional production value, some scenes might even be shot outdoors or on location and cross edited later into the studio scenes.

Actors who work for many years on a soapie or sitcom risk facing a career crisis in later life because they become so identified with the character they've been playing for so long – and with the formula type of acting they've locked into – that after the series has had it's run they're so typecast in the role they've created that they may have difficulty finding acting work in something different.

What's still more unsettling is that some actors have become so much a part of the specific role they've created, that they carry on the "personality" of their "TV character" into real life during its continuum and even after the series has run its course.

Acting by the Numbers

Different styles and methods of acting are taught by different drama schools. One is technical, relying on a "technique" or "formula" of acting rather than on a natural internalized approach.

It's a type of acting which is best described as expression by the numbers. If you watch this kind of acting for a while, you'll begin to sense that it's predictable and appears false. You'll know what the actor is going to do or say after they hit a sort of "acting pose" and "turn on" a specific expression that's supposed to communicate a particular "feeling" each time a specific type of reaction is required.

Each expression can be almost categorized. For example, there may be expressions 1, 2, 3 and 4 for certain types of smiles. And perhaps expressions 5, 6, 7 and 8 might suggest certain types of anger or sorrow emotions.

The reactions / expressions are *emotionless* and rather than *experiencing* the emotion, the actor's body language merely *imitates* it.

When you imitate something it is not your own and you are just going through gestures. You cannot feel the *emotion* of it, and therefore project it convincingly outwards to the audience.

These kind of broad expressions appear to be suited more to certain types of soapies, sitcom and theatre acting.

A true expression happens spontaneously as a direct consequence or result of a real emotion happening inside you in a situation.

As an exercise to awaken your perception about these different styles and techniques of acting, observe different types of soapies, sitcoms and movies and see if you can discern the differences.

Green / Blue Screen Acting

Many special effects that you see in the movies today are created in a controlled studio environment where the actors are photographed performing their scenes in front of a large wall or backdrop painted either green or blue.

The reason for this is that it gives a director a greater creative freedom. They can place any type of background or environment that they want to incorporate into the movie onto this backdrop.

Special effects are a complex subject which is a series of books in itself. The following is a brief summary of what this type of acting technique is about.

Special effects are also known as trick photography. They've been around since the beginning of photography and the invention of motion pictures.

Before the advent of green and blue screens, most special effects were created with two processes called (1) **matte photography** and (2) **back projection**.

Both of these methods are time consuming and use mechanically operated cameras and film projectors.

(1) **Matte photography** means that when a scene is photographed certain areas of the picture can be "matted out" (blocked or masked means the same thing) inside the camera, exposing only the areas of the scene that are not blocked out onto the film.

The action of the scene, which might also involve actors, is then photographed onto the exposed area of the film.

The exposed area of the film is then blocked out and the film is rewound inside the camera and the area of the film which was previously matted is now unblocked and photographed with new visuals which a director wants to incorporate into a scene.

The new visuals can be normal size action scenes involving actors or painted backgrounds, miniature models, sets, and portions of sets or other images.

They'll be photographed to blend in with the appropriate dimension and scale of the original photography and incorporated into the matted area.

The actors have to perform within clearly marked boundaries on the set during a matte photography shoot, and need to be careful not to cross over into those areas that have been matted out for the camera.

In 1939 much of the visual background and setting of the classic ground-breaking movie *Gone With The Wind* was achieved with matte photography. It was a long and tedious process done manually through the camera.

(2) **Back projection** is still used today in some places. The most common example of this is when you see actors in a scene sitting in a mock-up of a car and playing the scene with traffic moving outside seen through the windows of the car. This creates the *illusion* that it's the car with the actors in it that is moving. You can tell that it's back projection because the background behind the actors looks slightly diffused and grainy.

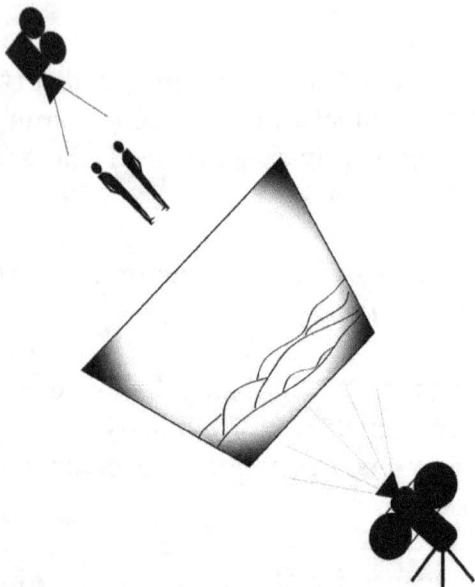

The actors perform **in front** of a specially constructed white movie screen which is slightly transparent to allow any image that's projected onto it **to also show on both the front and back** of the screen.

There is a movie projector **behind** the screen that projects onto it an appropriate scenic or action background which is chosen by the director to supplement the scene.

However, the image of the chosen background is projected onto the screen **in reverse.** Refer to our discussion earlier in this book on *Crossing the Line*.

The image that's projected onto the screen now appears **normal** as it faces the actors performing the scene on the other side of the screen. The camera then photographs the action of the actors performing the scene in sync with the image that's projected onto the screen.

Green or Blue screen – though not exactly the same – is sort of the same idea as matte photography and back projection combined, but it's an electronic-digital process. It does the same thing and allows special effects technicians to create even more interesting visual effects cleanly, quickly and efficiently. It also eliminates the technical problems of crossing the line and the background images behind the actors are sharper and cleaner. It was first introduced commercially in motion picture production during the 1970's.

Because of the way in which the chemistry of video, digital and film record an image, the specific colors of green or blue "neutralize" the area of the painted wall behind the action of the actor when it's photographed. It then allows the director to fill in the green or blue area of the wall electronically with any kind of visuals or backgrounds that they want to integrate into the action.

Today action movies like *Star Wars, Spiderman, Superman* and *Batman* use green or blue screen techniques to create special effects illusions like characters flying through the air, outer space settings, surrealistic buildings, city mock-ups, different environments or giant monsters causing havoc.

Miniature *models* of these sets, and props and characters are designed and built. These are then transmitted onto the green or blue screen and enlarged to the correct proportion of the live action photographed by the camera. It's easier, safer and cheaper to *simulate* these kinds of elements in the studio than to shoot them in the uncontrollable circumstances of real life space.

Green or Blue screen acting is a challenge for many actors. They perform in front of the screen in an imaginary space - usually with no real sets around them to play to. Sometimes a part of a set might be included to give a scene a three dimensional look. The rest of the environment information might then be edited electronically into the scene later, or simultaneously as the action is being photographed and happening in the scene.

It's also critical that the actors do not wear anything remotely green or blue, because what's inserted onto the green or blue screen behind them, will also appear on the green or blue clothing they're wearing.

Because of the instant playback capability of digital technology, once the principal photography in front of the green/blue screen has been done, and the special effects have been included into the scene, it allows the creative team to quickly review, assess and correct what has been shot instantly, rather than to wait for days for a roll of film to be processed and returned for viewing and modifications as it is done with matte photography and back projection technology.

You have to be disciplined to perform within the carefully laid out boundaries that are marked on the stark set or studio floor. It's an extremely technical working environment. If an actor moves away from those boundaries, they will infringe outside the green or blue screen layout. It takes some experience to adapt your performance to it.

Some actors who are also theatre trained and used to performing in artificial settings, seem to adapt more readily to the demands and technical requirements of green / blue screen acting. They're comfortable performing in imaginary space.

Green/blue screen technology has made the whole process of creating special effects a common and affordable feature in the production of commercials, TV programs and movies. TV studio newsrooms use it all the time and green screens are automatically incorporated into the design of a news anchor set.

Wardrobe Note: Some color clothing that you wear has a tendency to not always register well on video:

   Red bleeds   White reflects light   Black absorbs light

And some clothing that is designed with thin white stripes on a dark background is inclined to create an annoying strobe effect when you move. So it's always a good idea to not wear these colors by themselves. Break them up with other color combinations when you wear them, unless you're instructed otherwise by the people working on a production.

Cheating Camera Angles

Performing in real-life locations and sets, in unmanageable conditions, can be extremely difficult. The upside of this is that in a real-life space an actor's performance has a sense of realism about it.

However, when a director can't control a location or set in a real-life space they have to come up with ways to compensate for the problems that are faced in shooting a scene in such a situation, while still retaining the integrity of that scene.

There are various methods that a director can use to solve some problems. One of the most common is *to cheat a camera angle* to get the required effect of a shot if it's difficult to do in a normal, controlled setup. It's like creating a cheap and quick special effect.

As a movie actor it would be worthwhile for you to be aware of what will be required of you in a situation like this.

Look at the following three examples:

1]   What does a director do when they are committed for various reasons to shoot a Master Shot behind an actor in a tight location and forced to block a scene with a group of actors acting with their backs in front of a real brick wall while the other actor is facing them? What would the director do to get the

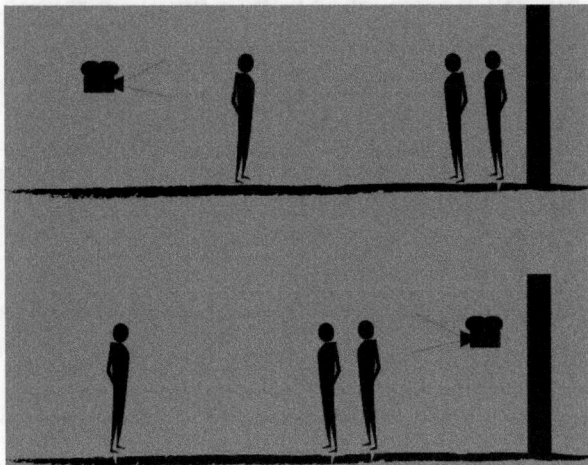

reverse shot of the actor facing the others who are performing in front of the wall?

The director can't break a hole into the wall to place the camera behind the other actors to get the shot of the actor facing them. So the director *cheats* the camera angle in a way that still creates the *illusion* of a successful reverse angle shot of the actor facing the others.

The director moves the actor *further back* and the other actors *forward* just enough to compensate for the change in distance between them, giving the camera crew enough space to place the camera behind the group of actors in the required position to get the shot, making sure that the background behind the actor facing them remains *neutral* and that they and the other actors are photographed in a relatively tightly framed shot.

2]   Or suppose you and character A are playing a part in an action movie and A has been in an accident and is lying in pain bleeding on the ground. You bend over to console A. After the Master Shot has been filmed, the director might then want a ***Close-up*** reaction of your face consoling A.

The director can't dig a hole in the ground to place the camera under you to film your closeup. There wouldn't be enough space between you and A and the ground to place the camera under you. So the solution is to set up a platform and to let you play your part on top of the platform instead of on the ground as you did in the Master Shot, allowing room for the camera to be placed low enough under you and the platform to photograph your reaction.

Looking up at you from this position, you will now probably be playing against the *neutral* background of the sky.

Your *eye-line* looking at A lying in pain on the ground will also need to *change* to compensate for the change in your position. Instead of looking at A's original position, you will probably be required to *fake your look to a new position* where A supposedly would also now be lying.

In these circumstances, the camera crew will guide you into your correct eye-line position. You will be playing your role in a combination of imaginary and real time space and you must stay focused and remain in the moment required by the scene in spite of this inconvenience.

3]   Or, you're in a scene in a Master Shot talking to actor A who is taking a bath and you're sitting on the edge of the bathtub which is also built against a tiled wall in a real-life space.

How would the director shoot the Reverse Shot of you talking to A which will also include the back of A's head in the shot looking at you? It would be impractical to place the camera and crew inside the bathtub with A sitting in it or breaking a hole into the wall to place the camera behind it in a position to capture the scene.

Instead, the director will *move both you and A outside the bathtub* allowing enough room for the camera to be placed at an enough distance away from you and A to shoot the Reverse Shot.

Both you and A will them be asked to sit on some sort of boxes to simulate the height and positions of where you both were at the bathtub. The scene then would probably be photographed in a relative tight shot against a *neutral* background in the bathroom.

Your *eye-line* looking at A's new position "in the bathtub" will also need to adapt to compensate for the change in both your position and A's.

Instead of looking at A sitting inside the original position of the bathtub, you will probably be required to *fake your look to a new position* where the bathtub with A sitting in it would supposedly also have moved.

In these circumstances, the camera crew will again guide you into your correct eye-line position.

Stunts

Safety on the Set

Visual action and stunt work has been a staple of the movies from the beginning. Action and stunts belong together, and the ground work of the sophisticated stunts that we see in the movies today, began way back in the silent era.

The chases, fights and stunts that are spectacular in movies like the *Star Wars, Indiana Jones, Jackie Chan* and *James Bond* series, are just a perfected version of what audiences already saw in the low budget movie serials and cowboy action "B" movies of the 1920's, 30's and 40's.

The studio that was most instrumental in turning this kind of action movie and its accompanying stunt work into a serious discipline and an art form, was the old Republic Pictures Studios located in Studio City near Los Angeles. Their famous trademark was the American eagle perched on a rock with wings outstretched, ready to take flight. It's a pity it no longer exists.

People who perform stunts are very special. There's usually a unique fellowship among them that's rare among movie people, because they live with danger and even the potential of a fatal accident happening if something goes wrong each time they do a stunt.

Don't try to do dangerous stunt work. Performing stunts is unsafe if you're not a professional. If something goes wrong you could be seriously injured and it could be the end of your career as an actor. Stunts are performed by people *who have been specially trained in this kind of work.*

Some years ago I was teaching drama at a film school in Cape Town. Inexperienced students who were studying directing often used our drama students to act in their student films. The students who were studying directing were never properly supervised, disciplined or trained in the safety procedures that are normal on a movie set.

One day word came back to me that one of our drama students was pressured by a directing student to jump out of a moving vehicle, because he thought that the action would look good in his movie.

The drama student cared enough about himself not to listen to the directing student, even though he was insulted and told he was not a good actor because "he didn't do what he was told to do".

Another time a student director threw kerosene on another drama student and set his hand on fire because he thought that kind of action "would look spectacular!"

Our student was badly scarred. His whole body almost caught alight before the fire was put out. I asked him why he allowed himself to be conned into doing such dangerous stunt work and he told me that he did it because he wanted to be a good actor and do what was asked of him.

I asked him what would have happened if he had been burnt so badly that it would have ended his career. He told me that it never occurred to him. I told him that what he did is not what acting is about. That's not the criteria of being a good actor. He was lucky to have survived that time.

In spectacular movie scenes where characters are set on fire, professional stunt people know what they're doing. They use fire repellent equipment and wardrobe, and perform under strictly controlled fire conditions with the fire department and first aid on standby on the movie set, ready to extinguish the fire if it goes out of control. That's standard safety procedure on all professional shoots involving inflammable material.

It's just common sense to understand the basics of safety when you do stunts. Stunts by professionals are planned precisely, rehearsed, choreographed and go through a dry run a number of times before they're performed and committed to camera.

Timing and safety is critical when professionals perform a stunt. When a stunt is ready to be shot, it will probably be photographed by two or more cameras that are set up at different camera angles to capture the action.

For example, wouldn't it be impractical and foolish if a terrifying car crash was shot with only one camera, and then to try and re-stage the whole scene again and repeat the same sequence over and over again from different camera angles once all the cars have ended up in a heap?

Professional stunt people are all rounders. They're accomplished in various activities. They know how to ride a horse the way real cowboys and equestrians do. They know how to race cars the way professional racing car drivers do. They're skilled in different styles of martial arts, and they know how to choreograph and perform amazing fight sequences the way real martial artists do. And if they're hired to double for an actor playing Tarzan they know how to swim the way an Olympic medalist does.

However, as an actor, you'll probably be required to perform a *basic* stunt perhaps once or even a number of times during your career. For example, if you're acting out a fight scene you should know how to throw and receive a punch. Fight scenes are one of the most common stunts you see in movies and TV series.

When you act out a fight and perform the stunt, you're the one on the receiving end of a hit when it's thrown at you. You have to make a well-timed, choreographed move *away* from the blow to avoid it coming at you.

At the same time you have to do "the acting" part to make it look real. And when you throw a hit back, you would need to know *where* and *how* to throw the hit *correctly* without harming the other actor or yourself.

It's therefore a good idea that if you're serious about acting, you get some basic stunt training from a reputable and professional stunt school if there is one in your area.

You'll also have to learn how to take, block and break a fall properly without getting hurt and not to fall at a wrong angle that could seriously injure you. If you're in a leading role and injured in a bad stunt – besides the physical harm it does to you – it will also cost the production company a lot of money.

It's unfortunate, but what matters to the production company is the possible financial loss they'll suffer and not your personal pain if your injury affects the outcome of the production in the wrong way.

That's why professional stunt doubles are hired to do the difficult and dangerous stunt work on a movie. They're chosen because of their ability to pull off a particular kind of stunt, and because they also physically resemble the actors they're performing the stunt for.

They perform the stunts in the *wider* or *master shots* in place of the actors. The action is then repeated in closer shots with the main actors who will then be required to mimic the action and choreography of the stunt people and act out the emotions required in the scene.

In your repertoire of talents you should also know how to do a variety of common things like riding a horse, a bicycle or driving a car.

It surprised me, but there are some actors out there who don't even know how to do a familiar thing like driving a car.

I once worked with one who didn't. I just assumed everyone knew how when I cast him in a small part. We were on location in a small town out in the country about forty kilometers outside Toronto. The scene involved him driving a car up to the general store in the town, get out and enter the building where the scene would continue from there. That's when he told me he didn't drive. Panic hit the set because of the tight budget and sensitive production conditions of the TV movie we were shooting.

We had established him already in two previous scenes so just replacing him with another actor who could drive was not an immediate option. We had to quickly hire a stunt man to double for him. According to the Screen Actors Guild rules at that time, driving a car was considered a stunt if a double was used for an actor in a scene.

The stunt double had to be transported from Toronto immediately, come onto the set, and dress and look like the actor and do the driving part of the scene for him.

It cost the production company more to hire the stunt man plus his transportation, than it did to pay the actor for the few days he was hired for the shoot. I never worked with him again.

If you're into action movies, you also need to be physically fit and nimble. Even when you do a basic stunt, the chances are that you could still get hurt if things go wrong even after a lot of preparation has been done. If your timing is off and you miss the rhythm of a move you could get badly hurt, or you can hurt the person you're working with.

However, some famous actors sometimes have insisted on doing their own stunts, which causes production companies some serious headaches. They don't like it, but the actors are powerful enough to get their own way.

Steve McQeen during the 1960's was someone like that. Besides being an accomplished actor, he was also a brilliant race car driver and motorcycle rider. In the movie *The Great Escape*, he did his own spectacular stunt work on a motorcycle during the escape sequence from a prisoner of war camp.

Another was Gene Kelly, who was a brilliant acrobat and dancer. He drove the top brass at MGM crazy during the 1940's and 50's when he did his own daring dance routines in very stunt like settings.

The late Bruce Lee was a Master martial arts expert and set the trend by performing his own spectacular fight stunts in his action movies, and in recent times Jackie Chan has even surpassed Bruce Lee in the daring and breathtaking stunts he performs in his movies.

Chasing "Stardom"

A movie star is not quite a human being...

- Marlene Dietrich

Glamour: *To charm; enchant; bewitch.*

- Oxford Dictionary

What is *"It"*? What is it about the *glamour, aura* or *star quality* which some people seem to possess that others don't? Is a screen "star" discovered and created by a particular role, or is the "role" created by the attitude and dynamics which the "star" actor projects?

Some actors seem to still possess *"it"* even as they begin to mature into middle and old age.

Actors like Tom Hanks, Meryl Streep, Sandra Bullock, Tom Cruise, Jodie Foster, John Travolta, Richard Gere, Denzel Washington, Gwyneth Paltrow and so many others - what makes *them* special? What attracts audiences to watch them and to keep watching them?

Is it one thing, or a combination of the things we've discussed in these pages?

Things like:

- The way they move physically and emotionally?
- Their sensuality? The way they talk and sound?
- The integrity and intense focus they have when they perform a role?
- The chemistry they give off when they interact with certain people?
- The way they're *alive*?
- Their natural style when we see them on the screen? Their relationship with the camera?

Thousands of great and wonderful actors around the world also have these same qualities. Many are just as good and talented as "the stars" audiences hook into, and some are even better. But they don't seem to have that "stardom" label attached to them?

So, what *is* "a star"?

A "star" is generally accepted as someone who excels at something, and it doesn't necessarily have to be only acting. There are a lot of people who also excel at things but are not recognized as "stars".

A "star" is someone who has an image and name that's instantly recognized by people around the world. But there also seems to be something more to it than that. For some reason, if you are a true "star" you have monetary "drawing power".

Your "image" sells product. You have influence. Your name becomes the main attraction to promote and publicize a movie, idea, belief or anything else. You are the main event and the person who *features* in a project, an event or entertainment situation of some kind.

You have "something" that attracts the media to you. Magazines and newspapers write about you. TV talk show hosts want you on their program. You're a hot topic because of the confidence you have in what you believe and in the way you communicate it.

It's what you do, and the way you do it on TV, on the screen, in your work and in your private life that makes you interesting to watch and to listen to. People talk about you. You can sway and influence people with your ideas. You "radiate" wealth, success and "glamour". You have celebrity. You have personality. You are famous.

Whether you deserve it or not, people treat you with respect, and perhaps they might even do so grudgingly. You're held in awe and maybe even looked upon with envy and fear. People are intimidated by you. They cater to your needs because of your *perceived* importance.

On the other hand, there's also a down side to being "a star". Your private life turns into public property. You become bait for gossip. You learn to live with little privacy because your every move is watched and analyzed. Some people thrive on this kind of scrutiny. Others can't.

You constantly have to work hard to keep up your image, or adapt it to suit the times when situations and circumstances change and you are no longer interesting to follow.

It might also be valuable for you to realize that there are different "levels" of stardom and different "types" of "stars". Even some people without any special talent sometimes achieve a sort of "star" status for no other reason than that they're famous for being famous and were born into wealth and a privileged position.

Fame is a powerful stimulant and it *attracts* ordinary people to someone famous, and people want to follow and imitate a famous person. Look at Paris Hilton. Her celebrity and lifestyle and the publicity she generates has given her a sort of "star" status.

The whole set-up of the British monarchy is built around wealth, pomp, pageantry, ceremony and glamour. It has a "show business" quality about it.

During the 1980's and 90's some members of the British Royal Family achieved a sort of "star" status because of their celebrity and the precariousness of their personal relationships. Princess Diana even achieved a "superstar" status because of her more dynamic personality, fame and independent lifestyle.

A "superstar" is someone who surpasses even a star image.

Yet members of other royal families in Europe, Asia and Africa may have some renown inside their own countries, but are generally unheard of anywhere else. They aren't recognized as radiating an *international* "star" quality.

Some sports "personalities" are "stars", others are "superstars" while many other sportspeople who are just as talented, are not.

Mother Theresa in her humble way emitted a "star quality" because of her charisma and the work she did amongst the poor. She reached an iconic stature and was a "star" to many people, even though she was a reluctant one.

The fame of what she did was known all over the world and her "name" helped to raise money which financed her work among the destitute.

The ritual and spectacle of the Catholic Church resembles theatre on a grand scale, and Pope John Paul II came across as a "superstar" – even to millions of non-Catholics – because of his position and forceful personality.

And yet, his successor Benedict VI, who was elected to the same position after the death of John Paul II, is so laid back that few people outside the church are aware of him. He doesn't radiate the same powerful and forceful presence.

Even people who you might personally dislike can display a "star quality" if they have some kind of special notoriety and a following of enough people who idolize them.

During the 1930's in Chicago some gangsters like Al Capone and Baby Face Nelson were "stars" in the minds of many people because of their infamy, the fear they generated, their exploits and the "glamorized" image the media created about them. Another example would be Bonnie and Clyde.

In a strange way, the legend that was built around the death of Che Guevara gave him a sort of "star status" because of the attention the adventure of his life received over a prolonged period of time.

Some American Presidents, like John F. Kennedy, Ronald Reagan, Bill Clinton and currently – to a lesser extent – Barack Obama, have been revered as "international stars", while the majority of leaders in other places might be "stars" in their own countries, but don't have the name recognition, influence and drawing power which even some members of the American Congress have.

For instance, look at someone like the late Ted Kennedy. His association with the legendary Kennedy "name" and his staying power as an American senator had elevated him into a sort of "star" category during his political career.

Just observe the world around you. There are "stars" in every field you can think of, but the ones most people are familiar with are the "stars" in the entertainment world, and especially in television and the movies.

How you *achieve* "movie stardom" is another matter. Many factors might contribute to making you a "star", and it's hard to know what the right formula is.

Study the experiences of some well-known actors to learn how they became "stars". Certainly luck and talent had a lot to do with it, and so was being in the right place at the right time. It was also helpful that they were able to connect with the kind of people who promoted their careers.

The story about how Harrison Ford was discovered goes that he was working as a carpenter doing some work at George Lucas' house around the time when Lucas was just beginning to make a name for himself as a producer-director. Lucas thought Harrison Ford could be a "star" actor. After he gave him a leading role in *STAR WARS*, the success of the movie turned him into a major "star".

Charlize Theron started her career as a model working in New York. The rumor is that she was in a bank one day and got into an argument with the management and threw a tantrum. An important actor's agent also happened to be in the bank and saw the forceful way she handled herself. He was impressed by her "performance" and was responsible for getting her started.

She began by appearing in some low budget movies. She worked hard to study acting and to change her South African accent into an American one. Her persistence won her bigger roles and she began to work with some big name stars which made her name more well-known. The high point of her career came when she hit superstardom after winning the Oscar for her riveting performance in *Monster*.

Marilyn Monroe was an unknown starlet at the beginning of the 1950's, ignored by both Columbia Pictures and 20th Century-Fox. Then she posed nude for a calendar. It was quite innocent by today's standards. There was no frontal nudity, but it was quite a shocking thing for someone to do at that time.

It created a lot of publicity and people talked about it. 20th Century-Fox suddenly noticed her and realized she was under contract to them as a minor bit player. And that's when they decided to go full out and promote her as a sex symbol.

The studio "created" her image. She was fashioned by publicity. Publicity brainwashed audiences into believing that she was sexy, and they bought it.

James Dean was set up by Warner Bros. Studios to become "the next Marlon Brando". After James Dean was killed in a car accident in the mid 1950's, the studios were looking for someone new to replace the *"James Dean"* image.

A youthful Paul Newman had the talent and looks and a comparable acting style that was popular with audiences at a time when he was just starting to break into the movies. So to cash in on the James Dean "idea", Paul Newman was groomed into stardom by 20th Century-Fox and he continued to remain a "star" until his death at 83.

Gene Wilder hit stardom in the 1970's. He was first noticed as a potential comedy "star" after he appeared in a short, humorous scene playing a cab driver chatting to Warren Beatty and Faye Dunaway as they were making a getaway in his cab in *Bonnie and Clyde.*

John Wayne has been a "star" forever. He was a football player as a young man and worked in the movies as an extra, as well as a set dresser and props man. He became a "B" movie cowboy in the 1930's because of his athletic abilities and physical presence, and then was "discovered" as a leading man in "A" feature films after he was given a leading role by director John Ford in his classic western movie *Stagecoach.*

The movie was a study of a group of characters travelling together on a long journey, who are confined in the small space of a stagecoach. The movie was built around the standard western formula which included action, the chase and the "hero" dealing with the bad guys.

The story sets up John Wayne as a mysterious stranger travelling with the group when it's revealed that he is a criminal, but ends up as the hero.

John Wayne still kept attracting audiences as he got older, and appeared in a variety of different genre movies. He's still a "superstar" legend even after his death more than three decades ago.

Clint Eastwood spent many years working as a television actor. He co-starred in a popular western series in the early 1960's called *Wagon Train.* During the 1960's it was difficult for "TV actors" to break into "big screen" movies because the major studios in Hollywood didn't take TV actors seriously as having "big screen" star potential. They also felt threatened by the rivalry from TV which was drawing audiences away from the theatres, and by some misguided logic, they banned "TV stars" that performed on the small screen from appearing in Hollywood "big screen" movies.

Clint Eastwood got an opportunity to work in Italy as a "big screen" movie star where he featured as *the man with no name* in some good, low budget and successful "spaghetti" westerns like *A Fistful of Dollars* and *The Good, the Bad and the Ugly,* which have since then become cult classics.

He returned to Hollywood with a "movie star" status and was one of the first "TV Stars" who made the transition from TV to the "big screen".

Today working in TV is seen as an excellent training ground for an actor and exposure in a successful TV series can be instrumental in achieving big screen stardom. Bruce Willis, Robin Williams, John Travolta, Burt Reynolds, Jennifer Aniston, Helen Hunt and Sally Field who are now important movie stars, were originally "stars" in popular television series.

Although the international character of the movie and TV industry has changed drastically since the 1960's, it seems that if you want to really make it into the big time it still has to happen through Hollywood, because the money and international distribution outlets for movies and television programs from there are still relatively powerful. It's all energized by hype, promotion and publicity and Hollywood is brilliant at it.

Many foreign actors know that only too well. Many work without international movie recognition for years in their own countries and may be recognized as "stars" locally, but because they are somewhat "unknown" world-wide, their international "star" potential is often under-estimated by Hollywood.

Actors like Nicole Kidman, Jeremy Irons, Michael Caine, Mel Gibson, Richard Burton, Sophia Loren, Gerard Depardieu, Colin Farrell, Laurence Olivier, Gwyneth Paltrow, Alec Guinness, Marcello Mastroianni, Emma Thompson, Peter Sellers, Ingrid Bergman, Peter O Toole, Juliet Pinoche and Julia Ormond had to appear first in "Hollywood" produced movies before they really became big "international stars".

It's not easy to sustain being a "star". Many actors might be "stars" for a while, but then they fade away into obscurity. For some reason their appeal is short-lived and diminishes. They don't have *staying power*.

Have you ever heard of "Fabian"? During the late 1950's and early 60's he was heavily promoted by 20th Century Fox as the next "Elvis", as was Pat Boone who made a series of teeny bop movies.

What about Hope Lange and Diane Varsi? They were "stars" in *Peyton Place* and *Ten North Frederick* which were two highly publicized movies promoting those actresses during the late 1950's. And Tuesday Weld? She was also an up and coming "star" during the early 1960's. But have you heard of any of them today? Maybe a few older people have.

Kim Novak was Columbia Pictures response to Marilyn Monroe. Many people considered Kim prettier, a better actress and more *naturally* sexy than Marilyn. She featured in some interesting movies like *Bell, Book and Candle* and Picnic, but does her name mean anything to you now?

So when you really have *"It"*, it's something that you'll radiate all your life. Some older actors have "it". You can see it and feel "it" when you watch them on the screen. There's a professionalism, confidence and glow about them.

Anthony Quinn was a secondary star in Hollywood movies for years, but became a "super" one in middle age when he played the leading role in a Greek made film directed by a little known director called Michael Cacoyannis. The film became a great international hit in the 1960's. It was called *Zorba the Greek*.

Olympia Dukakis became an international "star" later in life when she co-starred with Cher in *Moonstruck* and won an Oscar for Best Supporting actress. She did wonderful work for years but was never recognized before that as a "Hollywood star". When she was younger the circumstances and the roles she played just didn't seem to be right for her to reach "stardom".

After working and maturing as an actor in many supporting and co-starring roles Anthony Hopkins hit "big time stardom" and was "suddenly discovered", becoming an "overnight success" after he co-starred in *Silence of the Lambs*.

Jack Lemmon and Walter Matthau were still going strong in their seventies as *The Odd Couple II.*

George Burns, who was a star since the early years of TV, was "rediscovered" as a big screen movie star when he was in his 70's and played *"GOD"* in the movie. He then continued on as a "star" in *The Sunshine Boys.*

Were these actors lucky?

Perhaps they were, but in a way maybe they were also responsible for their own destiny because they worked hard and persevered through difficult times and made fortunate choices when the opportunities came their way.

Maybe the bottom line is that to some extent *you* create your own luck and path to "stardom".

And sometimes the timing of your circumstances and the importance of the position you find yourself in might elevate you to a "star" status.

Then, it's how you cope with that that will determine the degree by how much you succeed in holding onto your status as a "star".

Part 13

*Success in movies boils down to three things:
story, story, story*

> - Darryl F. Zanuck
>   *Co-founder / President*
>   *20th Century Fox*

Human beings cannot live without stories.

> - Anne Douglas
>   *Terrible Honesty*

Evaluating a Movie

A personal perspective

When I look at a movie, I try to see it objectively. I begin by viewing it from the historical perspective of the era in which it was made, and I consider the impact it had on audiences at the time when it was first released.

I look at various aspects such as:

- The country and physical environment in which it was produced.
- The social, political, economic, psychological, moral and cultural conditions prevailing at the time.
- Did it reveal an honest account of a specific era?
- The educational, cultural, social and spiritual development of the audience at which it was aimed.
- The creative and innovative ideas it introduced to uplift film into an art form in technical areas such as photography, sound, editing and visual style.
- New ideas it introduced in terms of film technique and acting for the screen.
- Its entertainment qualities and production value.
- How it contributed to cultural changes. The social and moral barriers it broke.
- The controversy it caused. How it may have changed peoples' perception of things. It's social, political, cultural and moral redeeming factors.
- The trends in fashion, style and thinking it introduced into society.
- How has it withstood the test of time? Does the film touch and entertain people today?

I think one should also appreciate *why* the movie was made and what was the objective of the people who made it? They may have had different motives which can determine how one should evaluate it.

Was its' purpose to entertain audiences? Or was it made primarily because the people who invested in its' production believed that it would be a commercial success and show a substantial profit?

Was it made as an experimental exercise in movie-making to satisfy some creative need for the producers and director, or was it made to make a valuable social, cultural, pious or political statement? Was it made with the intention of not showing a profit and to be declared as a tax write-off for wealthy investors? Or was it made for just plain fun? Was it for any one, or a combination of these reasons?

And

Did the movie achieve its objective?

Acting for the Screen: A concise history

How do the acting styles of screen "stars" from previous generations compare with the acting styles of movie and TV "stars" today?

Look at the movies of some famous actors who were *stars* in past decades and form your own opinion about this.

When people become aware of the historical roots of a particular discipline, it teaches those that are practicing that discipline what their place in it is.

So following that same principle, I believe that it's valuable for people who are studying to be screen actors, to become aware of how the experience of certain movie actors and directors from the past established and influenced the styles and film acting techniques that are practiced in different countries and cultures today. This is something you can learn from.

You'll begin to notice that about every couple of decades or so, changes have happened in *the way* that movies were made and presented.

You'll also see a pattern emerging of how film acting styles also *evolved* and changed over the decades.

You'll see how innovative directors, producers, writers and actors made an impact with their movies, which changed the way actors performed in them and how that altered the way audiences viewed movies in different decades.

Many groundbreaking films that influenced the evolution of the movies have been documented in other books and some research will give you a guideline as to which of these movies are worth looking at.

Outlined below are *some* of the movies that were made during the first seven decades of the 20th century that influenced my appreciation, knowledge and understanding of what was involved in the development of the movies and what acting for the screen is all about.

No doubt you probably will also have your own *special* choices.

1900 – 1929

The early years:

When the motion picture camera and movie projector were invented in the late 1800's, the first experiments with "moving picture" images that were shown commercially in the USA, France, Russia, Britain, Germany, Sweden and elsewhere in Europe were a simple phenomenon that attracted audiences who were *entertained* just by watching pictures of people and objects moving silently on a white background in a darkened room.

Then the first "movies" which touched audiences profoundly on an emotional level, were candid moving picture images that documented real life events of the pain and horrors of the Boer War in South Africa and the procession of Queen Victoria's funeral.

By the early 1900's this inspired a few creative people to begin trying out new ideas with moving picture images. They used "actors" in uncomplicated situations that entertained audiences on a more "emotional" level.

But in 1903 in the USA a short movie titled *The Great Train Robbery* caused a sensation.

It was made by Edwin S. Porter who was a cameraman who had been experimenting with the rudimentary principals of film editing by re-arranging and manipulating the separate moving picture images he photographed in a way that created excitement, tension and suspense.

The movie was a 'western' that for the first time told a *story* that had *a beginning, a middle* and *an end*.

It had the action of the bad guys robbing the train, a chase sequence of the good guys going after the bad guys, some simple but exciting stunt work and an outcome with the good guys winning over the bad guys. Even without sound, it mesmerized audiences and they wanted to see more. It set the stage for the movies as we know them today.

A few far sighted people from different walks of life sensed that a new and important industry could be created with this new technology, and they became "movie" producers who made more and more "story" oriented "moving pictures".

The movies were short, made up of uncomplicated story plots that had a running time of between ten and twenty minutes. They were mostly action westerns, melodramas, comedies and experiments in visual effects and science fiction.

This was *the silent era* of the movies. It was about telling stories on movie screens with pictures only because the technology to combine picture and sound hadn't been invented yet.

It involved "acting" without the *sound* of words. It was about communicating and expressing a character's emotions, thoughts and feelings through action and broad strokes of body language only.

Audiences began to enjoy the "image" that some of the "actors" projected when they appeared in those movies and an early "star" system began to emerge because the people who made the movies, particularly in the USA, realized that audiences would pay to go and see their favorite "actors" on the screen.

Ordinary people became "actors" just because they happened to be in the right place at the right time when this new industry was being created. They were all beginners who came from different occupations before they became involved in "the movies" which was a brand new and exciting business to get into.

Real life cowboys like Hoot Gibson, Tom Mix, William S. Hart, "Bronco Billy" and Buck Jones became western action "movie" heroes, and comedians like Charlie Chaplin, Harold Lloyd, Fatty Arbuckle and Mac Sennet's Keystone Cops became household names the world over wherever their movies were shown.

Some of the first dramatic "movie stars" with an appealing screen presence and sensuality were men and women like John Barrymore, Douglas Fairbanks, John Gilbert, Rudolph Valentino, Mary Pickford, Gloria Swanson, Lillian Gish, Pearl White and Sarah Bernhardt. Their names alone could draw paying audiences in to see a movie.

Their acting styles were what audiences today would consider "over the top".

They had no formal training in *film technique* when they started, because such a thing didn't exist. They were people who were learning a new type of work, and discovering new techniques as they went along.

That "over the top" style of acting was also influenced by professional actors coming out of vaudeville or a theatrical background, who were drawn to the new medium with it's attraction of potential fame and wealth. They projected their theatrical "acting experience" into "the movies".

When you look at the early comedies, dramas and action films during those early decades, you'll see that the performances are wooden with big expressions that also reflected the style of acting that was customary in theatre at that time, and this was also what the early film-makers thought "acting" was all about.

Those early styles of acting were acceptable because "the movies" were still a novelty and a cheap form of entertainment for mostly unsophisticated audiences. But a number of influential films from this period started to change that.

Some brilliant pioneering "directors" and "producers" appeared who were experimenters and entrepreneurs and they shaped the original movie techniques that are still the basis of how movies are made today.

From Hollywood, D.W. Griffith's *The Birth of a Nation* and later *Intolerance,* were feature length films running over two hours. They were landmarks in the development of the movies as a serious art form and commercial venture.
The Birth of a Nation was a story about the American civil war and the emotions it aroused in the audience were still fresh in the minds of people who had lived through it. Segregation between the races was still a precarious issue in the USA when the movie was released in 1915 and black actors could not work together with whites. So in the movie "black slaves" were played by white actors wearing black make-up and dressed as blacks. Many people today consider this movie racist and offensive.

Still, for spectacle and action the movie was in places brilliant and gripping even without the sound of dialogue. By today's standards it lacks a polished rhythm and technique and powerful closeups that would have captured the emotional detail in the actor's performances.

The acting is over-expressive and theatrical, but at times – during moments when the actors do become "pulled in" and underplay their roles – you can sense an emerging *film acting style.*

Intolerance was an action and dramatic spectacle cross-editing between four parallel stories centered on the theme of intolerance through specific historical periods from the fall of Babylon; to the time of Jesus; the persecution of the Huguenots in 16th century France, and into the persecution of a "modern" industrial working class family at the beginning of the 20th century.

It moved in and out of one story and into another like a jigsaw puzzle while still trying to keep the theme in focus. For that time, it was an experiment in innovative film editing and in spite of the still theatrical style of the actors it's an intensely emotional psychological study of human nature. You can feel its' attempt at trying to lift movie acting and movie story telling to another level.

By the 1920's people in other countries were also making movies with stories that reflected their cultural values and temperament and the social and political upheavals that affected them.

Abel Gance's *Napoleon* from France was a silent epic also running more than two hours. The action of the battle scenes in the movie was shot with a number of cameras. It was then projected onto three large screens with different images of the action happening simultaneously on each screen.

It was the prototype by more than four decades of the giant screen systems like Cinemascope and Cinerama, Panavision and IMAX which we have today. The battle scenes must have been especially mind-blowing to audiences at that time.

Like D.W. Griffith's The Birth of a Nation, the showings were accompanied by a full symphony orchestra that was set up in the theatre which followed and accented the action, and by sound effects created by a team of technicians working behind the screens.

In Germany, people were still locked into the emotions of defeat and the despair of the First World War, and those emotions were reflected in the kind of movies that were coming out of there.

There was *The Cabinet of Dr Caligari,* which is a psychological journey into the leading character's mind, culminating in horror and insanity. Though the performances are well over the top, there is still something dark, brooding, sinister and suspenseful about it. It's a masterpiece cinematographically and experimentally.

It resonated with a subliminal undertone of the German social condition and the emotional mindset happening to the nation after its defeat and humiliation in the First World War.

Sergei Eisenstein lived through the turmoil of the 1917 Russian Revolution, which influenced the emotional content in the way he made his epic movie *The Battleship Potemkin* in 1925. It's about oppressed sailors stationed on the Tsarist Black Sea. It's based on an earlier historical incident in 1905, when the sailors mutinied and took over their ship. It's about revolution and counter-revolution and the tragedy of the sailors who are finally mowed down by Cossack troops.

It's considered one of the ten best movies ever made. It's still gripping to look at today. It contains drama, action, emotional intensity and suspense. There's almost a documentary real-life flavor about it in the way it was shot, performed and edited. Sergei Eisenstein was one of the first movie pioneers who experimented with editing techniques that are still used in the movies today.

Through his experiments with editing and directing actors in movies, he realized the difference between a theatrical performance and the subtleties of performing for the screen. As a result of this, the performances of his actors are more pulled in and cinematically powerful.

There were many movies made during this period with actors who were establishing themselves specifically as "movie actors" and "stars". Among them were Harold Lloyd, Buster Keaton and Charles Chaplin with his famous alter ego "tramp" character in *The Gold Rush, City Lights* and *Modern Times.*
These pioneers began to understand how the cinema worked and were brilliant

in creating action and comedy. Their experiments in cinematography were crude by today's standards, but they produced some amazing special effects sequences in their movies.

They also realized that somehow the style of acting that worked in theatre just didn't come across that well when performed on the screen.

The movies were still silent, but some people were already experimenting with the idea of putting sound into movies. The big change came about in 1928 and again it happened in the USA when the first commercially successful, partly sound movie called *The Jazz Singer* was released by the Warner Brothers studio in Hollywood.

It starred Al Jolson who was debatably the most successful singer and entertainer on Broadway at that time. He wasn't particularly handsome, in fact he was rather plain looking, but he radiated an incredible performance energy and "star quality". With him in the lead role, this movie ushered in the sound era.

The film was mostly silent, with brief moments of Jolson singing his most popular songs and speaking a few words here and there. The movie was partly based on his own life story as a Jewish rabbi's son who was passionate about becoming a jazz singer, which was in conflict with the wishes of his orthodox, cantor father.

The acting was still wooden, melodramatic and over the top, but the movie had heart and must have had an enormous impact on *mass audiences* who experienced Al Jolson's lively performance, his singing and ad lib dialogue for the first time in a way that was never seen before.

About halfway through the movie he improvised a short scene speaking to "his mother". Then he said the words, "You ain't heard nothin' yet..." And that changed movie history.

The movie was a box office hit and convinced the movie studios that picture and sound was the way of the future.

The introduction of sound created new problems for the people who made movies. The recording equipment was clumsy and experimental and unlike the free flowing way in which silent movies were made, the cameras now became immobile.

They had to be placed in specially constructed "sound booths" so that the noise from the camera mechanism wouldn't be picked up by the microphones and that required directors to shoot scenes from *locked* positions close to where the microphones were positioned on the set.

For a while audiences were fascinated by the novelty of only *hearing* their favorite actors speak. The "movies" became the "talkies" and what became important was for actors to "talk" instead of to "move" on the screen.

The transition to sound wasn't easy for many actors who were popular "stars" in the silent era. Some were able to make the transition to sound, others were not.

Those who didn't just had bad voices and bad speaking habits which irritated audiences. Suddenly they didn't look so appealing or glamorous when they spoke. Their voices were weak and raspy and just didn't *sound* good on the screen.

They resonated strangely to the audience, and combined with their over-the-top style of acting, appeared ridiculous. They were unable to adapt to the new developments that were happening, and they faded away into obscurity.

In those early days no one really understood how to adjust their voices and acting styles to the new technical requirements of sound. With the actor's voice becoming an increasingly important feature of the movies, efforts were made to teach actors how to strengthen their voices and to train them in a method of acting that was more suitable for the "talking" screen.

So the first "sound movies" were rather like theatrical productions projected onto a screen. Most of them were static, talky, over written and boring. As audiences began to loose interest in the novelty of sound, producers and directors began to realize that new recording techniques and equipment had to be developed for the way sound movies were made.

A new style of writing was also needed that was less "talky" and a new method of acting had to be developed that was more subtle and suited to the movies.

1930 – 1939
The first decade of sound:

The thirties was a time of immense technical and creative advancement.

Under the guidance of inventive directors, the movies became more sophisticated, and sound and picture were finding a way to bond together technically with new and better inventions in sound equipment. The cameras were released from the limitation of the "sound booths" and became versatile again and began to move cinematically the way they were intended to be used.

You can see these changes happening in movies like *Hell's Angels* with its spectacular air combat sequences directed by Howard Hughes and in social conscience movies like *All Quiet on the Western Front* with Gary Cooper, which were both stories about the First World War. Also in the prison drama *I Am a Fugitive from a Chain Gang* with Paul Muni and in passionate, high energy show biz story musicals like *42nd Street* with Ruby Keeler and *Gold Diggers of 1933* with Ginger Rogers.

And from Germany, combining social conscience with decadent show biz, there was *The Blue Angel* with Marlene Dietrich who later came to Hollywood as a refugee from Nazi Germany and became a big star.

Movie people were also beginning to experiment with a very particular style of "screen" acting, writing and dialogue delivery. Look at the tight, snappy acting, dialogue delivery and action in movies like *Little Caesar* with Edward G. Robinson and in *The Public Enemy* with James Cagney.

It was an era of great films that vividly reflected the social environment of the 1930's in America and the need for escapism and a subliminal cultural history that audiences craved for. It was "a golden age" of the movies and introduced a new generation of movie stars, idols and character actors.

Look at the films of Douglas Fairbanks Jr., Bette Davis, Joan Crawford, George Arliss, Wallace Beery, Tyrone Power, Cary Grant, Victor McLaglen, Ronald Colman, Robert Donat, Spencer Tracy, Katherine Hepburn, Jean

Harlow and W.C. Fields.

May West's sexually suggestive comedies were banned for being too risqué by the censorship board that controlled the content of the movies that came out of Hollywood from the 1930's right up to the late 50's. Today we wouldn't even blink an eyelid about that, but at that time it was groundbreaking stuff.

There was Fred Astaire and Ginger Rogers who introduced a stylish, high class approach to ballroom dancing in "escapism" musicals like *Top Hat*. And Eleanor Powell who radiated stylized dance energy so spontaneously and oozed sexuality so naturally that she made it seem effortless.

For adventure there was Johnny Weissmuller, a five time Olympic medal winning swimming champion who became the definitive Hollywood *Tarzan* and by popular consensus the greatest Tarzan ever. There was also the original *King Kong,* where the real "stars" of the movie were the special effects and the giant ape.

For sophisticated romantic comedy there was *Ninotchka* which starred Greta Garbo in what is probably her best role. It was directed by Ernst Lubitsch, and written by Billy Wilder before he also became a legendary director.

All three began their film careers in the film centers of Europe before they immigrated to America.

The Great Dictator is Charles Chaplin's first talking picture. It's a social comment and made fun of the Nazi and Italian fascist dictatorships just before the start of the 2nd World War.

For horror and scaring audiences of that time, there was Boris Karloff and Bella Lugosi in a series of over the top but amusing *Frankenstein* and *Dracula* movies and the poignant *The Hunchback of Notre Dame* which was sensitively, although somewhat theatrically, portrayed by Charles Laughton.

Definitely worth looking at are the Shirley Temple movies of this decade in which she co-starred with the brilliant, black tap dance man Bo Jangles. There are dazzling song, dance and dialogue sequences performed by a six to ten year old Shirley partnering the veteran Bo Jangles. The movies leave you breathless, experiencing absolute entertainment with talent that radiates exceptional high performance energy.

Most of the movies that were produced up to this time were shot in black-and-white. There were experiments in color cinematography going on even during the silent era, but the process of producing a feature length movie in full color was economically impractical until the 1960's unless the movie was produced with a big budget.

For action-adventure, have a look at Errol Flynn in the original *The Adventures of Robin Hood* and Judy Garland for fantasy in *The Wizard of Oz,* which made her a "star". Both these movies were shot in the new Technicolor process which added a fresh visual quality to the screen.

The end of the decade saw the premiere of what is probably the most talked about movie of all time and the most successful financially. It had an all star cast, visual impact and special photographic effects that made the film economically possible. It was a movie that was in essence made famous by publicity and the spectacle of the production.

It was called *Gone with the Wind* and was based on a best selling novel by one time author Margaret Mitchell. By today's standards the movie is overlong and seems to drag on. The acting seems forced and rather melodramatic in places and the dialogue seems too "talky" because it follows much of the way the novel is written.

But it made "superstars" of Clark Gable, Leslie Howard, Olivia De Havilland and Vivien Leigh who was an unknown actress in America. She was from England and married to Laurence Olivier who was making a movie in Los Angeles at the time.

She just "happened" to be visiting the Hollywood studio back lot where "the burning of Atlanta" sequence of the movie was being filmed, and was "discovered" when she was introduced by her agent to David O. Selznick who was the producer of the movie and looking for the right actress to play Scarlett O' Hara. A role that was coveted by just about every actress in Hollywood.

Vivien Leigh's agent also just "happened" to be David O Selznick's brother and when he presented her he said, "David, I'd like you to meet Scarlett O' Hara..."

And the rest is movie history.

What's interesting about this groundbreaking movie is that like "The Birth of a Nation" which was made more than two decades before, it was also a story of the American civil war. The black slaves were now played by black actors, but they were still subservient.

It was a reflection of the racial discrimination that still prevailed in the white culture of America and didn't show black people making a heroic contribution in the conflict which would have been historically accurate if the movie had done so.

However, Hattie McDaniel was a black character actress who broke ground in 1939 by winning the Academy Award for best supporting actress playing a role as Scarlett O'Hara's black maid.

1940 – 1949
The glory days of the American movie studios:

By the start of this decade, seven major movie studios in Hollywood dominated the film industry around the world. They were Warner Brothers, MGM, Columbia, 20th Century-Fox, Paramount, RKO and Universal. Each one was in the business of selling dreams and fantasies to mass audiences and they dictated *the way* movies were made and *where* and *how* they were shown.

Europe was at war for a second time, so the studios there couldn't produce much. Their economies were a wreck and what movies did come out of Europe were mostly war stories, some thought provoking social conscience movies, low budget comedies and propaganda films. The money and much of the top talent had already migrated to America and more specifically, to Hollywood.

The Hollywood movie studios had become so rich and powerful that they could attract the best talent from everywhere. Each studio their own directors and writers under contract and they created their own stars and promoted them internationally.
Under the American studio star system of the 1930's, 40's and 50's it was

mostly the popularity and screen presence of the actors that was important, and most of the studio "stars" basically just played themselves in the movies they made.

The studios regarded their stars as an asset, so movies were made to fit specifically around the image and drawing power of these actors who continued to have an enormous influence world-wide on the social, moral, political and cultural values of society.

Each star projected a personal style that was all glitz, polish and professionalism. They seemed to have an inborn understanding about working in front of the camera and for the most part developed a film acting technique which looked like it was unburdened by any academic theory.

Because America was still the main market for the movies produced by the studios, the studios were also strongly influenced by powerful religious groups that supported the morals and family values of America's puritanical heritage.

So the studios made certain that nothing would damage or scandalize the image of their stars in the eyes of the movie going public, to the point where they even dictated the way their stars lived their private lives.

In Europe and Asia it was different. There the main focus of the actors and studios was not so much on the actor's personality and private life but rather on story, character interpretation and realism.

With each American studio promoting its own roster of stars, you could even begin to discern a particular style in the movies that each studio produced. You could tell a Warner Bros. picture by the studios choice of story material, the way it was presented and by the "stars" that performed in it. Their basic formula was high action developed around tight, well written scripts that were economically and quickly produced into movies. The scenes and performances were efficiently paced, getting on with the story without wasting time.

Their movies were also given an edge with brilliant directors like Michael Curtiz and interesting character actors like Walter Huston playing opposite the star image of Humphrey Bogart in *Treasure of the Sierra Madre,* Peter Lorre and Sydney Greenstreet who appeared in supporting roles opposite

Humphrey Bogart and Mary Astor in movies like *The Maltese Falcon* and again with Humphrey Bogart, Ingrid Bergman, Paul Henreid and Claude Rains in *Casablanca*.

Each one of these movies has become an enduring classic.

MGM was famous for its production spectacle and was publicized as the studio that "had under contract more 'stars' than there were stars in heaven". It was a pretty bold statement to make, but it did make interesting PR copy. Their specialty was musicals and they were brilliant at it.

An MGM musical had a definite MGM "look" about it. You can see it in the movies of Gene Kelly and underwater swimming ballerina Esther Williams who appeared in a bathing costume in just about every movie she was in, which usually culminated in one or two spectacular swimming pool ballets involving a gigantic and sexy cast of bathing ballerinas.

Controlled like a personal fiefdom by co-founder Louis B. Mayer, as in Metro Goldwyn *Mayer,* MGM was probably "the" prestige studio of the 30's, 40's and 50's. They really did have a vast pool of actors to draw from that could fit into just about any genre of movie.

Look at the movies of cool and stylish actors like Spencer Tracy and Katherine Hepburn, and larger than life "stars" like Joan Crawford or young and talented child actors like Mickey Rooney, Judy Garland and Elizabeth Taylor.

Columbia was sort of an upper class "B" picture factory with stars like Glenn Ford, Evelyn Keyes and sex symbol Rita Hayworth. Under the rule of movie tyrant Harry Cohn, Columbia was always trying to win respectability up there with MGM and the other class "A" studios. Still, Columbia did turn out some wonderful classic movies under their "star" in-house director Frank Capra. It's worth reviewing some of his social conscience and "feel good" movies.

20th Century-Fox was dominated by the personality and creative style of co-founder and Executive in Charge of Production, Darryl F. Zanuck. Before he co-founded 20th Century Fox, he was originally the Executive in Charge of Production at Warner Brothers Studios and was mainly responsible for overseeing the success of the first groundbreaking, partially sound film, *The*

Jazz Singer.

While he was at Warner Bros. he also created some early high energy musicals for the studio, as well as a string of innovative and popular gangster movies that reflected the gangster lifestyle in America during the time of prohibition. It was then that the manufacture, sale and distribution of alcohol was banned, which opened the way for criminals like Al Capone to take over the alcohol industry.

Under Zanuck during the mid 1930's and throughout the 40's, 20th Century-Fox produced a series of prestigious and commercially successful movies and it was a toss-up between Fox and MGM as to which of the two was the most admired studio.

His influence can be seen in pioneering social conscience movies like *The Grapes of Wrath,* a story of the hardship of an American family of migrant workers crossing the American Midwest during the 1930's, trying to find their place in the promised land of California, and in *How Green Was My Valley,* which touched on nostalgia and looked at family life in a Welsh coal mining town.

All about Eve explored personal relationships and life in the theatre. *Pinky* touched on racial issues and *Gentleman's Agreement* on anti Semitism at a time when these themes were still risky topics. The original *The Mark of Zorro,* placed in the days of early Spanish California, was a classy action fable that set a mysterious masked hero against the forces of greed and corruption.

Paramount was the personal realm of co-founder, producer and director Cecil B. De Mille. He started in Hollywood before any movies were made there with Adolph Zukor and Samuel Goldwyn, who also co-founded MGM as in Metro **Goldwyn** Mayer. Goldwyn quit Paramount because he couldn't get along with Zukor and De Mille, then he quit MGM because he couldn't get along with Mayer. He then founded his own studio and called it Samuel Goldwyn Studios and over the years produced some classic independent movies.

De Mille's specialty was historical spectacles, especially of the biblical kind. The research and historical accuracy in his movies was questionable, which mixed religion with a good measure of sex, but that never stopped him from manipulating history and rewriting it for the sake of entertainment and drama. All his movies made money.

He was not an actor's director. He let the actors "act" in whatever way they wanted in his movies. His philosophy was, "I hired you to act, and that's what I expect you to do".

He first made *The Ten Commandments* during the silent era and his second version of it in sound and color was made in the mid 1950's when he was in his 70's. It was spectacular for its special effects and the parting of the Red Sea and the transformation of "Moses", played by Charlton Heston after he speaks to God on Mount Sinai.

As in all of De Mille's movies, the writing is ponderous and the performances from an all star cast are theatrical, wooden and predictable, but De Mille was a great PR man. He personally played the voice of God in the movie.

By contrast, director Billy Wilder made some sophisticated comedies and dramas for Paramount. Check out some of his movies. *The Lost Weekend* with Ray Millard stands out as a study of alcoholism and is still shown today at drug addiction clinics and *Double Indemnity* with Barbara Stanwyck and Fred MacMurray is a classic study of fraud in the insurance industry.

Witness for the Prosecution with Tyrone Power, Charles Laughton and Marlene Dietrich is a memorable courtroom thriller about how a clever criminal mind can deceive the justice system.

Some like it Hot is a risqué comedy touching on homosexual undertones with Jack Lemmon and Tony Curtis posing as two girl musicians trying to escape from gangsters who are after them after they witness a murder. It also co-starred Marilyn Monroe as Tony Curtis' love interest in what was probably her best comedy role.

The humorous *Irma la Duce* set in the early 20th century in Paris with Shirley MacLaine as a soft hearted prostitute and Jack Lemmon as an uptight policeman who falls in love with her is another memorable comedy that has the Wilder touch.

RKO was probably the one studio that took more creative risks than the others, and often financed untried movie talent. It was once one of the top five studios in Hollywood, but it's been out of existence since the 1950's.

Actor, writer and director Orson Welles, still in his mid twenties, would perhaps not have been able to make *Citizen Kane* if it had not been for RKO. *Citizen Kane* is still considered by many critics to be one of the greatest films of all time.

At this point, it's also worth looking at what makes a bad movie. Many critics will look at a movie called *Planet 9 from Outer Space* by Ed Woods Jr. They consider this to be the worst movie ever made that was actually released world wide. It's a perfect example in lessons of what not to do in acting and directing a movie.

Perhaps because it is so bad, it's become a cult movie. Ed Woods Jr. admired Orson Welles who was his role model and was obsessed with the innovative style of Citizen Kane, but Woods just didn't have the talent of Welles or the finesse of pulling through what he produced.

Universal is the largest movie studio in the world. It's so huge in area it's registered as a city. During the 40's it was considered a "B" class movie factory. Universal was known primarily for turning out *Deanna Durbin* musical operettas which were commercially popular and horror fare like *Frankenstein* and *Dracula* movies as well as *Abbot and Costello* comedies which have become a part of Hollywood's mythology.

Universal operated under an assembly line formula and like Columbia and Republic Pictures, also churned out dozens of Saturday matinee westerns, detective yarns and movie serials.

But there was also a grade "A" side to Universal. Alfred Hitchcock later made some of his most memorable suspense movies there like *Rear Window, North by Northwest, Psycho* and *The Birds*.

Disney was still a small time studio struggling to survive, catering to family fair with Mickey Mouse and the gang as the main attraction keeping it together. Its specialty was cartoons and animated movies.

But the one thing the studios had in common was the superficial flavor of most of the movies they made. You could tell they had a "studio look" about them.

Everything about their movies was just technically too perfect and without reasoning why, you just knew it. What was particularly irritating and often unnecessary by today's production standards, was the constant drone of background music which was intended to drive the action in the movie.

Often it was just overkill.

However, with all those "stars" and others like William Holden, Lauren Bacall, Jean Arthur, Susan Hayward, Ava Gardner, Van Johnson, Deborah Kerr, Lana Turner, Henry Fonda, James Stewart and Gregory Peck the movies from this era were entertaining and touched audiences.

Then around 1950 Director Elia Kazan and Marlon Brando from *The Actors Studio* in New York introduced an emotionally internalized "method" of acting which influenced the way a new generation of actors would perform on stage and in the movies.

It was not glitzy and artificial. It came from a real place within the actor and vibrated with a deeper intensity. Look at their creative collaboration in *A Streetcar Named Desire, Viva Zapata* and *On the Waterfront* and Brando's performances with other directors in *The Men, Julius Caesar* and *The Wild One.*

Although he was hindered to some extent by a theatrical background and a theatrical style of writing in the dialogue of these films, Brando's delivery is honest and raw. And yet, although that method style of acting seemed to be so real, by today's standards, when you view it, it seems at times to be somewhat over intense and clinical for the camera, but it laid the foundation for the more natural and spontaneous performance style we are accustomed to today. It was another step in the evolution of acting for the movies.

Compare Brand's more natural and relaxed acting style in the films he made during the last two decades of his life to these earlier works and you will see the evolution more clearly.

It has also been suggested that Brando's movie acting style was also influenced to some extent by Montgomery Clift who was a brilliant actor who first made an impression in 1948 in director George Stevens' classic movie *A Place in the Sun*.

It's also worth looking at some of Montgomery Clift's other films such as *From Here to Eternity* and *The Young Lions*. You can see the similarity between Clift's and Brando's film acting styles.

Twilight of the cowboy action heroes and movie serials

The western movie made Hollywood. Without the western movie there would have been no Hollywood.

- James Horwitz
"They Went Thataway"

For a ten year old growing up in a small town in the middle of South Africa in the late 1940's and early 50's, the weekly cliff hanger serials and the action cowboy heroes on horses who chased the bad guys and who saved maidens from runaway stagecoaches was great, grand and exciting.

Today, they do the same thing in space ships and instead of riding horses, the heroes and bad guys are transported by exotic extra-terrestrial creatures. In some ways the basic formula of the action movie hasn't changed much. Only the image of the characters has and the stories, situations and special effects have become more sophisticated.

But back during the grand years of the action hero cowboys, there was Tom Tyler, Bob Steele, Tim McCoy, Alan 'Rocky' Lane, Johnny Mack Brown and Ken Maynard who was one heck of a stunt rider and a real cowboy who could do just about anything riding his "wonder horse" Tarzan.

William Boyd as Hopalong Cassidy and the singing cowboys Gene Autry with his horse Champion and Roy Rogers with Trigger "the smartest horse in the movies" and that other singing cowboy Tex Ritter – who each took time out to play their guitar and sing a song in between sorting out the bad guys.

But my all time favorite cowboy hero was without a doubt Charles Starrett as

The Durango Kid. Like *Zorro* he was also a masked man in black, but who rode a white horse named Raider and he scared the shit out of the bad guys each time he appeared to save the downtrodden.

His sidekick was overweight and clownish Smiley Burnett who wore a funny hat and the same checked shirt and sang a song in a voice that sounded like a croaking frog in every movie of the Durango Kid series.

Another was Wild Bill Elliott as *Red Ryder* with his Red Indian sidekick *"Little Beaver"* played by child actor Bobby Blake.

Bill Elliot's standard line each time a bad guy provoked him was, "I'm a peaceable man". Then, you just knew that a fabulous fight sequence would follow, where he would take on more than one bad guy and beat them all.

These cowboys appeared in a number of 40 minute Saturday matinee curtain raisers, followed by a movie serial which lead up to the feature film attraction at the local movie house. This combination brought the fans back to the movies week after week for more action and excitement.

For my money, one of the best movie serials ever was *Captain Marvel,* a comic book character who was better, stronger, more striking and more popular than Superman.

In the 1940's he was a serious commercial threat to the Superman brand and Dell comics took Marvel comics to court to force an end to the Captain Marvel character.

Dell won out and Captain Marvel disappeared. Many years later he was resurrected as *"Shazam"* on television. The special effects, action, pacing and flying through the air sequences of this Black and White serial were superb and still generate excitement watching the special reruns today.

Fans would sit for fifteen minutes through each chapter for twelve weeks to find out who *The Crimson Ghost* was. Each chapter led you into the next, and would end in a cliffhanger which would leave you wondering until the next week how it would be resolved.

Then there was *Rocket Man* and *The Indian Rider* who was a serial hero wearing a mask that resembled the face of an Indian warrior. The bad guys were always too dumb to figure out who he really was.

The people who played those roles weren't great actors, but they generated pure cinema. It was fun to follow them, though the movies and serials were rated "B" and sometimes even "C".

Nothing much was expected of them other than that there was plenty of action, great stunts and the anticipation that in the end the heroes triumphed over the bad guys.

They were pure escapism and reviewing those movies and serials today it was incredible what the people who made them achieved technically and creatively at that time with limited resources and minimal shooting schedules.

Those movies and serials were a training ground for a new generation of talent who in the next decade learnt how to make movies efficiently and were ready to take on making movies for the new medium of television.

1950 – 1969
Years of panic (The impact of TV on big screen movies):

Television was introduced in the USA in the early 1950's and had a profound impact on the way movies were made and presented. Acting styles and other movie disciplines were again affected as a result of performing in the high pressure environment of TV production.

The introduction of television was the most serious threat to the movie studios up to this time because people now stayed home to be entertained for free by the small TV screen and patronized the movie houses less often.

The studios tried to ignore this threat from television by refusing to supply the new medium with product and with the acting talent they controlled and the more they ignored it, the more it contributed to the erosion of their absolute power over the next two decades.

They tried 3-D gimmicks in movies like *The House of Wax* and *Bwana Devil* to lure paying customers back into the theatres, and with new giant screen dimensions like Cinemascope, Cinerama, Vistavision, Technoscope and Panavision which won out over the others and is still in use today.

There was even a system called Smell O Vision which sprayed exotic smells into the theatre as audiences watched the movie.

On those huge screens the actors looked gigantic and larger than life and the movies were more lavish, in color and spectacular to look at. At a time before the current trend to build movie complexes in shopping malls – where the screens actually became smaller – the movies during these decades were projected onto massive screens that were almost two floors high and just as wide, in "movie palaces" which could seat hundreds of patrons in one sitting in one large space.

It didn't seem to matter whether the movies were bad or good, as long as the message got across that watching a movie in a theatre was bigger and better than what you could see on a small screen at home.   The reasoning of the studios was that if the budget was more costly, the sets richer, the production more impressive and the "stars" more famous, it would lure back the paying customers.

And in the beginning it did.

It started with a movie called *The Robe,* which was shot in Cinemascope. It was a story revolving around the crucifixion of Christ. It starred a young Richard Burton as a Roman military commander who falls in love with a "Christian" Jean Simmons and is converted to the new religion. It wasn't a new theme and it had certainly been done before. It was very similar to MGM's *Quo Vadis* which was produced some years earlier. But it was the novelty of the giant screen that attracted audiences.

Muscleman Victor Mature played Richard Burton's "slave", who ends up obtaining the miraculous robe of Christ after the crucifixion. The movie made a fortune at the box office.

There was also Mike Todd, a producer who was known as "the big promoter" who developed his own big screen gimmick, Todd A-O, just to make a movie based on Jules Verne's *Around the World in Eighty Days.* It boasted an assembly of American and international "stars" in cameo roles. If you were famous, you were in it.

However, in spite of the gimmicks, audiences still paid to experience some really good movies. Fred Zimmerman's *High Noon* with Gary Cooper and George Stevens' *Shane* with Alan Ladd and *Hondo* with John Wayne are considered to be among the best westerns ever made.

The Third Man directed by Britain's Carol Reed and starring Joseph Cotton and Trevor Howard, with a brief appearance by Orson Welles as the mysterious third man, is still gripping and visually powerful after more than fifty years after it was made.

Warner Bros. found a lifeline in James Dean when they starred him in *East of Eden, Rebel without a Cause* and *Giant.* James Dean was briefly promoted as another "Marlon Brando" and became idolized after he was killed before the age of thirty in a car accident.

The original movie *Moulin Rouge,* directed by John Huston, dramatized the tragic career of the artist Toulouse Lautrec. The story was set in Paris around the atmosphere of the Moulin Rouge nightclub which made the Can Can dance famous. Jose Ferrer played the artist who was a dwarfed cripple.

He performs throughout the whole film walking on his knees to recreate Lautrec's dwarflike image. The physical demands on the actor to perform like this for weeks on end, was agonizing, but that's what actors are sometimes expected to do in special circumstances.

Contrast this with the French produced film *Can Can* which was about the birth of the dance at the Moulin Rouge but done with a uniquely Gallic flare.

The African Queen, also directed by John Huston, starred Humphrey Bogart and Katherine Hepburn who were at war with themselves and the Nazis in deepest Africa. They were both into middle age when the movie was made, and it was a wonderful character study of an uptight spinster who is forced through circumstances to put her trust in a loser alcoholic river captain and his boat.

Around this time Elvis Presley took the world by storm and Paramount

Pictures were further bolstered financially by contracting him to a series of musical action-romance movies which were built specifically around his rock and roll popularity. His *Love me Tender* (20th Century-Fox) and *Jailhouse Rock (MGM)* are entertainment milestones in the history of the movies.

But with the competition from TV becoming increasingly more intense, the studios had to re-evaluate their fear of television, and Universal was the first major studio to fully embraced TV as a new source of income.

Universal moved quickly to work with the three major TV networks in the USA. With their "B" picture "assembly line" system of movie making, the studio had the know-how and infra-structure to make TV oriented movies economically, efficiently and fast. They created a TV production subsidiary and called it Revue Studios, which churned out drama and comedy series that were made specifically for TV.

They reworked the old western and detective story formulas into a more sophisticated and refined form, with more mature story themes that captured the interest of audiences and entertained them again for free week after week in the comfort of their own homes. By ignoring the new medium and technology of TV from the beginning, the other studios were placed in "catch-up" mode.

Revue Studios opened acting opportunities for a new generation of actors who were not given a chance at the major studios to make it onto the big screen, but who became immensely popular as TV stars on the small screen. In the 1960's enormous changes took place in the industry as well as on the American political landscape. It was a time of massive turmoil and those circumstances also began to turn against the studios.

Slowly, serious competition emerged from countries on the other side of the Atlantic and Pacific which began to challenge the way movies were made and distributed by Hollywood. The most influential European producers were arguably Pathe in France, UFA in Germany and in Britain Alexander Korda's London Films and the J. Arthur Rank Organization.

Annual film festivals were held at Cannes, Venice, Berlin and Moscow and were established as a venue to compete with Hollywood to sell European and other internationally produced movies world-wide, and as they gained recognition and prestige, they opened up new markets for producers to showcase their movies.

However, a movie still had to be successful commercially in America and with few exceptions most foreign movies had limited runs in the USA. They were confined mostly to the "art house" circuit, which was a specialized theatre outlet in the major American cities that showed exceptional foreign films to more sophisticated movie goers.

It's interesting that most British movies which were seen in the USA at that time were also considered to be "foreign" because they "looked different" even though the actors spoke English. Although British films had favorable distribution outlets throughout the British Empire and Commonwealth, they weren't popular in the USA because they weren't regarded as being as glitzy and as polished as American movies.

They were more "real" and slower moving, which didn't appeal to the "escapism" taste of most Americans. That generation was brought up during the cold war, and wasn't into realism. They wanted action and fantasy when they went to the movies.

Different examples of the style of British films from that era are *Great Expectations* adapted from Charles Dickens novel, and directed by David Lean, starring John Mills and Jean Simmons. There was *Hobson's Choice,* also with John Mills who plays a subservient cobbler's assistant who marries the boss's strong-willed daughter, who changes his life for the better, and *A Kid for Two Farthings,* which starred buxom blond Diana Dors, who was Britain's version of Marilyn Monroe.

And there was *Where no Vultures Fly,* which was a story about the senseless slaughter of big game hunting in Africa and was decades ahead of its time in bringing eco awareness stories to the screen.

Also worth reviewing are the early movies of Alec Guinness and Peter Sellers before they became accepted as "international stars in American movies". *The Lavender Hill Mob, Kind Hearts and Coronets, The Man in the White Suit, Our Man in Havana, The Lady Killers, I'm Alright Jack* and *The Mouse that*

Roared, all reflect the wry British humor and the English genius for understatement.

Other well made British films, based on the British experience of the 2nd World War, include *A Matter of Life and Death* (released in the USA as *Stairway to Heaven).* It's a psychological fantasy with David Niven as a British pilot who is shot down and while reviewing his circumstances under anesthesia – during surgery to save his life – is confronted with a personal decision of whether he should live or die.

The Wooden Horse and *The Colditz Story* dealt with escapes from Nazi POW camps by British soldiers and influenced more lavish American World War 2 movies like:

Stalag 17, which is a riveting study of trust and betrayal in a Nazi POW camp.

The Dirty Dozen led by Lee Marvin is about a bunch of misfits who go on a suicide mission behind enemy lines in Nazi Germany.

The Train starred Burt Lancaster as a cunning train driver who uses his wits to save French art treasures that are being stolen by the retreating Nazis.

The Great Escape – with an all star cast – explores the way different prisoners from different countries attempt to escape from a Nazi POW camp.

The Young Lions featured Marlon Brando as a Nazi soldier with a sense of humanity who becomes tragically disillusioned about the war. Dean Martin and Montgomery Clift played his American counterparts with May Britt as the romantic interest.

Where Eagles Dare. Richard Burton and Clint Eastwood are dropped behind enemy lines to try to discover the traitor in British military intelligence who has been passing information to the Nazis.

David Leans' *Bridge on the River Kwai* and *Lawrence of Arabia* were mainly produced with British talent. They were enormously successful both critically and financially, but they were financed and distributed by an American studio and included a cast of international and American stars.
Sean Connery didn't want to be locked into the 007 role he created in the

original James Bond series, so he wisely changed his image completely in a little known but powerful British movie titled *The Hill.* It focused on the themes of brutality, sadism and revenge in a British army camp.

Real Eurasian:

From Japan there was director Kurasawa's *Rashomon,* which is a character study of a crime seen from the point of view of three different people. *The Seven Samurai* is about peasants in a feudal village in Japan who hire seven samurai to protect them from a feudal warlord who was terrorizing their village.

The Americans re-made it into a successful western called *The Magnificent Seven,* which was about seven misfit gunfighters hired by poor peasants to help them get rid of bandits who were terrorizing their village. It was set somewhere on the border between the USA and Mexico.

Looking back at Kurosawa's movies from today's perspective, the acting seems labored. One even suspects a slight hint of the kabuki theatre's rhythmic, ritualistic style of acting that influenced the performances.

Produced in Sweden, Ingmar Bergman's *The Seventh Seal* and *Wild Strawberries* attracted a lot of acclaim from people inside the movie industry, but his work wasn't popular with average movie goers who found his style rather theatrical, intellectually too talky, moody and slow moving, which also reflected the heaviness of the cold Swedish environment.

From Italy, Federico Fellini's *Nights of Cabiria, La Strada, La Dolce Vita, 8½* and Vittorio De Sica's *Bicycle Thief* have become cinema classics.

In France there were movies by a "new wave" of directors like Jean Renoir, Roger Vadim and Jean Luc Goddard.

These foreign directors achieved an international recognition and "stardom" which even surpassed the importance of the actors who were cast in their films.

Their focus was on realism, relationships, interpretation and stylization in story telling. Like the low budget B movie American studios, their movies were made with limited resources and were shot mainly on location in real life environments with small and efficient crews.

What was especially striking about the films of Fellini, De Sica and the new wave of French directors, was that there was nothing artificial about the acting that appeared in their movies.

There is a documentary flavor about it. It seemed that for the first time, foreign actors in the movies looked more natural and real, and their movies inspired a new generation of young directors and actors graduating from the film schools and hands-on training grounds of America.

With this foreign influence, Hollywood started to get more serious about exploring human relationships in movies that were made with less glitz but with more substance. It can be observed in *Separate Tables* and *Marty* which was made on a shoestring budget but won the Academy Award in 1955.

Also in movies like:

The Caine Mutiny – was about a navy court martial. The crew of an American warship turn against their captain and prove his incompetence. Humphrey Bogart turns in a powerful performance as a sad and pathetic figure who breaks down emotionally because of stress.
The Blackboard Jungle – which explored inner city turmoil and teenage school violence.

The Moon is Blue – which looked at sexual issues. It was tame compared to what audiences are used to today, but controversial for it's time.

12 Angry Men - about trial or mistrial in the American jury system.

Ship of Fools – is about prejudice, racism, anti-Semitism and fear. It's a character study of a motley group of passengers seeking refuge in a safe port on a German tramp steamer on the eve of the start of World War II.

The Snake Pit - looks at insanity and psychological trauma.
The Naked City - realistically dramatized crime and punishment in a major

American city.

The Nun's Story – was about a woman's conflict between her shifting beliefs, faith and religion.

Papillon – was based on a true escape story and dealt with the mistreatment of prisoners at an isolated French prison colony, and the triumph of the human spirit.

The emergence of black empowerment:

Pressured by the American civil rights movement, the decade of the 60's was also a turning point for black actors who were finally accepted for their talent and were empowered to work in the industry on an equal footing with white actors. They were no longer cast to play subservient roles in the movies or on TV.

Sydney Poitier opened the way with his Academy Award winning performance in *Lillies of the Field,* where he plays a traveling black handyman who comes across a flock of white, conservative Catholic nuns who con him into doing odd jobs for them. It's a begrudging relationship at first because of their racial prejudices, but they learn to accept and respect each other for who they are and not because of their skin color.

Interestingly, Sidney Poitier was a little known young American actor in 1948 when he was cast by Britain's Alexander Korda to play a lead role in the first film version of Alan Patton's memorable novel, *Cry The Beloved Country.*

It looked at the hardships suffered by black people in apartheid South Africa. Ironically, it was allowed to be shot and shown in South Africa by the then white government when apartheid was just beginning to become formulated into a national policy.

Television during the 1960's was also largely instrumental in opening stardom opportunities for black actors. It eased the white American public into accepting black actors working with white actors as equals on the nations TV screens.

One of the first black actors who played a prominent role on TV was Bill Cosby who co-starred with Robert Culp as covert secret agents in the original TV series *I Spy*. Their cover to get them to travel from one assignment to the next was that Robert Culp was an international tennis pro, with Bill Cosby posing as his manager.

It was shot on the road at different locations across America and what was particularly innovative about the series was its acting style which appeared so natural that it seemed effortless. It was ground-breaking because of the on-screen energy that occurred between Bill Cosby and Robert Culp and the interjection of spontaneous and humorous ad lib dialogue, which was usually initiated by Bill Cosby. Their timing played off each other and it was perfect.

It had an improvisational quality, and their ad lib dialogue would happen at just the right places at just the right moments in the action. It inspired a new way for movie and TV actors to interact on screen with each other.

One should also not under-estimate the influence that the TV series *Star Trek* had in breaking down cultural and racial barriers. Every episode of Star Trek was created around stories that included aliens, ethnics and people of color.

It made it easier for mixed racial groups to be accepted as less threatening by most of the TV viewing audience watching those characters on TV every week.

Two other groundbreaking TV series that contributed to the rise of black actors and social consciousness was *All in the Family* and its offshoot *The Jeffersons*. Both series tackled the delicate themes of narrow mindedness, racial prejudice and bigotry forcefully and with humor.

Sanford and Son was a sophisticated situation comedy series starring Redd Foxx and Demond Wilson. It revolved around the generation gap between an aging, eccentric but street-wise black man and the give and take relationship he has with the "modern" views of his hardworking adult son.

They ran a salvage business, which was a nice way of saying that they dealt in junk. The series was insightful for its time, because it showed that black families also faced the same issues and dealt with the same everyday problems that white families confronted.

The decline of the major studios:

As the decade came to a close, interest in Cinemascope and the other big screen gimmicks began to wane. It started with *Cleopatra*, which was the most expensive and most publicized movie made up to that time. It starred Richard Burton, Elizabeth Taylor and Rex Harrison.

Elizabeth Taylor was the first female star to be paid one million dollars for her part in the movie. This was big money at that time. She demanded it and got it. But the movie was a financial disaster and almost destroyed 20th Century-Fox. It also proved that big names and big everything else was no guarantee of a box office success.

And then there were other movies made during that time that also had spectacle, but with heart. Like *Spartacus* starring Kirk Douglas and directed by Stanley Kubrick who came from the new generation of movie-makers. Compare the performances and action of *Spartacus* to *The Gladiator* with Russell Crowe which had the same story-line and was made at the beginning of the 21st century.

Stanley Kubrick is considered by many movie people to be a uniquely original movie director. His *Dr. Strangelove* with Peter Sellers, made at the height of the cold war nuclear paranoia between the USA and Russia, has become a black comedy classic. His landmark *2001: A Space Odyssey* is also acclaimed by many space scientists as the best sci-fi movie ever made.

After working on a short lived TV series called *The Green Hornet,* legendary martial arts expert Bruce Lee left Hollywood and went to Hong Kong to star in a series of low budget martial arts action movies. He was largely responsible for beginning a new genre of movies that were focused around the martial arts, which became popular and profitable and are still successful today, starring a new generation of martial arts experts.

By 1970 many of the people who were foremost in creating the American movie industry began to retire or die off. Lawyers, actor's agents and business people who had no special interest in the creative side of movie making took control of the industry.

Most of them were more interested in the allure of power and big profits which the "image" of the movie industry implied rather than inspiring innovative movie making and indirectly, this was also one of the causes of the downward spiral of the major studios.

Big stars began to break away from the stranglehold of the studios and became independently influential. Some formed their own production companies and became directors, producers, writers, partners and stakeholders who starred in their own movies. They demanded - and got - a large percentage share of the box office receipts of the movies they made.

A low budget movie that was independently produced and which had an unexpectedly enormous impact world-wide during this time was *Easy Rider* made by and starring Peter Fonda and Dennis Hopper. It was about two young men who travel on motorcycles across the country to discover the soul of America through that turbulent period in its history.

Its story was timely because it played out the political, social, cultural and racial unrest that was happening in America and audiences, especially young people, identified with it.

Peter Fonda and Dennis Hopper both came out of movie families, but got their opportunity to make movies working for Roger Corman. He was an independent producer and a living legend in Hollywood, and a master at making low budget, quickly shot movies.

He was responsible for starting the careers of a number of people, including actors like Jack Nicholson and directors like Martin Scorcese, who became famous after gaining experience on Roger Corman films.

The new generation of creative people who emerged over the next thirty years had less classical theatre training but more of a movie and television background. This is reflected in the quality and style of the movies they produced. Look at some of the remarkable made for TV movies and the feature films that have been made since the mid 1970's through to the present.

The writing is tighter and more film orientated. The dialogue flows more naturally and the actors make their performances look less obvious and less dramatized. It's subtly different from the acting styles that came before.

Motion picture production became more global leading into the 21st century. Beginning around the early 1980's places like Australia, Canada, Holland, Spain, China and India also started gaining an international reputation as indigenous film centers, each reflecting their own culture in the movies and TV programs they produced.

Today, India produces more feature films each year than any other country in the world. "Bollywood" based in Mumbai, has became world famous as India's movie capital, and in many ways it has rivaled the image that Hollywood had during its peak as the movie capital of the world.

Large scale movies have become more costly to produce and the bigger and grander that they are, the more they cost, and the more a movie costs to produce, the more difficult it becomes for it's investors to recoup their original investment.

As a general rule, a movie needs to earn back at least two and a half times its original cost before it will even begin to show a profit. So if it cost millions and millions of dollars to produce it will be so much harder for it to break even financially.

The current trend is for the major studios to collaborate with independent producers and with other studios domestically or world-wide, to form co-production partnerships to finance a movie and to distribute it together. The downside for the studios is that they also have to split their corporate credits and profits, and usually they have to wait a long time for the profits to come in.

Old style movie theatres are being patronized less and less by audiences and many have closed down. But when the movie *home market* started to expand and became economically feasible in the late 1980's, new distribution outlets for movies became possible through video and DVD rentals and sales, as well as with movie releases to cable and satellite TV.

Movies released through the internet are still in the experimental stage, but this seems to be another direction the industry is exploring to attract paying audiences in the future.

No one can honestly predict what will make a movie successful. Much depends on the timing of its release and whether or not people are ready to see it. However, if a movie can be made economically enough with an interesting story, craftsmanship and credible performances, the chances are that it can recoup its original investment and make a reasonable profit for its investors.

And what are the predictions for the future and the direction that the movies might take in the 21st century?

To begin with, the movie and television industry has certainly become more global and more 'little guy' friendly, and although the American studios still have a hold on the industry, their grip is becoming less powerful.

Video and digital technology makes things possible today that were difficult to accomplish a few years ago. New electronic hardware is being invented all the time that makes it practical and affordable for just about anyone to experiment and to go out and make a simple movie relatively cheaply, and through the internet to even find audiences to see to it. People are doing it all the time.

On a larger, more elaborate scale, work is already being done internationally on innovations like:

- Virtual reality and re-invented full scale 3 Dimension for both films shown in theatres and on TV, allowing the audience to participate in the action of the movie and become part of the story "experience", interacting with the characters on the screen.
- Where the audience can manipulate the direction of the story to suit the individual tastes and mindset of the people watching it.
- Full scale cinema's designed inside the home as part of a comprehensive entertainment system with movies being shown to individual paying customers at their convenience on demand.
- With computerized and digital technology there are predictions that old time movie actors can be recreated electronically and be recast to "star" in new and unimagined types of movies.

Improvements will constantly re-shape the way movies are made and experienced but still, as long as an actor continues to work from a real place inside themselves, they will hold the audience spellbound no matter what the innovations are.

Summary

WHAT ARE THE INGREDIENTS OF A GOOD MOVIE?

A personal view

THE STORY / SCRIPT

This is about the emotions that the narrative touches which would incorporate strong writing that includes aspects of engrossing drama, humor, suspense, intriguing characters and flowing dialogue.

STRUCTURE

This is in the way the story unfolds in:

- The rhythm, timing and pacing of the dialogue and action.

It would include an appropriate balance between drama, humor and suspense.

PERFORMANCE

This is about the way the actors play the story, *become* the characters and generate emotions and action appropriately.

THE VISUAL LOOK

It's the way in which photography, lighting and camera movement capture the atmosphere, drama, humor, suspense, emotion, action and location of the story. It's about an appropriate balance between photography, action and drama, so that the one doesn't dominate the other.

FLOWING CONTINUITY

In this context it means avoiding disturbing elements that jar or disrupt the progression and mood of the action and narrative.

GOOD DIRECTION

This is about the way the story is conceived and brought to life on the screen by the director. It includes:

-   The interesting way in which the director stages the action and captures detail in telling the story and how the actors are directed to *become* the part.

CREATIVE EDITING

It's about how the photographed sequences, scenes and performances are physically connected and structured in the final presentation, in a way that moves the story, sound and action forward in exciting and appropriate ways. Its how the rhythm, timing and pacing of the scenes create a visual and emotional impact in telling the story.

ORIGINALITY AND CINEMATIC INNOVATION

It's in the way the technical, artistic and aesthetic elements are brought together and used imaginatively in telling the story. It's about presenting the movie in exciting new ways.

IT'S STAYING POWER

This is about looking at the movie from the time-frame when it was originally made. Does it still touch a new generation of viewers? It's about its commercial and artistic success through the years. There are many such movies. The two most famous are arguably *Gone With the Wind* and *The Wizard of Oz* made in the late 1930's which still impact on audiences today.

SET DESIGN

It's about how real life locations are used, or how sets are designed and constructed to create the right mood and feeling for the story. It's about the care, detail and authenticity that's been taken to create a convincing story atmosphere – or fantasy.

THE USE OF PROPS

It's how the actors apply them as a natural part of the action and the character they are playing.

COSTUME / WARDROBE / GROOMING

How well or innovatively do these reveal the nuances of a characters personality and enhance the mood and atmosphere of the story?

BACKGROUND ATMOSPHERE

In this sense, how well are background extras, animals, vehicles and other business placed and directed to give a natural ambience to the setting of the story.

MUSIC / SOUND

In this context, that would also include the appropriate use of *silence*. It's how these elements are used in an efficient way – not too much and not too little – to complement the mood and emotion of the story.

ITS UNIVERSAL APPEAL

Finally, it's in the way the movie *informs* and *entertains* people across cultural, social, ethnic, linguistic, economic and religious barriers. This would include:

-   The *statement* it makes.
-   The *influence* it has on art, culture, social issues, values, fashion and the *evolution* of entertainment in general.
-   It's cleansing, cathartic value.

Part 14

Ars Gratia Artis
(Art gratifies the artist)

Inscription above the roaring lion on the MGM trade mark

End Notes

If an opportunity presents itself, I think it would be a worthwhile experience for anyone who is serious about pursuing a career as an actor in the movies or on television to work on a professional production for a short time, or even on a student film in some assistance capacity.

The *experience* of working "on the other side" of the camera is invaluable. It will benefit you as a screen actor. It will sensitize you to the problems that crews and production companies deal with every day during the making of a movie or television program.

By *observing* other actors at work in a practical and especially in a professional environment, you'll learn about the subtlety of screen acting techniques that are not taught in drama schools.

You'll see how unanticipated performance difficulties are resolved by watching different directors at work, and how different actors cope with challenges. You'll also be in a position to make some valuable contacts in the industry.

If you are cast in a part, try to sit in with the editor while your scenes are edited. By looking at yourself and studying your positive points as well as the mistakes you've made during a shoot, you'll learn more about acting for the movies in one day than acting theories will teach you in weeks.

In theatre, student actors are expected to become involved behind the scenes in different capacities when their drama school produces a play. They gain experience by becoming engaged in activities like painting and building sets, organizing props and helping to solve production problems. The result is that they become more focused in their roles and they better understand the responsibility they have with the setting and the other characters in the play.

By becoming involved in the production details of the play, they begin to recognize the intricacies of the performance. It makes them appreciate what it takes to make their performance on stage look good. It's human nature that when you appreciate something and are totally involved, you tend to perform it better.

By the same token, I think it's important that a similar training should apply to film schools which teach students acting for the screen. They should involve their drama students in all phases in the making of a student film.

Acting, writing, directing, producing and editing for the movies are all inter-connected disciplines. The same psychology and basic structural rules apply, so it seems reasonable to me that people studying directing, writing, editing and producing, should at least also take a short course in *acting for the screen* to understand how an actor thinks, what the actors needs are, how an actor communicates and the discipline that is required from the actor to become good at it.

That's the way I was trained when I studied film production and directing at the 20th Century-Fox Talent School in Hollywood in 1958.

There are directors today, especially those working in TV, who as a general rule are only technically trained. They often don't understand how to connect with actors. In film school they learn the technical features of making a movie or television program, but *not* how to direct actors to achieve a good screen performance.

"When they work with actors in a professional capacity, it's almost like they cross their fingers after they've cast an actor, and then hope like hell that he/she will be good enough to carry the performance through".

You'll hear comments like this from experienced actors who've worked with some directors on TV series and even on feature films.

They'll tell you that there are different types of directors.

There are those whose concentration is the visual and technical side of making a movie and some are brilliant at it.

Others, who have been trained primarily as screen writers, are focused on the way the story develops and how the characters evolve on the screen.

Still others who've been trained predominantly as actors, have a greater understanding of how to work with actors but don't have a grasp of the technical side of movie making, and they leave that up to the experience of efficient crews, a skilled cameraman and a talented editor to carry them through.

And there are those who have a broad overview in the making of a movie because they've been trained and have experience in both the performance as well as the technical aspects of making a movie.

Experienced actors will also tell you that different directors use various "methods" to achieve results from both the actors and crew. Some are lewd, rude, bullies and abusive. Others are subtle, observant and encouraging. Some might flatter and pamper you, or just ignore you altogether. Others are very precise in what they want and might even "act" out the part in a scene for you to imitate.

Others are uncertain and might look insecure on the set. Some give you leeway and freedom to perform your part creatively, or they might intimidate you to have complete control over you. And there are those who are so laid back in the way they draw out a performance that you don't even realize you're being directed.

So during your acting career you're bound to work with directors with different personalities, who have a variety of different directing styles. In either case, the bottom line is for you to maintain a professional attitude and *take note* of the direction they give you and then accept what you feel is valuable for your performance. Maintain your integrity and self respect no matter what goes on around the set and stay focused on what *you* know. *Trust* what you do best and you'll have the support of the crew.

Today, if you want to work in the top brackets of film and television production, you should be well-rounded in the creative, performance, technical, post-production and even the distribution phases of the industry whether you want to be an actor, writer, director, producer, editor, promoter or distributor.

The people who have a working knowledge and an understanding of all those facets, will most likely be successful in a very competitive industry. They're the ones who will have the edge over others who will be trying to play catch-up.

Postscript:

Not every person has the opportunity to become the "main attraction" in a movie.

However, there are other ways that you can become involved as an actor in the industry if you truly care about acting. Many people who've been trained as actors have found it rewarding to play secondary or supporting roles or even minor parts to the "main attraction".

Some people might have other primary jobs and do professional acting as a part-time or secondary career.

I've known some actors who worked solely as bit players or character actors in movies, TV series or commercials and found that rewarding creatively and financially. Some did it as a source of extra income. Others who didn't need the money did it for the exposure and emotional high they got by appearing in the movies.

People do it for many reasons.

There was a restaurant proprietor in Hollywood way back in the 1930's who started acting part-time in bit parts in the movies because he wanted to connect with important people in the industry.

As important people got to know him, he became part of the Hollywood "in" group and formed friendships with many famous people who patronized his restaurant and it became world-famous and exclusive. His name was Mike Romanoff and his restaurant was called *Romanoff's* which is now part of Hollywood's mythology.

I knew a policeman in Los Angeles who worked in the movies and on television series during his days off from police duty. He studied acting as a hobby and started doing movie work part-time to earn a little extra cash, but mostly he did it for the 'high' of working in a "glamorous" industry.

There was also a professional plumber I knew who loved acting and worked as a movie and TV character actor part-time, and an electrician who did the same, who was originally trained as a Shakespearean actor at the British Royal Academy of Drama in London.

Working part-time in the movies gave these two people an opportunity to make contact with some important people who passed onto them the plumbing or electrical jobs they required. They became known in Los Angeles as the plumber and electrician to the stars and they made a small fortune from their full time electrical and plumbing business in between their part-time acting jobs.

A multi-millionaire stockbroker also did that. He did acting part-time as a bit player because he said it gave him the opportunity to free his blocked emotions and to accept his deepest desires through role playing different characters in the movies and on TV. He also made some high powered contacts in the industry and added them to his stock-market portfolio.

And there are housewives who studied acting as a hobby to improve their self confidence and communication skills, but turned it into a part-time occupation to earn some extra cash and to break away from the boredom of staying at home.

A few years ago a practicing psychiatrist took a short course on acting for the screen at our studio. He calls it a cathartic experience, and recommends it to some of his patients to take an acting course to get in touch with their feelings and play out *their* fantasies in a safe and controlled environment.

The bottom line then is that when people are passionate and serious enough about acting for whatever reason, they persevere and find a way to reach their goal.

It's not unusual for young people who are trained as actors to work as waiters and waitresses or do other jobs to earn survival money while they're trying to enter the industry. And that first opportunity usually comes by being cast in even a minor part.

Vocabulary

Film, TV and Theatre Words

ACTOR: The person who plays a story character in front of people, cameras, the stage or talks into microphones in order to tell a story.

ACTION: A command used by a Director to start a scene or a shot - usually on a film or TV production; a movement of some kind that is done or being done; in the process of doing; an act happening.

ADVANCING A STORY: To progress the plot, action or characters of a story forward.

ANGLE: The direction or place from which a picture or action is recorded or filmed, with reference to the subject being photographed; the point of view from where the camera is placed to film or record a scene.

BEAT: As in music, the rhythm or tempo used in timing a motion picture, TV production or stage action.

BEAT CHANGE: The change of rhythm or tempo in a scene.

BIT PLAYER: An actor playing a small part or character role in a scene; usually performing it with limited dialogue.

BLOCK: To work out the action of a scene on a stage or movie set; to stop or balk at another person's suggestion; to stand in front of another actor, covering and/or diminishing his/her performance to the camera or the audience. For example, as in *UPSTAGING* someone.

BOOM: A long, adjustable metal arm with a microphone connected to it, used by a soundperson to position the microphone close to the actor's action to better capture his/her dialogue during a movie or TV shoot.

BUSINESS: Movie talk for an actor's general physical actions in a scene.

CAMERA CRANE: A movable support with a long arm that can be raised high up, down or sideways in any direction. At the top end it holds a platform onto which a movie or TV camera can be locked. The platform also holds seats for the camera operator, the director and a space to attach lights if required.

CAMERA OPERATOR: The person responsible for working the camera moves and photographing the story action.

CHARACTER: The part played by an actor, usually created and written into a script by a writer; the peculiar and distinctive traits of a person.

CHARACTER ANIMATION: The art of making an animated figure move; sometimes described as "acting through drawings". The **animator** needs to understand how the character's personality and body structure will be reflected in the figure's movements.

CLAPPERBOARD/CLAPSTICKS: Two boards, either of wood or plastic, hinged together at one end that are slapped together with a loud "clap!" by the CLAPPER PERSON on a movie or TV set - used to indicate the start of a film or taping session. Contained on the clapperboard is certain information indicating the scene number being filmed, sound and film roll numbers, the director's name and title of the production. This information is used by the film or video editor as a reference during editing and in post production to identify the placement of the various "takes" of the scenes in the story that were filmed or taped during shooting.

CLOSEUP (CU): The detail of a subject photographed from a short distance so that only a small portion of the subject fills the frame. For example: such as a very close view of a subject's face or other story details in the scene.

EXTREME CLOSEUP (ECU): Same as above but photographing the subject even closer and much more in detail.

COMMUNICATION: The exchange of ideas and words between two points or two people. Sometimes this might include physical action.

CONFLICT: Opposing intentions; the reasons of a quarrel, a disagreement or a fight between characters in a drama. For example: a war, an argument, etc.

CONTINUITY: It's a daily, detailed description of the *content* of every shot of a scene that is filmed or recorded during a shoot. It ensures that no discrepancies occur between all the scenes, camera angles, takes, visual elements and the actor's actions and dialogue in a movie. The person on the set responsible for documenting all this information is the CONTINUITY PERSON.

CREDITS: Titles of acknowledgement or recognition of the people who worked on a production.

CROP: To alter the size of an image either electronically, physically or photographically.

CUT: A command generally used by the director to stop the operation of the camera, action or sound recording of a scene; the instantaneous change in a movie from one scene to another; to sever, splice or piece together a section of film or video tape during editing.

CUTTING: Another word for "editing"; the selection and assembly of the various scenes or sequences of a reel of film or video. This is the responsibility of the editor, sometimes overseen by the director during post production. Also see *EDITING*.

DAILIES / RUSHES: The picture and sound assembly of a days shooting, viewed each day by the key production people, so that the best takes of the day's performances and action can be checked and selected for editing.

DEFINITION: The clarity with which picture and photographic detail can be perceived.

DIALOGUE: The lines spoken by an actor during a scene, usually interpreted from a movie, TV or stage scrip; the portion of a sound track that is recorded by voice artists from a script and spoken by characters on the screen.

DIAPHRAGM: The large, muscular partition separating the abdomen from the chest. With practice, the richness and power of an actor's voice resonates from here; also relating to the camera's mechanism controlling the opening for light; a disk with a fixed or variable opening that manages the amount of light that enters the camera.

DIRECTOR: The creative person who interprets the written text or script; the person responsible for bringing the script to life. He/she works closely with the actors and oversees all the technical aspects of the production. A director might have any number of assistants, referred to as *Assistant Directors* or *A.D's.* *A.D's.* usually function in an organizational capacity on the set.

DISTRIBUTION: In movie language this refers to the specialized business whereby a film is publicized, circulated, rented or sold to an appropriate venue for showing. *The distributor* is the person, corporation or entity who organizes and disseminates the film to an appropriate venue for showing.

DOLLY: (Noun) a *device* with wheels built to carry a movie or TV camera and the camera operator, which facilitates the movement of the camera toward or away from the subject when shooting a scene. For a smoother movement, the dolly is sometimes pushed or pulled on metal tracks.

(Verb) The *action* of physically moving the camera toward or away from the subject when shooting.

DRAMATIC NARRATIVE: A story containing some kind of conflict.

DUOLOGUE/TWO HANDER: A scene or play for two characters.

DUBBING: The combining and sound balancing of two or more sound components into a single recording.

EDITING: To change a script by adding, eliminating or rearranging scenes, dialogue or text into a new or different order; to organize the various shots and scenes photographed during production, as well as the sequences and elements of the soundtrack, into a story order which creates the finished film.

EDITOR: The creative or technical person responsible for selecting, arranging and placing the shots, sequences and elements of the soundtrack together to produce a finished film. Often works with an *assistant editor*, whose job is usually to prepare and organize the components for the editor to edit.

EXHIBITOR: relates to the person, organization or entity that owns or rents the venue where the movie is shown. For example: a movie theatre.

EXT: Exterior - shot outdoors.

EXTENDING THE STORY: To further develop the characters and the plot.

FILM: A thin, flexible celluloid material used inside a still or movie camera to photograph, capture and produce still or moving images; and once the film has been processed in a film processing laboratory, to project back onto a screen the photographed images. It comes in different formats - 16mm, 35mm, 65mm, IMAX, etc.

FOCUS: To direct one's total and undivided attention to a specific point; to adjust the camera lens so that it produces the sharpest visual image possible on film or video during photography, playback or projection.

FOLEY: Background sounds which are added during audio editing to heighten realism in a scene. For example: footsteps, bird sounds, natural room tone, heavy breathing, etc. Also referred to as SFX - sound effects.

GATE / CHECK THE GATE: A term used to describe what the *Camera Assistant* does, which is to open the camera after each "take" to ensure that no dust, hair or dirty matter has collected inside the mechanism.

HAIR & MAKEUP: The production departments responsible for the hairstyling and visual appearance of the actors.

IMMEDIATE OBJECTIVE: What a story character wants on an immediate basis.

IMPROVISATION: To do, produce, prepare or respond to something on the spur of the moment, without intellectualizing the result or the consequences. Also referred to as an *IMPROV*.

IN THE CAN: A term used to describe a scene or shoot which has been completed.

INT.: Interior - shot indoors.

LIP SYNC: The simultaneous, precise re-recording in a recording studio of a character's dialogue which an actor does watching the action on a screen, so that the sound is accurately superimposed on the lip movements of the character. This is usually done when the original recorded soundtrack has been distorted or damaged for some reason during a shoot, which sometimes happens in uncontrollable situations on location.

LIVE ACTION: The filming or videotaping of real life or documentary scenes of people, props and locations without the benefit of a script or rehearsed set-ups; real life actors performing in a scene as opposed to animated situations.

LOCATION: The setting of a scene. For example: a forest, street, house, kitchen, bedroom, stairway, swimming pool, etc.

LONG SHOT (LS): Photographing a scene or action from a far distance, or with a full view.

MASTER SHOT (MS): A wide shot which captures all the action taking place in a scene; also referred to as an ESTABLISHING SHOT. It's usually the first shot of a scene and sets up the continuity and rhythm of all the other shots and 'takes' that are set up to cover the scene.

MEDIUM SHOT (M.S.): A scene that is shot from a medium distance. When used with people in a scene, it generally sees them from the waist up.

MESSAGE: The director or writer's intention/idea of what he/she wants to get across to an audience; sometimes also referred to as the SUBTEXT, UNDERTONE or BOTTOM LINE of a scene.

MID CLOSEUP (MCU): Not so closeup.

MONOLOGUE: Dialogue written for one person, usually reflecting the inner thoughts of a character, or someone telling a story; a long speech.

MULTI CAMERA SETUP: A situation when two or more cameras are used in a movie shoot, usually on big budget action productions and in *studio sitcom* and *soapie series*.

NARRATION: An off-screen commentary also referred to as a VOICE OVER.

OBJECTIVE: A character's goal or purpose in a scene.

PAN: From panoramic (a complete view) – usually incorporating a scenic when camera movement follows the action up, down or sideways anywhere through 180 to 360 degrees.

PLOT: The sequence of events or happenings which take place in a story.

POST PRODUCTION: The work done on a film, video or TV production after the major photography has been completed. For example: editing, mixing, post sync, marketing, distribution, publicity, etc.

PROPS: General objects which an actor might use in a scene to add depth and character to his/her performance.

PROMPT: The person responsible for monitoring the dialogue of an actor during a theatrical performance. Usually sits off-stage. On a movie set, the prompt is normally handled by the continuity person.

PRODUCER: The person responsible for the financing, budgeting, staff, legal contracts, distribution, etc. of a production; the person who oversees the overall smooth flow of the production. He/she may sometimes also make a creative contribution.

A production might also have various associates or assistants with titles such as Executive Producer, Associate Producer, Co-Producer, Production Assistant, etc.

A Line Producer is normally someone in an executive capacity who oversees the smooth running of the production on the set. Sometimes they might also be referred to as Production Managers.

RUNNER: Normally the lowest member of a production team who is a production trainee learning movie making skills through practical experience from the bottom up; an all-round go-getter, often referred to as a "Go-fer", as in "go fer fetching what's needed on the set…"

SCENE: A single, complete sequence of dramatic, comic or documentary action.

SCRIPT: The text of a performance piece, outlining the story dialogue and in a condensed form visual descriptions of a scene's placement, setting, background, the story characters and if required, certain action and camera moves.

SEQUENCE: A series of shots from different camera angles usually placed in the same time frame and location that tell a particular part of the story. For example: a car chase / action situation, a barroom brawl, a love scene, etc.

SET: The "setting" or set up of a scene where the action and performance happens. It can be in a natural location such as the outdoors, on a city street, inside a building - or it can be a "setting" designed and re-constructed on a movie sound stage.

SHOT: The basic component of a scene. It may be captured or "shot" on film, videotaped or digitally photographed; the position of where the camera is placed; the photographic composition of a scene.

SHOW REEL: A collection of film, video or digital clips showing samples of an actor, director's or other creative person's best movie, TV, commercial and stage work plus a CV and other relevant information; used for self promotion/advertising and usually packaged on a DVD.

SIBILANCE: An excessive amount of vocal hiss when unvoiced consonants such as "s" are uttered. Usually occurs with untrained voices in performance.

SITCOM: An abbreviation for *Situation Comedy*; a style of entertainment that's mainly produced for television usually in half hour, weekly time slots and features a series of situations that revolve around a cast of running characters who are locked into the series.

SOAPIE: An abbreviation for *Soap Opera*; a style of mellow-drama; an on-going, daily running TV serial, normally a half hour long with continuing characters. Soapies evolved out of the tear jerking daily serials called "soap operas" heard on American radio before the introduction of television. They were named this way because in the early days of radio and television soap manufacturing companies were the primary commercial sponsors for this type of programming.

SPECIAL EFFECTS / SFX: A term used broadly to denote any special sound or visual effects created either in a laboratory, the studio or during a live action setup.

SPOTLIGHT: A lighting unit, capable of being focused to produce a harsh, centered light. When articulated, is called a FOLLOW SPOT because it can be moved to follow the action.

STAGING: The director's setting or planning of how camera, sound, lighting and the actor's action will take place in a scene; also referred to as BLOCKING.

STAGE DIRECTIONS: Information which tells the actor's where and how to move on the set. (In theatre: Upstage, Downstage, Stage Left, Stage Right, etc.).

STEADY CAM: A portable camera mount that stabilizes the camera from shaking during movement. The camera is strapped onto the camera operator who can follow the action of a scene in one smooth continuous movement. For example, it allows the operator freedom of movement to follow the actors in a scene from one room into another in one uninterrupted action, or to move with the actors all the way up a stairway and into another room in one continuous shot.

STORYBOARD: A series of drawings or cartoons which suggest camera angles, with captions which outline the story and other details of the production. Used in PRE PRODUCTION (before the actual shooting begins) as a visual aid to create a common vision amongst the key people involved in the production.

SUBTEXT: Also referred to as UNDERTONE. The writer's hidden meaning and intention in a scene, not written explicitly in the script. Left open to be interpreted by the actors and director.

SYNCHRONIZE: To align the soundtrack with the images of a movie; to match the soundtrack of the movie with the action, lip movements and dialogue of the actors; primarily recorded at the same time that the camera photographs the scene.

TALKING HEADS: A production style usually seen on soapies and interview shows. The performance is usually visually static, shot from the waist or head up, eliminating much of the sense of geography or background in a scene. It's a cost effective and cheap way to produce a show, and practical in circumstances where production budgets are limited.

TRI POD: A portable camera mount with three adjustable legs. The camera is secured onto the mount in a locked position to prevent it from shaking when a scene is being shot.

VOICE ARTIST: An actor who performs the voices for characters during a recording for animation, radio, film or digital productions. These recordings are also known as VOICE OVERS.

WARDROBE: Sometimes referred to as the COSTUME DEPARTMENT. This is where the performance clothes for the actors are created, kept, distributed, repaired and cleaned. The person in charge of wardrobe is referred to as the *Wardrobe Person / Master / Mistress*; may have a number of assistants, depending on the budget of the production.

WILD ONE: A sound recording only, recorded unsynchronized to the camera. It's done or re-done after a shot has been filmed; it's usually re-recorded cleanly without the actors on camera action as "insurance" due to a technical sound problem during the take.

ZOOM: A continuous camera lens movement either IN towards a subject, or OUT away from the subject; To *ZOOM IN* or *ZOOM OUT*.

The photographs in this book are clips from video scenes performed at the Screen Actors Studio, Cape Town.

Thanks to all of you who appeared in these pages.

About the author

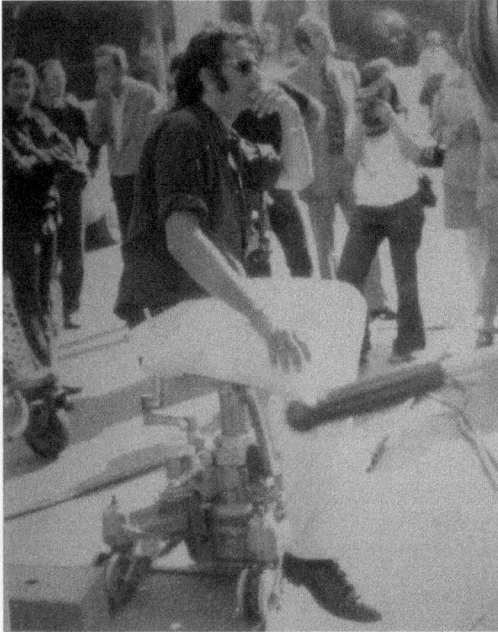

Tony Perris grew up in Bloemfontein, South Africa and has been involved in the film and television industry since 1958 when he was invited by the President of 20th Century-Fox to study directing and film production in Hollywood. He has directed television series, drama, documentary and educational films for over forty years.

He has worked as a writer, producer and director in Johannesburg and Los Angeles and in Toronto, Canada.

He returned to South Africa in 1992. He taught acting for the screen for four years at a film and media school in Cape Town. In 2004 he co-founded *The Screen Actors Studio* with Aletta Bezuidenhout, which specializes in training actors for the screen.

For further information visit our website at:

www.screenactstudio.com